Wheat-Free, Gluten-Free
Dessert Cookbook

Connie Sarros

Contemporary Books

Chicago   New York   San Francisco   Lisbon   London   Madrid   Mexico City
Milan   New Delhi   San Juan   Seoul   Singapore   Sydney   Toronto

The **McGraw-Hill** Companies

Library of Congress Cataloging-in-Publication Data

Sarros, Connie.
    Wheat-free, gluten-free dessert cookbook / Connie Sarros—1st ed.
       p.   cm.
    Includes index
    ISBN 0-07-142372-9
    1. Wheat-free diet—Recipes. 2. Gluten-free diet—Recipes. 3. Desserts. I. Title.

  RM237.87.S27   2003
  641.5'63—dc21   2003012696

1 2 3 4 5 6 7 8 9 0   AGM/AGM   2 1 0 9 8 7 6 5 4 3

ISBN 0-07-142372-9

Interior design by Sue Hartman
Interior illustrations by Jacqueline Dubé and Dean Stanton, copyright © 2000, 2001 Birch Design Studios

McGraw-Hill books are available at special quantity discounts to use as premiums and sales promotions, or for use in corporate training programs. For more information, please write to the Director of Special Sales, Professional Publishing, McGraw-Hill, Two Penn Plaza, New York, NY 10121-2298. Or contact your local bookstore.

This book is printed on acid-free paper.

To my father, who has celiac disease,
and to my mother,
who is always trying to find new desserts
to make for my father

Contents

Preface

$\mathcal{S}$ince you are looking at this cookbook, it is likely that you or someone you know has a wheat intolerance or celiac disease (CD). To explain the condition in simplified terms, if you have celiac disease and eat gluten, your body won't absorb the nutrition from the foods you eat. This will not only cause you lower-tract distress, but it could also lead to further serious health problems.

Medical terms for celiac disease are *celiac* (or *ceoliac*) *sprue* and *gluten-sensitive enteropathy*. This disease is a lifelong condition in which the water-soluble protein component in grains (gluten) combines with tissue-type antigens found on the surface of the intestinal cells, creating an immune reaction that destroys the intestinal-lining cells. Once the immune system is activated in this way, there is progressive destruction of the surface cells that are normally responsible for absorption in the small intestine.

The symptoms of CD vary widely from person to person. Most common are diarrhea, weight loss, gas, severe cramping, bloating, fatigue, anemia, and/or severe skin rashes. When a person with celiac disease first goes on a gluten-free diet, the time it takes to notice a significant improvement in health also will vary greatly from one individual to another. The process may take two days or two weeks—or longer. But by adhering to a strict gluten-free diet, the person with celiac disease may enjoy a symptom-free life and feel healthy and energetic. If you have celiac disease, warn your offspring: this condition tends to be inherited.

Gluten is protein found in most cereal grains, primarily wheat, barley, rye, and oats (either directly or from cross-contamination). When someone is diagnosed with CD and advised to eliminate gluten, what immediately comes to mind is eliminating all traditional pastas, breads, cakes, and cookies from the diet. But once you are familiar with your diet guidelines, you will find there are many suitable and delicious alternative ingredients and foods, so you do not have to sacrifice eating bread, pastries, and pasta. They'll just be made a bit differently now.

There are so many hidden sources of gluten. Beer contains such forbidden ingredients as malt, barley, and hops, so it is taboo. Malt flavoring (gluten) is found in many commercial puddings and cereals. Many soy sauces, horseradish, and some jelly candies are no-nos. A chocolate candy bar may be gluten-free, but the conveyor belt may have been dusted with flour to keep the candy from sticking to the belt. But if you ask, candy companies will send you a list of their gluten-free products. You will learn which turkeys to buy and which have been injected with broth that contains modified food starch. By writing to food companies, you will discover which brands are "safe." By constantly reading updated lists of acceptable foods to educate yourself, you may keep your system operating properly.

To add to the confusion, a food producer may not add gluten to one batch of a product and then does add gluten to the next batch of the same product. (This is especially true with frozen nondairy whipped toppings.) Some producers get their supplies from varied suppliers that cannot guarantee that the raw product is gluten-free. And some companies sell gluten-free products, but their legal departments have advised them to issue disclaimers, so the person with celiac disease has no way of knowing whether the items are safe for them or not.

Become an avid, educated label reader. There is no need to become discouraged, because many brands and substitutions are gluten-free. No specific brand names are listed here, because companies are constantly changing their ingredients or procedure for processing. What is gluten-free today may not be gluten-free tomorrow. Companies are usually willing to send you a list of their gluten-free products if you just call them. You may also get lists of acceptable foods and join support groups through national celiac disease organizations, online support groups, or by going to celiac disease sites on the Internet. Helpful online resources include celiac.com and clanthompson.com. You can call the Celiac Sprue Association/USA, Inc. (CSA/USA) at 1-402-558-0600. Subscribe to the St. John's Celiac Mailing List on the Internet at list serv@maelstrom.stjohns.edu.

It is essential to read labels regularly because ingredients constantly change. This point cannot be emphasized enough. The ingredients listed in this book are, at the time of printing, all gluten-free. However, ingredients in any given processed product may change. For this reason, the recipes in this book use no packaged mixes.

This book is devoted to desserts. People who must limit their diet as much as those who have celiac disease certainly deserve to satisfy their sweet tooth. Enjoy!

Hints for Successful Gluten–Free Cooking

Most traditional recipes containing gluten may be converted to gluten-free versions with excellent results. Cooking "gluten-free" is not difficult, but it does require some adjustments to ingredients and methods of preparation.

The Myth of the Mystery Flour Mixture

Baking without wheat flour is really no mystery and takes no additional time. Plenty of alternative flours may be used. The problem is that the alternative flours are often more gritty and heavier than wheat flour. This may be combated by mixing a variety of gluten-free flours. Combining the correct proportions of the various flours helps reduce the heaviness of one and the grittiness of another. Readily available at health food stores and even many traditional grocery stores are rice flour, sweet rice flour, potato flour, potato starch flour, tapioca flour, buckwheat flour, and a variety of bean flours. Cornmeal, corn flour, and cornstarch

1

are frequently combined with those flours. The secret (if there is one) is to find a combination of flours that will result in a lighter, less grainy texture. Gluten-free pastries tend to crumble, so xanthan gum (a white powder sold in a pouch) is often added to help hold the mixture together and keep it from crumbling.

In this cookbook, many desserts are made with "gluten-free flour mixture." Gluten-free baking will be easier and more convenient if you make up a large batch of the following recipe for Gluten-Free Flour Mixture, and freeze it in a plastic freezer bag. The mixture will be loose enough to measure straight from the freezer each time you need it. Let the measured amount come to room temperature, then sift again before mixing it with other ingredients.

ℐluten-Free Flour Mixture

2½ cups rice flour

1 cup potato starch flour

1 cup tapioca flour

¼ cup cornstarch

¼ cup bean flour

2 tablespoons xanthan gum

Sift the rice flour, potato starch flour, tapioca flour, cornstarch, bean flour, and xanthan gum together in a large mixing bowl. Store the flour mixture in a reclosable plastic bag. Refrigerate up to 1 week. For longer than a week, store in the freezer. *Makes 5 cups.*

You have several options for the bean flour. Mung bean flour is available at Asian grocery stores and is a wonderful addition to the light-textured dessert recipes. Chick-pea or garbanzo bean flour also is light. Fava bean flour, found at health food stores, is a nice addition for denser desserts, like pound cakes, fruitcakes, and sweet breads. Additional flours that are gluten-free are sweet potato flour, sweet rice flour, sorghum flour, buckwheat flour, and pea flour. If you are allergic to corn, omit the cornstarch.

Additional Baking Hints

Baking with Gluten-Free Flour Mixture will be most successful if you follow these additional hints:

- Gluten-free flours have less taste than wheat flour. If you are converting a wheat recipe to a gluten-free one, it helps to add something with significant flavor to the batter or dough. Some flavorful additions are orange juice, cinnamon, raisins, chocolate chips, extra vanilla, and almond extract.
- If you don't have xanthan gum, you may substitute double the amount of gluten-free unflavored gelatin (1 teaspoon xanthan gum = 2 teaspoons gluten-free unflavored gelatin), or fold in 1 stiffly beaten egg white.
- Add 1 tablespoon of gluten-free mayonnaise or sour cream to cake and bread recipes to make them lighter.
- If you are converting a traditional wheat flour recipe to a gluten-free version, replace the flour with Gluten-Free Flour Mixture, then add 1 extra egg and half again as much baking soda or gluten-free baking powder as the recipe calls for.
- Gluten-free flours contain no preservatives. Keep them refrigerated or frozen.
- Bake gluten-free products longer and at a lower temperature than conventional recipes.

- If baking with rice flour exclusively, combine it with the liquid called for in the recipe, and heat till warm, stirring (do not boil), then cool. This will help eliminate most of the grittiness.
- You may want to substitute other ingredients for the liquid specified in a conventional wheat recipe. Using carbonated drinks or buttermilk tends to make baked products lighter. Fruit juices add flavor and moistness.

Cooking Basics

$\mathcal{B}$aking gluten-free is not difficult, but it does require some adapting and converting of conventional recipes. Not all traditional recipes that contain gluten can be converted to gluten-free versions with satisfactory results. Fortunately, most can. The following lists of measurement equivalents, substitutions, and terms and guidelines, along with their explanations, will help you better understand gluten-free cooking and terms used throughout this book.

Measurements

1 tablespoon = 3 teaspoons
1 fluid ounce = 2 tablespoons
1 jigger = 3 tablespoons
¼ cup = 4 tablespoons
⅓ cup = 5⅓ tablespoons
½ cup = 8 tablespoons
1 cup = ½ pint = 16 tablespoons
1 cup = 8 fluid ounces

same day they are prepared. Most may be frozen, but freeze them right away to retain freshness.

Chocolate: Whenever chocolate chips are listed as an ingredient, use semisweet chocolate chips. If the recipe calls for gluten-free bar chocolate, substituting chocolate chips may alter the finished product.

Chopped Dates: Most chopped dates sold in grocery stores have been coated with sugar to prevent the pieces from sticking together, but a few brands use flour for coating. If you buy whole, pitted dates and chop them yourself, the easiest way to do this is to cut the dates with clean scissors dipped in hot water or sprayed with gluten-free nonstick spray.

Cocoa: Whenever cocoa is listed as an ingredient, it means unflavored, powdered, natural cocoa. Do not substitute hot chocolate mixes, because they contain sugar, and many contain gluten.

Eggs: Due to the increasing concern about salmonella, no recipes in this cookbook use raw eggs. The many refrigerated desserts and frostings that use raw egg whites have been rejected for use in this book. Before baking, let eggs come to room temperature. Set them out on the counter for 1 hour before using them in a recipe, or place them in a bowl of warm water for 15 minutes. This is especially important when making whipped egg whites.

Equipment: If you have a mixer and a blender, you can make all of these recipes. In lieu of a blender, you may use a food processor. No fancy gadgets are required. Some recipes call for using a pastry bag or microwave, but the recipes may be made without these.

Flours: Because alternative flours are heavier than wheat flour, it is necessary to sift the flours together before adding them to liquid ingredients. Even if you are using only a small amount of flour mixture, take the time to sift it.

Do not confuse "sweet rice flour" with "rice flour." Sweet rice flour is used as a thickener, like cornstarch, but cannot be substituted for rice flour in recipes. Likewise, do not substitute "potato flour" (a thickener) for "potato starch flour" (used in baking).

Gluten-Free Bread: Some recipes call for gluten-free bread cubes or bread crumbs. The commercial rice or tapioca breads sold in health food stores are too solid for these recipes. You need a type of bread that is more porous. You may use homemade gluten-free bread, or you may purchase lighter breads from health food stores or mail-order catalogs. Using a more porous bread will allow moisture to saturate the bread better. When using gluten-free bread in a recipe, cut off and discard the crusts and end pieces.

Greased Pans: Greasing a pan means coating the pan with shortening to prevent the baked product from sticking. You may safely coat your pan in one of two ways: (1) With a small piece of paper towel, rub a small amount of butter along inside of pan. (2) Spray the pan with a gluten-free nonstick cooking spray. (Before purchasing cooking spray, check the label to make sure it is gluten-free.)

Natural Ingredients: The recipes in this book use as many "natural" ingredients as possible. However, a few recipes use substitutes (such as gluten-free margarine) to lower cholesterol.

These recipes call for fresh eggs. If you plan to use an egg substitute, check with the manufacturer first to be certain it does not contain gluten.

In an effort to stay away from foods with a lot of added chemicals, these recipes use no sugar substitutes.

Preheated Oven: It is essential to preheat the oven to the desired temperature before baking. A cold oven takes approximately 10 minutes to reach the temperature of 350 degrees. Preheating the oven may mean the difference between the success or failure of a dessert.

References to Other Recipes: Some recipes use a sponge cake as a base for the dessert. Rather than duplicate the sponge cake recipe over and over again, the ingredients lists for these recipes include a cross-reference to the recipe for Sugar Sponge Cake. In Chapter 6, "Pies," the piecrusts are first; the pie fillings follow. The recipes for the pie fillings list with the ingredients the recommended piecrust, referring to the specific recipe. When you see these references, merely turn to the original recipe. (Check the Index to find the page number.)

Whipping Cream: Whipping cream, or heavy cream, is used the majority of the time in this cookbook. Nondairy frozen whipped toppings may or may not be gluten-free, depending on how they are manufactured. It is recommended that you check with the manufacturer when using nondairy frozen whipped toppings. As of this printing, Cool Whip is gluten-free, but remember: what is gluten-free today may not be gluten-free tomorrow.

Xanthan Gum: The first time you see this term, you may feel intimidated. Don't. When alternative flours replace wheat flour in baked goods, the finished product—whether it is bread, cookies, or a cake—tends to fall apart. Wheat flour binds ingredients better than the alternative flours. Xanthan gum is a powder added to many gluten-free baked goods to help with this binding. It is a light powder that comes in a pouch or other small package and may be readily purchased at almost all health food stores. Usually, anywhere from ¼ teaspoon (for small batches of cookies) to 2 or 3 tablespoons (for large loaves of bread) is enough to bind the baked product together.

1

Cakes

ho doesn't like a good piece of cake? There are cake recipes included here for any occasion, whether it be a birthday, anniversary, or luncheon. The end of this chapter features recipes for additional frostings and fillings. For many of the cakes, the nutritional information is broken down for each component of the recipe—cake, filling, frosting—so you may determine these values for different recipe combinations.

Glazed Chocolate Fantasy

Baked in a 9″ × 13″ pan, this is the perfect cake to take to a family picnic.

- ¼ cup butter, softened
- 1 cup sugar
- 6 eggs, separated
- 1 teaspoon vanilla
- ⅓ cup ground almonds
- 3 ounces (3 squares) gluten-free semisweet chocolate, melted

1 cup Gluten-Free Flour Mixture (See the Hints chapter.)

¾ teaspoon gluten-free baking powder

½ teaspoon baking soda

½ teaspoon salt

¾ cup plus 2 tablespoons milk

Chocolate Torte Glaze (Recipe follows.)

Preheat oven to 350°F, and grease a 9″ × 13″ pan. Cream the butter with ¾ cup of the sugar. Add the egg yolks and vanilla; beat well. Stir in the almonds, then the chocolate. Sift together the flour mixture, baking powder, baking soda, and salt. Add the dry ingredients to the creamed mixture alternately with the milk, blending well after each addition. In a separate bowl, beat the egg whites until frothy; gradually add the remaining ¼ cup of sugar, and beat until stiff peaks form. Carefully fold the egg whites into the chocolate mixture, and turn into the greased pan. Bake 25 minutes or till a toothpick inserted in the center comes out clean. While the cake is still warm, pour the Chocolate Torte Glaze over the top. Spread quickly. Leave uncovered until the glaze has set. *Makes 24 3- by 1¼-inch servings.*

One serving—Calories: 106; Total fat: 5.6 g; Saturated fat: 1.3 g; Cholesterol: 59 mg; Sodium: 90 mg; Carbohydrates: 11.8 g; Fiber: 0.6 g; Sugar: 7.5 g; Protein: 2.9 g

Chocolate Torte Glaze

2 ounces (2 squares) gluten-free
   semisweet chocolate

2 tablespoons butter

1 tablespoon light corn syrup

1 cup sifted confectioners' sugar

2 tablespoons hot water

Mix the chocolate, butter, and corn syrup in the top of a double boiler over simmering water. Stir in the sugar and hot water. *Makes 24 2-teaspoon servings.*

One serving—Calories: 45; Total fat: 1.7 g; Saturated fat: 0.4 g; Cholesterol: 3 mg; Sodium: 12 mg; Carbohydrates: 7.1 g; Fiber: 0.1 g; Sugar: 6.2 g; Protein: 0.1 g

Walnut Syrup Cake

Not overly sweet, this Grecian cake stays moist for several days if kept well covered.

½ cup butter, softened

¾ cup sugar

4 eggs

¾ cup Cream of Rice

3 teaspoons gluten-free baking powder

Dash salt

1 teaspoon cinnamon

1 tablespoon gluten-free mayonnaise

¼ cup milk

1 teaspoon vanilla

¾ cup finely chopped walnuts

Cinnamon Syrup (Recipe follows.)

Glazed Walnuts (Recipe follows.)

Preheat oven to 350°F, and grease a 9″ × 13″ baking pan. Cream the butter. Add the sugar, and continue beating till fluffy. Add the eggs slowly, and continue beating till light. Stir together the Cream of Rice, baking powder, salt, and cinnamon; add alternately to the butter mixture with the mayonnaise and milk. Add the vanilla, and beat till smooth. Fold in the walnuts. Pour into the greased pan, and bake 30 minutes or until a toothpick inserted in the center comes out clean. Remove from oven, and score the top of the cake into diamond-shaped pieces. Pour the warm Cinnamon Syrup slowly over the cake. When the cake is cool, cut it into the diamond-shaped pieces, and cover with foil. Allow the cake to set several hours for the syrup to be absorbed. Just before serving, place a glazed walnut half on each piece. *Makes 24 3- by 1¼-inch servings.*

Cinnamon Syrup

½ cup sugar

1 cinnamon stick

1 cup water

1 tablespoon orange juice

Combine the sugar, cinnamon stick, water, and orange juice in a saucepan; bring to a boil over medium heat, stirring constantly to dissolve the sugar. Let the mixture boil 10 minutes without stirring. Cool 5 minutes before pouring over the cake. *Makes 24 1-tablespoon servings.*

One serving (cake with syrup)—Calories: 121; Total fat: 7.6 g; Saturated fat: 0.7 g; Cholesterol: 46 mg; Sodium: 60 mg; Carbohydrates: 11.7 g; Fiber: 0.3 g; Sugar: 6.5 g; Protein: 2.2 g

Glazed Walnuts

2 cups sugar

1 cup water

1 pound walnut halves

Combine the sugar and water in a saucepan. Heat slowly, stirring constantly, until the sugar dissolves, then cook rapidly without stirring to 300°F (or until a few drops of syrup poured into a cup of cold water form hard, brittle threads that break when pressed). Remove the pan from the heat, and stir in the walnuts, ½ cup at a time; and toss to coat evenly. Remove the nuts from the syrup with two forks, and place them on wire racks lined with waxed paper. Cool until the glaze is firm. Store in an airtight metal tin. *Makes 24 3-tablespoon servings.*

One serving—Calories: 163; Total fat: 12.2 g; Saturated fat: 1.1 g; Cholesterol: 0 mg; Sodium: 1 mg; Carbohydrates: 12.6 g; Fiber: 1.2 g; Sugar: 10.1 g; Protein: 2.8 g

Orange Syrup Cake

This moist cake is best when baked early in the morning and eaten that evening.

½ pound butter, softened
¾ cup sugar
1 cup Cream of Rice
6 eggs
1 cup Gluten-Free Flour Mixture (See the Hints chapter.)
2½ tablespoons gluten-free baking powder
¼ teaspoon salt
Grated zest of 1 orange
⅔ cup orange juice
1 cup ground almonds
Orange Syrup (Recipe follows.)

Preheat oven to 350°F, and grease an 8″ × 12″ baking pan. Beat the butter and sugar together till creamy. Gradually add the Cream of Rice. Add the eggs, one at a time, beating well after each. Sift the flour mixture, baking powder, and salt; add to the mixture alternately with the orange zest and juice. Stir in the almonds. Pour into the greased pan; bake 30 minutes. Score the top of the cake lightly into diamond shapes. Pour the slightly cooled Orange Syrup slowly over the cake. When the cake is cool, cut into the diamond-shaped pieces, and cover with foil. Let the cake set several hours for the syrup to be absorbed. *Makes 12 3- by 4-inch servings.*

Orange Syrup

2 cups water
2 cups sugar
Juice of 1 orange

Mix the sugar and water together in a saucepan. Add the orange juice. Boil for 15 minutes or until the syrup is slightly thickened.

Cool 5 minutes before pouring slowly over the cake. *Makes 12 3-tablespoon servings.*

One serving (cake with syrup)—Calories: 441; Total fat: 22.7 g; Saturated fat: 1.1 g; Cholesterol: 146 mg; Sodium: 122 mg; Carbohydrates: 26.8 g; Fiber: 1.4 g; Sugar: 32.3 g; Protein: 3.4 g

Zucchini Cake

If you have any of this cake left over from the previous evening's dessert, try it sliced and toasted for breakfast.

1 cup corn oil

2 cups sugar

3 eggs

1 tablespoon gluten-free mayonnaise

2 cups grated zucchini (about 2 medium zucchini)

2¼ cups Gluten-Free Flour Mixture (See the Hints chapter.)

2¼ teaspoons baking soda

½ teaspoon gluten-free baking powder

¾ teaspoon salt

2 teaspoons cinnamon

2 teaspoons vanilla

1 cup chopped walnuts

Maple Butter Glaze (Recipe follows.)

Preheat oven to 350°F, and grease a 10-inch tube or Bundt pan. Beat the corn oil and sugar. Whip in the eggs, mayonnaise, and zucchini. Sift together the flour mixture, baking soda, baking powder, salt, and cinnamon; stir into the oil mixture. Stir in the vanilla and nuts. Pour the batter into the greased pan. Bake 1 hour or until a toothpick inserted in the center comes out clean. Cool in pan 20 minutes; invert onto a serving platter. Drizzle the Maple Butter Glaze over the cooled cake. *Makes 16 1⅛-inch-thick servings.*

Maple Butter Glaze

½ cup butter

2 cups sifted confectioners' sugar

2 tablespoons pure maple syrup

2–3 tablespoons hot water

Heat the butter in a saucepan over medium heat until golden. Remove from heat. Stir in the sugar and syrup. Stir in the hot water until the icing spreads smoothly. *Makes 16 1-teaspoon servings.*

One serving (cake with glaze)—Calories: 424; Total fat: 25.8 g; Saturated fat: 2.5 g; Cholesterol: 55 mg; Sodium: 190 mg; Carbohydrates: 45.6 g; Fiber: 1.2 g; Sugar: 31.4 g; Protein: 4.2 g

ℒemonade Cake

This light, refreshing cake makes an excellent base for other desserts.

4 large eggs

2 cups sugar

1 6-ounce can gluten-free frozen lemonade concentrate, thawed

1¼ cups milk

1 tablespoon gluten-free mayonnaise

2 tablespoons butter, softened

2 cups Gluten-Free Flour Mixture (See the Hints chapter.)

2½ teaspoons gluten-free baking powder

½ teaspoon salt

Lemonade Topping (Recipe follows.)

Preheat oven to 350°F, and grease a 9″ ×13″ baking pan. Beat the eggs until light and fluffy. Beat in the sugar, 1 tablespoon of the lemonade concentrate (reserving the remainder for the topping), and the milk, mayonnaise, and butter. Sift together the flour mixture, baking powder, and salt; blend into the egg mixture. Pour into the greased pan; bake 30 to 35 minutes till golden brown. Cool. Cut into squares, and serve with warm Lemonade Topping. *Makes 24 3- by 1½-inch servings.*

Lemonade Topping

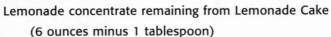

1 cup sugar

1½ tablespoons cornstarch

2 eggs

2 tablespoons butter

¼ teaspoon salt

Lemonade concentrate remaining from Lemonade Cake

    (6 ounces minus 1 tablespoon)

Combine all ingredients in a small, heavy saucepan. Cook, stirring, over medium heat till mixture thickens. *Makes 24 1½-tablespoon servings.*

One serving (cake with topping)—Calories: 149; Total fat: 2.9 g; Saturated fat: 0.7 g; Cholesterol: 57 mg; Sodium: 111 mg; Carbohydrates: 27.9 g; Fiber: 0.4 g; Sugar: 15.5 g; Protein: 3 g

*P*istachio Nut Cake

To cover the bare spots, pick up nuts with a wadded piece of damp paper towel, and press the nuts lightly to the side of the cake.

9 eggs, separated

¼ teaspoon salt

1 teaspoon cream of tartar

1 cup plus 2 tablespoons sugar

Grated zest of 1 orange

¼ cup frozen orange juice concentrate, thawed
1¾ cups Gluten-Free Flour Mixture (See the Hints chapter.)
⅔ cup chopped pistachios
Orange Filling (Recipe follows.)
Pistachio Frosting (Recipe follows.)

Preheat oven to 300°F, and lightly butter a 10-inch angel food cake pan. Beat the egg whites with the salt until foamy; add the cream of tartar, and beat till stiff peaks form. Add ⅔ cup of the sugar gradually, beating well after each addition. In a separate bowl, beat the egg yolks until very thick. Add the remaining ⅓ cup plus 2 tablespoons of sugar to the yolks, and beat well. Add the zest and juice to the yolk mixture, beating well. Fold the egg white mixture into the yolk mixture. Sift the flour mixture over the egg mixture, then fold in until blended. Fold in the nuts. Pour into the buttered pan, and bake 1 hour. Cool, inverted, on a cake rack. When cool, remove the cake, and cut it horizontally into three layers. Fill the layers with the Orange Filling; frost with the Pistachio Frosting. Refrigerate the cake 3 hours to set the frosting before serving. *Makes 16 1¼-inch-thick servings.*

One serving—Calories: 153; Total fat: 5.2 g; Saturated fat: 1.2 g; Cholesterol: 119 mg; Sodium: 72 mg; Carbohydrates: 20.8 g; Fiber: 1 g; Sugar: 8.1 g; Protein: 6.1 g

Orange Filling

1 egg
¾ cup sugar
Grated zest of 1 orange
Juice of 1 orange
1 tablespoon lemon juice
2½ tablespoons cornstarch
1½ cups (¾ pint) whipping cream

Beat the egg. Add the sugar, orange zest, and orange and lemon juices. Stir in the cornstarch. Cook in a double boiler over simmering water, stirring, until thick. Cool. Whip the cream until stiff peaks form. Fold into the cooled egg mixture. Spread between layers of Pistachio Nut Cake. *Makes 4 cups.*

One serving—Calories: 112; Total fat: 8.7 g; Saturated fat: 5.4 g; Cholesterol: 45 mg; Sodium: 14 mg; Carbohydrates: 7.8 g; Fiber: 0.01 g; Sugar: 6.2 g; Protein: 0.9 g

Pistachio Frosting

> 4 tablespoons butter, melted
> 3½ cups confectioners' sugar, sifted
> 2 tablespoons orange juice
> Grated zest of 1 orange
> 2 tablespoons light cream
> 2 cups ground pistachios

Pour the butter over the sugar; cream together. Add the orange juice and zest. Stir in the cream. Beat well to form a smooth frosting. Add more sugar if too thin or more cream if too thick. Frost the sides and top of a cake. Sprinkle the nuts over the top and sides of the cake, pressing them lightly into the frosting. *Makes 16 2½-tablespoon servings of frosting, plus 2 tablespoons nuts.*

One serving—Calories: 222; Total fat: 10.2 g; Saturated fat: 0.9 g; Cholesterol: 8 mg; Sodium: 33 mg; Carbohydrates: 30.9 g; Fiber: 1.6 g; Sugar: 26.8 g; Protein: 3.4 g

Carrot Cake

If you need to make a cake ahead of time, this is the cake to select because it will stay moist for several days.

> 2 cups Gluten-Free Flour Mixture (See the Hints chapter.)
> 3 teaspoons gluten-free baking powder

1¾ teaspoons baking soda

1 teaspoon salt

1 teaspoon cinnamon

2 cups sugar

¾ cup plus 2 tablespoons corn oil

4 eggs, slightly beaten

1 tablespoon gluten-free mayonnaise

2 cups grated carrots

½ cup chopped walnuts

1 8½-ounce can crushed pineapple, with juice

Cream Cheese Frosting (Recipe follows.)

Preheat oven to 350°F, and grease a 9″ × 13″ baking pan. In a large bowl, sift together the flour mixture, baking powder, baking soda, salt, and cinnamon. Add the sugar, corn oil, eggs, and mayonnaise; stir well. Stir in the carrots, nuts, and pineapple. Spread in the greased pan, and bake 30 minutes or till a toothpick inserted in the center comes out clean. Cool; frost with the Cream Cheese Frosting. *Makes 18 3- by 2¼-inch servings.*

One serving—Calories: 220; Total fat: 14.2 g; Saturated fat: 1.9 g; Cholesterol: 47 mg; Sodium: 156 mg; Carbohydrates: 21 g; Fiber: 0.8 g; Sugar: 14.8 g; Protein: 2.7 g

Cream Cheese Frosting

½ cup butter, softened

8 ounces gluten-free cream cheese, softened

2 cups confectioners' sugar

1 teaspoon vanilla

Whip all ingredients together till fluffy. If the frosting is too thick, add a few drops of milk. *Makes 18 3-tablespoon servings.*

One serving—Calories: 143; Total fat: 9.7 g; Saturated fat: 2.8 g; Cholesterol: 27 mg; Sodium: 91 mg; Carbohydrates: 13.7 g; Fiber: 0 g; Sugar: 13.2 g; Protein: 0.7 g

Sugar Sponge Cake

This cake is used as a base for many other desserts throughout this book.

    6 eggs, separated
    ½ teaspoon cream of tartar
    1½ cups sugar
    ½ cup water
    1 teaspoon vanilla
    1¼ cups Gluten-Free Flour Mixture (See the Hints chapter.)
    Pinch salt
    Butterscotch Honey Topping (Recipe follows.)

Preheat oven to 325°F, and grease a 10-inch tube pan or a 9″ × 13″ baking pan. Beat the egg whites with the cream of tartar until stiff peaks form. Cook the sugar and water in a small saucepan over medium heat until it threads. (This only takes a few minutes; watch closely so it doesn't start to crystallize.) Slowly pour the sugar water over the egg whites, beating constantly. In a small bowl, beat the egg yolks until thick; add the vanilla, and fold into the egg whites. Sift together the flour mixture and salt; carefully fold into the egg white mixture. Pour into the greased pan, and bake 1 hour for a 10-inch tube pan or 35 to 40 minutes for the rectangular pan, or until a toothpick inserted in the center comes out clean. To serve, spoon the Butterscotch Honey Topping (warm or cold) over slices of cake. *Makes 18 1¼-inch-thick or 3- by 2-inch servings.*

One serving—Calories: 93; Total fat: 1.7 g; Saturated fat: 0.5 g; Cholesterol: 71 mg; Sodium: 21.3 mg; Carbohydrates: 16.3 g; Fiber: 0.3 g; Sugar: 9.9 g; Protein: 2.9 g

Butterscotch Honey Topping

This topping is also terrific over gluten-free chocolate ice cream with toasted almonds sprinkled on top.

¼ cup sugar

¾ cup honey

¼ cup butter

¼ teaspoon salt

⅔ cup evaporated milk

Combine the sugar, honey, butter, salt, and ⅓ cup of the milk in a saucepan. Cook over medium heat, stirring frequently, to soft-ball stage (238°F). Stir in the remaining ⅓ cup of milk; cook over medium heat until thick and smooth, about 3 minutes. Serve hot or cold. *Makes 18 4-teaspoon servings.*

One serving—Calories: 80; Total fat: 2.7 g; Saturated fat: 0 g; Cholesterol: 7 mg; Sodium: 71 mg; Carbohydrates: 14.2 g; Fiber: 0 g; Sugar: 13.4 g; Protein: 0.7 g

𝒫umpkin Ring

For a finishing touch, drizzle the top of this cake with a confectioners' sugar glaze to which you add a hint of cinnamon.

1½ cups Gluten-Free Flour Mixture (See the Hints chapter.)

¾ teaspoon salt

¼ teaspoon gluten-free baking powder

1¼ teaspoons baking soda

¼ teaspoon cloves

½ teaspoon cinnamon

1 cup sugar

1 large egg

⅓ cup butter, melted

1 tablespoon gluten-free mayonnaise

⅓ cup plus 2 tablespoons water

1 cup canned pumpkin

½ cup chopped nuts

⅔ cup raisins

Preheat oven to 350°F, and grease a 10-inch angel food cake pan or Bundt cake pan. Sift the flour mixture, salt, baking powder, baking soda, cloves, and cinnamon into a large bowl. Add the sugar, egg, butter, mayonnaise, water, and pumpkin; beat till blended. Stir in the nuts and raisins. Pour the batter into the greased pan, and bake 40 minutes or till a toothpick inserted in the center comes out clean. Invert the pan, and cool on a rack. *Makes 16 1¼-inch-thick servings.*

One serving—Calories: 132; Total fat: 4.4 g; Saturated fat: 0.4 g; Cholesterol: 16 mg; Sodium: 136 mg; Carbohydrates: 20 g; Fiber: 1.2 g; Sugar: 11.3 g; Protein: 2.8 g

Orange Almond Cake

Ground almonds and eggs are the base for this totally flour-free cake.

6 eggs

1½ cups finely ground almonds

1 cup granulated sugar

Pinch salt

1 teaspoon gluten-free baking powder

1 teaspoon cinnamon

½ cup orange juice

3 tablespoons confectioners' sugar

Fresh orange slices

Preheat oven to 350°F, and grease a 9-inch springform pan. Beat the eggs until thick. Add the almonds, granulated sugar, salt, baking powder, cinnamon, and orange juice; mix well. Pour the batter into the greased pan; bake 35 minutes or until firm to the touch. Cool. Remove the sides of the pan. Sift the confectioners' sugar over the top of the cake, and garnish with orange slices. *Makes 16 1-inch-thick servings.*

One serving—Calories: 121; Total fat: 6.4 g; Saturated fat: 1 g; Cholesterol: 79 mg; Sodium: 25 mg; Carbohydrates: 12.1 g; Fiber: 1 g; Sugar: 10.3 g; Protein: 4.3 g

Mandarin Cake

Mandarin oranges are blended right into the cake batter to give you a moist, tender cake with a taste of the tropics.

1 ⅓ cups Gluten-Free Flour Mixture (See the Hints chapter.)
½ teaspoon salt
1 ¼ teaspoons baking soda
½ teaspoon cinnamon
1 cup sugar
1 11-ounce can mandarin oranges, drained well
1 egg
⅔ cup ground walnuts
Glazed Topping (Recipe follows.)

Preheat oven to 350°F, and grease a 9-inch square pan. Sift into a large bowl the flour mixture, salt, baking soda, cinnamon, and sugar. Add the oranges and egg; whip 3 minutes. Stir in the nuts. Pour the batter into the greased pan, and bake 25 to 30 minutes or till a toothpick inserted in the center comes out clean. While the cake is still warm, pour the Glazed Topping over the cake. Cool on a wire rack. *Makes 9 3-inch-square servings.*

Glazed Topping

¾ cup light brown sugar
3 tablespoons butter
3 tablespoons milk

Combine all the ingredients in a saucepan, and bring to a boil. Boil 2 minutes. *Makes 9 2-tablespoon servings.*

One serving (cake with topping)—Calories: 249; Total fat: 9 g; Saturated fat: 0.6 g; Cholesterol: 34 mg; Sodium: 184 mg; Carbohydrates: 40.9 g; Fiber: 1.3 g; Sugar: 27.4 g; Protein: 3.3 g

Chocoholic's Dream

The name speaks for itself. When you sit down to enjoy this dessert, forget counting cholesterol or calories!

2½ ounces (2½ squares) gluten-free unsweetened chocolate

3 eggs, separated

⅓ cup sugar

½ cup butter, softened

1 teaspoon vanilla

7 tablespoons Gluten-Free Flour Mixture
    (See the Hints chapter.)

Decadent Filling (Recipe follows.)

Decadent Glaze (Recipe follows.)

Preheat oven to 350°F, and grease two 9-inch round cake pans. Line the bottoms with waxed paper, and grease the paper. Melt the chocolate in a small bowl placed over hot water; cool to luke-warm. Whip the egg whites until foamy. Beat in 3 tablespoons of the sugar, 1 tablespoon at a time, until the meringue forms soft peaks. Beat the butter in another bowl until creamy; whip in the remaining 2⅓ tablespoons of sugar and the egg yolks until fluffy. Beat in the vanilla and cooled chocolate. Sift the flour mixture, then stir into the butter mixture. With a whisk, fold in the meringue, one-third at a time, until no streaks of white remain. Divide the batter evenly into the prepared pans, and smooth the tops. Bake 15 minutes or until the centers spring back when lightly pressed with a fingertip. (The cake layers will be very thin.)

Cool in the pans for 10 minutes; remove from pans, and cool completely on wire racks. Wrap and chill the layers for 1 hour. Place a cake layer on a cookie sheet; spoon Decadent Filling over the top. Top with the second layer, pressing down on the top lightly. Smooth the sides with a spatula. Chill again before glazing. Decorate with the Decadent Glaze. *Makes 12 1¼-inch-thick servings.*

One serving—Calories: 146; Total fat: 11.2 g; Saturated fat: 2.3 g; Cholesterol: 68 mg; Sodium: 97 mg; Carbohydrates: 8.1 g; Fiber: 1 g; Sugar: 3.1 g; Protein: 2.6 g

Decadent Filling

    8 ounces (8 squares) gluten-free semisweet chocolate

    2 ounces (2 squares) gluten-free unsweetened chocolate

    1 cup whipping cream

    ¼ teaspoon vanilla

Chop the chocolates coarsely; place in a saucepan with the cream. Cook, stirring constantly, over medium heat until the chocolate melts and the mixture *just* comes to a boil. Pour into a bowl, and stir in the vanilla. Cool, stirring frequently; refrigerate until the mixture starts to thicken and set, about 45 minutes. Beat the mixture at high speed until it is fluffy and double in volume, about 3 to 5 minutes. *Makes 3 cups.*

One serving—Calories: 184; Total fat: 15.7 g; Saturated fat: 9.5 g; Cholesterol: 28 mg; Sodium: 11 mg; Carbohydrates: 13.7 g; Fiber: 1.8 g; Sugar: 11.2 g; Protein: 1.7 g

Decadent Glaze

    4 ounces (4 squares) gluten-free semisweet chocolate

    ½ cup whipping cream

    3 teaspoons hot gluten-free coffee

    2 tablespoons butter, softened

    3 tablespoons chopped pistachios

Heat the chocolate, cream, and coffee in a small pan over low heat, stirring constantly, until the chocolate is melted and the mixture just comes to a boil. Remove from heat; cool to lukewarm. Add a little more hot coffee if too thick or the mixture separates. Transfer the chilled cake to a rack over a pan to catch excess glaze. Spread the glaze over the cake with a spatula, letting the glaze run down the sides of the cake to coat it completely. Chill the cake until the glaze is set, about 1 hour. Place the cake on a serving platter. Beat the butter with the excess chocolate glaze until stiff enough to pipe onto the cake. Chill for 15 minutes. Spoon into a pastry bag, and pipe small rosettes in circles over the center of the cake. Sprinkle the pistachios around the outside of the rosette circle. *Makes 12 2-tablespoon servings.*

One serving—Calories: 160; Total fat: 15.2 g; Saturated fat: 4.1 g; Cholesterol: 34 mg; Sodium: 85 mg; Carbohydrates: 6.7 g; Fiber: 0.7 g; Sugar: 5.8 g; Protein: 0.9 g

Chocolate Spice Chiffon Cake

This flourless cake is an excellent base for Trifle (see Chapter 8), or top it with sliced fresh strawberries and chocolate sauce.

- ¾ cup butter
- 12 ounces gluten-free bittersweet chocolate
- 2 tablespoons unsweetened cocoa
- ¼ teaspoon cinnamon
- ⅛ teaspoon nutmeg
- ⅛ teaspoon ground cloves
- 10 eggs, at room temperature
- ¾ cup sugar

Preheat oven to 350°F. Grease a 10-inch springform pan, and cut parchment to fit the sides and bottom. Butter the parchment once it is in the pan, then dust with cornstarch. Melt the butter in a small pan. Remove from heat, and stir in the chocolate, cocoa, cinnamon, nutmeg, and cloves until well blended. Set aside to cool. Separate the eggs. In a large bowl, whip the egg whites until frothy. Add the sugar slowly, and continue beating until stiff peaks form. Whisk the egg yolks into the cooled chocolate mixture, then gently fold into the egg whites until thoroughly blended. Pour the batter into the pan, and bake 40 minutes or until the center is almost set. (The top may begin to crack slightly.) Do not overbake. Cool the cake on a wire rack. *Makes 16 1¼-inch-thick servings.*

One serving—Calories: 259; Total fat: 30.2 g; Saturated fat: 7.9 g; Cholesterol: 155 mg; Sodium: 132 mg; Carbohydrates: 12.3 g; Fiber: 3.4 g; Sugar: 5.4 g; Protein: 6.2 g

Mississippi Mud Cake

Cocoa, coconut, pecans, and marshmallow creme all in one bite—life doesn't get any better than this!

> 5 eggs
> 2 teaspoons gluten-free mayonnaise
> 2 cups sugar
> 1½ cups Gluten-Free Flour Mixture (See the Hints chapter.)
> ⅓ cup unsweetened cocoa
> 1 cup butter, melted
> 1 teaspoon vanilla
> 1 cup flaked coconut
> ½ cup chopped pecans
> 1 7-ounce jar gluten-free marshmallow creme
> Sugared Cocoa Icing (Recipe follows.)

Preheat oven to 350°F, and grease a 9″ × 13″ baking pan. Beat the eggs and mayonnaise until thickened. Gradually beat in the sugar. Sift together the flour mixture and cocoa into a large bowl. Stir the melted butter, vanilla, coconut, and pecans into the dry ingredients; add to the egg mixture, and stir well. Pour the batter into the greased pan, and bake 35 minutes or until a toothpick inserted in the center comes out clean. Remove the cake from the oven, and immediately spread with the marshmallow creme. Prepare the Sugared Cocoa Icing and spread over the warm marshmallow creme layer. *Makes 18 3- by 2-inch servings.*

Sugared Cocoa Icing

½ cup butter, melted

⅓ cup unsweetened cocoa

1 teaspoon vanilla

6 tablespoons milk

1 pound (4 cups) sifted confectioners' sugar

Stir together all ingredients in a bowl until smooth. *Makes 18 3¾-tablespoon servings.*

One serving (cake with icing)—Calories: 425; Total fat: 20.6 g; Saturated fat: 2.4 g; Cholesterol: 93 mg; Sodium: 173 mg; Carbohydrates: 59.3 g; Fiber: 2.1 g; Sugar: 44.5 g; Protein: 3.9 g

Sweet Cream Cake

If you have your own favorite filling recipe, try spreading it between the layers of this white cake.

2 eggs

1 cup plus 1 tablespoon sugar

1 teaspoon vanilla

1 tablespoon gluten-free mayonnaise

1¾ cups Gluten-Free Flour Mixture (See the Hints chapter.)
¼ teaspoon salt
2 teaspoons gluten-free baking powder
1 cup whipping cream
1 teaspoon cinnamon
Cocoa Buttercream Filling (Recipe follows.)

Preheat oven to 350°F, and generously grease two 9-inch round cake pans. Beat the eggs until thick. Gradually beat in 1 cup of the sugar. Blend in the vanilla and mayonnaise. Sift the flour mixture, salt, and baking powder; add alternately with the cream to the egg mixture. Pour the batter into the greased pans, and bake 25 minutes or until a toothpick inserted in the center comes out clean. While the cake is baking, stir together the remaining 1 tablespoon of sugar and the cinnamon. Sprinkle the cinnamon sugar over one of the layers 5 minutes before the cake is done baking and continue to bake till done. Let layers cool in pans for 5 minutes, then remove cakes to a wire rack to finish cooling. When the cake is cool, place the plain layer on a serving dish, and spread with the Cocoa Buttercream Filling. Place the cinnamon-sugar layer on top. *Makes 1¾ cups.*

One serving—Calories: 194; Total fat: 8.7 g; Saturated fat: 5 g; Cholesterol: 63 mg; Sodium: 78 mg; Carbohydrates: 26.1 g; Fiber: 0.6 g; Sugar: 14.1 g; Protein: 3.2 g

Cocoa Buttercream Filling

6 tablespoons butter, softened
½ cup unsweetened cocoa
¾ cup sifted confectioners' sugar
⅓ cup milk
1 teaspoon vanilla

Cream the butter until fluffy. Sift together the cocoa and sugar; add to the butter alternately with the milk. Add the vanilla. Whip till light and of spreading consistency. *Makes 1¾ cups.*

One serving—Calories: 95; Total fat: 6.7 g; Saturated fat: 0.4 g; Cholesterol: 16 mg; Sodium: 65 mg; Carbohydrates: 9.8 g; Fiber: 1.2 g; Sugar: 7.6 g; Protein: 0.9 g

Lemon Pudding Cake

This combination of cake and pudding is sweet enough that it doesn't need a frosting.

    1 ½ tablespoons butter, softened

    ¾ cup granulated sugar

    2 teaspoons grated lemon zest

    1 teaspoon gluten-free mayonnaise

    3 eggs, separated

    3 tablespoons Gluten-Free Flour Mixture (See the Hints chapter.)

    ½ teaspoon cornstarch

    Pinch salt

    ¼ cup freshly squeezed lemon juice

    1 cup milk

    3 tablespoons confectioners' sugar, sifted

Preheat oven to 350°F, and grease a 1-quart casserole. Cream the butter with the granulated sugar until fluffy. Whip in the lemon zest and mayonnaise. Add the egg yolks, one at a time, beating well after each. Sift the flour mixture, cornstarch, and salt into a separate bowl; add to the butter mixture alternately with the lemon juice and milk. With clean, dry beaters, whip the egg whites and salt until stiff peaks form; fold into the batter. Pour the batter into the buttered casserole, and place the casserole in a pan of hot water. Bake 1 hour or until no imprint remains when the top of the cake is touched gently. Dust the top of the cooled cake with the sifted confectioners' sugar. *Makes 6 ⅓-cup servings.*

One serving—Calories: 182; Total fat: 6.8 g; Saturated fat: 1.7 g; Cholesterol: 119 mg; Sodium: 87 mg; Carbohydrates: 22.7 g; Fiber: 0.1 g; Sugar: 18 g; Protein: 4.9 g

Cherry-Chocolate Charm

White chocolate is the secret ingredient that makes this cake so magical.

¼ cup butter, softened

¾ cup sugar

1 tablespoon gluten-free mayonnaise

1 egg

1 tablespoon gluten-free light rum

1 cup Gluten-Free Flour Mixture (See the Hints chapter.)

¼ teaspoon salt

¾ teaspoon baking soda

⅓ cup unsweetened cocoa

½ cup buttermilk

1 16-ounce can gluten-free cherry pie filling

½ cup coarsely grated white chocolate

Chocolate Frosting (Recipe follows.)

Preheat oven to 350°F, and grease a 9-inch round cake pan. Cream the butter and sugar till fluffy. Whip in the mayonnaise and egg well; blend in the rum. Sift together the flour mixture, salt, baking soda, and cocoa; add to the butter mixture alternately with the buttermilk. Stir in 1 cup of the pie filling and ¼ cup of the white chocolate. Pour into the greased pan, and bake 30 to 35 minutes or until a toothpick inserted in the center comes out clean. Cool the cake in the pan for 10 minutes; remove from the pan, and cool on a wire rack. Place the cake on a serving plate. Frost the sides and top with the Chocolate Frosting. Spoon the remaining pie filling in the center of the top; sprinkle with the remaining ¼ cup of white chocolate. *Makes 9 1¾-inch-thick servings.*

One serving—Calories: 288; Total fat: 10.2 g; Saturated fat: 2.4 g; Cholesterol: 39 mg; Sodium: 168 mg; Carbohydrates: 46.5 g; Fiber: 1.9 g; Sugar: 15.9 g; Protein: 3.9 g

Chocolate Frosting

> 1 ounce (1 square) gluten-free unsweetened chocolate
>
> 2 tablespoons butter
>
> 2 tablespoons milk
>
> 1 cup sifted confectioners' sugar
>
> ½ teaspoon vanilla

Place the chocolate and butter in the top of a double boiler. Heat over hot water (not boiling) until the chocolate is melted. Stir in the milk and sugar until well mixed. Cover and continue to cook 10 minutes. Remove from heat, and stir in the vanilla. Beat until glossy. If too thin, add a little more confectioners' sugar. If too thick, add a few drops of milk. *Makes 9 2½-tablespoon servings.*

One serving—Calories: 95; Total fat: 4.5 g; Saturated fat: 1.1 g; Cholesterol: 7 mg; Sodium: 30 mg; Carbohydrates: 14.4 g; Fiber: 0.5 g; Sugar: 13 g; Protein: 0.4 g

Filled Chocolate Chiffon Mousse Cake

To ensure proper volume and consistency, let the eggs warm to room temperature 1 hour before whipping them. Save the scooped-out cake pieces and let them air-dry overnight; then place them in a blender and make cake crumbs to be used in a pie crust or to sprinkle on puddings and ice cream.

> ½ cup sifted unsweetened cocoa
>
> ¾ cup boiling water
>
> 1¾ cups Gluten-Free Flour Mixture (See the Hints chapter.)
>
> 1¾ cups sugar
>
> 2¼ teaspoons baking soda
>
> ½ teaspoon salt
>
> 8 eggs, separated
>
> ½ cup corn oil
>
> 1 tablespoon gluten-free mayonnaise

2 teaspoons vanilla

½ teaspoon cream of tartar

Chocolate Mousse Filling (Recipe follows.)

Put the cocoa in a bowl, and stir in the boiling water till smooth; cool 30 minutes. Preheat oven to 325°F. Sift together the flour mixture, sugar, baking soda, and salt. Make a well in the center of the dry ingredients, and pour in the egg yolks, corn oil, mayonnaise, vanilla, and cocoa. Beat with a wooden spoon just till smooth. Beat the egg whites and cream of tartar until very stiff peaks form. (Do not underbeat.) Pour the batter over the egg whites; with a wire whisk, gently fold to combine. Turn the batter into an ungreased 10-inch tube pan. Bake 1 hour or until the top springs back when pressed with a finger. Invert over the neck of a bottle; cool 1½ hours. With a knife, loosen the sides of the cake, and remove from pan. Cool on a wire rack. Cut a 1-inch horizontal slice from the top of the cake; set aside. With a sharp knife, cut a cavity in the cake, leaving 1-inch-thick walls around the center, side, and bottom. With a spoon, very carefully remove cake from the inside of this area. Fill the cake cavity with 2½ cups of the Chocolate Mousse Filling. Replace the top of the cake. Frost the top and sides of the cake with the remaining filling. *Makes 16 1¼-inch-thick servings.*

One serving—Calories: 203; Total fat: 10 g; Saturated fat: 1.9 g; Cholesterol: 106 mg; Sodium: 113 mg; Carbohydrates: 24.6 g; Fiber: 1.3 g; Sugar: 13.2 g; Protein: 5 g

Chocolate Mousse Filling

¾ cup unsweetened cocoa

1½ cups confectioners' sugar

3 cups heavy cream

2 teaspoons vanilla

¼ teaspoon salt

1 teaspoon unflavored gelatin

Sift together the cocoa and sugar. Stir in the cream, vanilla, and salt. Refrigerate 1 hour. Sprinkle the gelatin over 1 tablespoon of cold water to soften. Heat, stirring, over hot water to dissolve; cool. Remove the cream mixture from the refrigerator; add the gelatin, and whip until stiff; refrigerate again for 45 minutes. *Makes 5 cups.*

One serving—Calories: 210; Total fat: 17.3 g; Saturated fat: 10.8 g; Cholesterol: 63 mg; Sodium: 56 mg; Carbohydrates: 14.7 g; Fiber: 1.3 g; Sugar: 12.1 g; Protein: 1.8 g

Fruit Sponge Cake

Colorful assorted fruits may include mandarin oranges, sliced strawberries, kiwi, peaches, grapes, and blueberries. If you use any canned fruit, drain it thoroughly before placing it on the cake.

> 2 eggs
>
> ⅓ cup sugar
>
> ¼ teaspoon salt
>
> 5 tablespoons Gluten-Free Flour Mixture (See the Hints chapter.)
>
> ¼ cup cornstarch
>
> 2 cups assorted fruit
>
> Apple Glaze (Recipe follows.)

Preheat oven to 350°F, and grease a 9-inch round cake pan. Line with waxed paper, then grease the waxed paper. Beat the eggs until fluffy. Gradually add the sugar and salt; beat until the mixture is double in bulk and mounds slightly (about 5 minutes). Sift the flour mixture and cornstarch over the egg mixture, and fold in. Pour the batter into the prepared pan, and bake 25 minutes or until the cake springs back when lightly touched. Cool 10 minutes; remove from the pan, and cool completely on a wire rack. Place on a serving plate. Arrange the fruit on the cake. Spoon the Apple Glaze evenly over the fruit. Let set 30 minutes. *Makes 8 2-inch-thick servings.*

One serving (varies somewhat, depending on the fruit used)—Calories: 84; Total fat: 1.4 g; Saturated fat: 0.4 g; Cholesterol: 53 mg; Sodium: 91 mg; Carbohydrates: 15.6 g; Fiber: 1 g; Sugar: 6.8 g; Protein: 2.3 g

Apple Glaze

- 1 tablespoon cornstarch
- 1 tablespoon lemon juice
- 1 cup apple juice
- 2 tablespoons sifted confectioners' sugar

Put all the ingredients in a small saucepan. Bring to a boil, stirring constantly, and boil 1 minute. Cool to room temperature. *Makes 8 2½-tablespoon servings.*

One serving—Calories: 25; Total fat: 0 g; Saturated fat: 0 g; Cholesterol: 0 mg; Sodium: 3 mg; Carbohydrates: 6.4 g; Fiber: 0 g; Sugar: 5.1 g; Protein: 0 g

*D*ate Nut Cake

This dessert is low in cholesterol and dairy free. For best results, use a porous gluten-free bread.

- 3 egg whites
- 1 cup sugar
- 1 teaspoon vanilla
- 3 slices gluten-free bread, diced into ¼-inch cubes
- ⅔ cup mini semisweet chocolate chips
- 1 cup chopped walnuts
- ¾ cup chopped dates

Preheat oven to 325°F, and spray an 8″ × 12″ baking pan with gluten-free cooking spray. Beat the egg whites till soft peaks form. Gradually add the sugar, then the vanilla. Beat until stiff but not dry. Fold in the bread, chocolate chips, walnuts, and dates. Spread the batter in the greased pan, and bake 20 minutes or until lightly browned. Do not overbake. Cool. If desired, top each serving with a scoop of gluten-free vanilla ice cream. *Makes 12 2-inch-square servings.*

One serving—Calories: 184; Total fat: 8.2 g; Saturated fat: 1.5 g; Cholesterol: 0 mg; Sodium: 41 mg; Carbohydrates: 27.1 g; Fiber: 1.9 g; Sugar: 13 g; Protein: 3.3 g

Fresh Apple Pound Cake

By selecting baking apples (such as Rome or Golden Delicious), you will assure that your cake is moist.

   1 cup butter, softened

   2 cups sugar

   4 eggs

   1 tablespoon gluten-free mayonnaise

   1 teaspoon vanilla

   3 cups Gluten-Free Flour Mixture (See the Hints chapter.)

   1½ teaspoons cinnamon

   1 teaspoon allspice

   ½ teaspoon nutmeg

   ½ teaspoon salt

   2 teaspoons baking soda

   ¾ cup buttermilk

   1 cup peeled, minced baking apples

   ¾ cup chopped pecans

   Apple Icing (Recipe follows.)

Preheat oven to 325°F, and grease a 10-inch tube pan. Cream the butter and sugar. Add the eggs, one at a time, beating well after each addition. Whip in the mayonnaise and vanilla. In a separate bowl, sift together the flour mixture, cinnamon, allspice, nutmeg, salt, and baking soda. Add the dry ingredients alternately with the buttermilk to the butter mixture. Beat till smooth. Stir in the apples and nuts till blended. Pour into the greased pan, and bake 1¼ hours or till a toothpick inserted in the center comes out clean. (Do not overbake.) Let the cake set in the pan 10 minutes; remove to a wire rack to cool. Spread with Apple Icing while cake is still warm. *Makes 16 1¼-inch-thick servings.*

One serving—Calories: 311; Total fat: 17.9 g; Saturated fat: 0.8 g; Cholesterol: 83 mg; Sodium: 224 mg; Carbohydrates: 34 g; Fiber: 1.5 g; Sugar: 16.5 g; Protein: 4.8 g

Apple Icing

1 cup sugar

½ cup water

1 tablespoon butter

¼ cup grated apples

½ teaspoon vanilla

½ teaspoon cinnamon

Combine all the ingredients in a saucepan, and bring slowly to a boil, stirring constantly. Boil 1 minute. Spread over a warm cake. *Makes 16 2-tablespoon servings.*

One serving—Calories: 38; Total fat: 0.7 g; Saturated fat: 0 g; Cholesterol: 2 mg; Sodium: 8 mg; Carbohydrates: 7.7 g; Fiber: 1.1 g; Sugar: 7.5 g; Protein: 0 g

Chocolate Almond Torte

Instead of flour, finely ground almonds and cornflakes serve as a base for this torte.

5 eggs, separated

⅛ teaspoon salt

½ cup granulated sugar

¼ teaspoon cinnamon

2 cups ground almonds

¼ cup ground gluten-free cornflakes

2 ounces (2 squares) gluten-free semisweet chocolate, grated

1 tablespoon grated lemon zest

Chocolate Glaze (Recipe follows.)

50 blanched whole almonds

1 cup whipping cream

¼ cup confectioners' sugar

Allow the egg whites to come to room temperature. Preheat oven to 350°F, and grease a 9″ × 5″ loaf pan. Whip the egg whites with the salt till soft peaks form. In a separate bowl, beat the egg yolks until thick; gradually add the granulated sugar and cinnamon, beating until the mixture is smooth and well blended. Gently fold the egg yolk mixture, ground almonds, cornflakes, chocolate, and lemon zest into the egg whites just until blended. Pour into the greased pan, and bake 45 minutes or until the cake is golden and springs back when gently pressed with a fingertip. Cool 10 minutes; loosen the edges with a knife. Turn the cake out on a wire rack to cool completely. Place the cake on a serving plate; spoon the Chocolate Glaze evenly over the cake. Press the whole almonds upright onto the top of the cake, 5 almonds across, 10 lengthwise. Refrigerate, covered, until serving time. Whip together the cream and confectioners' sugar till fairly firm peaks form. To serve, slice the loaf so that each serving has a row of almonds and spoon a dollop of the whipped cream on each slice. *Makes 10 1-inch-thick servings.*

One serving—Calories: 369; Total fat: 28.8 g; Saturated fat: 8.5 g; Cholesterol: 140 mg; Sodium: 85 mg; Carbohydrates: 21 g; Fiber: 4 g; Sugar: 15.3 g; Protein: 11.6 g

Chocolate Glaze

2 tablespoons unsweetened cocoa

1 tablespoon plus 2 teaspoons water

1 tablespoon corn oil

1 tablespoon light corn syrup

1 cup confectioners' sugar, sifted

Combine the cocoa, water, corn oil, and corn syrup in a saucepan. Cook, stirring constantly, over low heat till smooth. Remove from heat. Beat in the sugar till smooth. *Makes 10 2-tablespoon servings.*

One serving—Calories: 68; Total fat: 1.5 g; Saturated fat: 1.3 g; Cholesterol: 0 mg; Sodium: 3 mg; Carbohydrates: 14 g; Fiber: 0.3 g; Sugar: 11.6 g; Protein: 0.2 g

Cinnamon Chocolate Cake

The light texture of this cake is from pecan meal instead of flour.

2 cups chopped pecans

½ cup melted butter

1¼ cups granulated sugar

¼ cup unsweetened cocoa

¼ plus ⅛ teaspoon cinnamon

¾ teaspoon gluten-free baking powder

4 eggs

1 teaspoon vanilla

¼ cup confectioners' sugar

Preheat oven to 350°F, and grease a 9-inch springform pan. Place the pecans in a food processor or blender, and process until very fine. Add the butter, granulated sugar, cocoa, ¼ teaspoon of the cinnamon, the baking powder, eggs, and vanilla; process 30 seconds. Scrape down the sides, and process another 30 seconds. Pour the batter into the greased pan, and bake 40 minutes or until a toothpick inserted in the center comes out clean. Let cool 15 minutes; removes the sides of the pan, and let the cake cool on a rack. When cooled, place a paper doily over the top of the cake. Combine the confectioners' sugar and cinnamon, and sift over the top of the cake; remove the doily. *Makes 12 1¼-inch-thick servings.*

One serving—Calories: 291; Total fat: 23.8 g; Saturated fat: 1.8 g; Cholesterol: 73 mg; Sodium: 102 mg; Carbohydrates: 18.4 g; Fiber: 2.5 g; Sugar: 15.3 g; Protein: 4 g

⒪range Sponge Cake

To achieve the right consistency, be sure the eggs are at room temperature before you prepare this cake.

    7 eggs, separated
    1¾ cups Gluten-Free Flour Mixture (See the Hints chapter.)
    ½ teaspoon salt
    1½ cups granulated sugar
    1 tablespoon grated orange zest
    2 tablespoons plus 1 teaspoon orange juice
    2 tablespoons confectioners' sugar

Place the egg whites in a large bowl and the yolks in a small bowl; let the egg whites come to room temperature. Preheat oven to 350°F, and very lightly grease a 10-inch tube pan. Sift the flour mixture with the salt. Beat the egg whites until foamy. Gradually beat in ½ cup of the granulated sugar; continue beating until soft peaks form; set aside. Beat the egg yolks at high speed until slightly thickened and paler; gradually beat in the remaining 1 cup of granulated sugar. Continue beating on low speed until very thick. Add the orange zest and juice; mix just until combined. Blend in the flour mixture just until combined. With a wire whisk, fold the yolk mixture into the egg whites until well blended. Pour the batter into the greased pan, and bake 35 minutes or till a toothpick inserted in the center comes out clean. Invert the pan, and let cool 1 hour. Loosen the edges of the cake from the pan with a knife, and unmold. Sprinkle the top with confectioners' sugar. *Makes 12 1⅓-inch-thick servings.*

One serving—Calories: 230; Total fat: 3 g; Saturated fat: 0.9 g; Cholesterol: 124 mg; Sodium: 136 mg; Carbohydrates: 30 g; Fiber: 0.7 g; Sugar: 16.8 g; Protein: 5.4 g

Apple Pie Cake

The canned pie filling helps keep this cake moist and tender.

1 21-ounce can gluten-free apple pie filling

½ cup corn oil

2 eggs, slightly beaten

1 teaspoon vanilla

1 cup granulated sugar

2 cups Gluten-Free Flour Mixture (See the Hints chapter.)

1 teaspoon cinnamon

1¼ teaspoons gluten-free baking powder

1 teaspoon baking soda

⅛ teaspoon salt

½ cup chopped walnuts

½ cup raisins

3 tablespoons confectioners' sugar, sifted

Preheat oven to 325°F, and grease a 9-inch round cake pan. Stir together the pie filling, corn oil, eggs, and vanilla. Sift the sugar, flour mixture, cinnamon, baking powder, baking soda, and salt; stir into the apple mixture, blending well. Stir in the walnuts and raisins. Pour the batter into the greased pan, and bake about 1 hour or until a toothpick inserted in the center comes out clean. Let the cake cool, and sprinkle the top with the confectioners' sugar. *Makes 8 2-inch-thick servings.*

One serving—Calories: 470; Total fat: 19.8 g; Saturated fat: 2.6 g; Cholesterol: 53 mg; Sodium: 89 mg; Carbohydrates: 69.1 g; Fiber: 2.7 g; Sugar: 26.6 g; Protein: 6.1 g

Peanut Butter Cupcakes

If you love the taste of chocolate with peanut butter, add ½ cup of mini semisweet chocolate chips to the batter before baking.

¼ cup gluten-free peanut butter

¼ cup butter, softened

2 teaspoons gluten-free mayonnaise

¾ cup light brown sugar

1 egg

¼ teaspoon salt

½ teaspoon vanilla

1 cup Gluten-Free Flour Mixture (See the Hints chapter.)

1 ½ teaspoons gluten-free baking powder

½ cup milk

Creamy Frosting (Recipe follows.)

Preheat oven to 375°F. Cream the peanut butter, butter, and mayonnaise till fluffy. Beat in the brown sugar, egg, salt, and vanilla. Sift together the flour mixture and baking powder; add alternately with the milk to the butter mixture. Place paper baking cups in muffin tins, and fill each two-thirds full with batter. Bake 20 minutes or till a toothpick inserted in the center comes out clean. Cool in the pans 15 minutes; remove the cupcakes, and cool on a wire rack. Frost with the Creamy Frosting when cool. *Makes 12 cupcakes.*

One cupcake—Calories: 145; Total fat: 7.6 g; Saturated fat: 0.8 g; Cholesterol: 29 mg; Sodium: 126 mg; Carbohydrates: 16.3 g; Fiber: 0.7 g; Sugar: 8.5 g; Protein: 3.3 g

Creamy Frosting

1 cup light brown sugar

½ cup granulated sugar

Few grains salt

⅓ cup whipping cream

2 tablespoons butter

1 tablespoon light corn syrup

½ teaspoon vanilla

Mix the brown sugar, granulated sugar, salt, cream, butter, and corn syrup in a saucepan. Bring to a boil, stirring constantly. Boil 1 minute, then cool to lukewarm. Stir in the vanilla. Beat the frosting until thick enough to spread. *Makes 12 2½-tablespoon servings.*

One serving—Calories: 104; Total fat: 4.3 g; Saturated fat: 1.5 g; Cholesterol: 14 mg; Sodium: 26 mg; Carbohydrates: 16.4 g; Fiber: 0 g; Sugar: 14.7 g; Protein: 0.2 g

ℋoney Gingerbread

For a quick treat, top each slice with a canned peach half and whipped cream instead of the Lemon Sauce, and your taste buds will delight in the experience!

2 cups Gluten-Free Flour Mixture (See the Hints chapter.)

¼ cup sugar

2 teaspoons gluten-free baking powder

1 teaspoon baking soda

½ teaspoon salt

1 teaspoon ground ginger

½ teaspoon cinnamon

½ teaspoon ground cloves

1 egg, well beaten

½ cup plus 1 tablespoon honey

½ cup plus 2 tablespoons buttermilk

2 teaspoons gluten-free mayonnaise

4 tablespoons butter, melted

Lemon Sauce (Recipe follows.)

Preheat oven to 350°F, and grease a 9-inch round cake pan. Sift together the flour mixture, sugar, baking powder, baking soda, salt, ginger, cinnamon, and cloves. In a separate large bowl, beat the egg, honey, buttermilk, mayonnaise, and butter. Beat in the dry ingredients until thoroughly combined. Pour the batter into the greased pan, and bake 30 to 35 minutes or until a toothpick inserted in the center comes out clean. To serve, spoon warm or cold Lemon Sauce over the warm cake. *Makes 9 1¾-inch-thick servings.*

Lemon Sauce

  ½ cup sugar
  1 tablespoon cornstarch
  1 cup water
  1 tablespoon butter
  1 tablespoon grated lemon zest
  1 tablespoon lemon juice

Mix the sugar and cornstarch in a saucepan. Gradually stir in the water. Cook over medium heat, stirring constantly, until the mixture thickens and boils. Boil and stir 1 minute. Remove from heat, and stir in the butter, zest, and juice. Serve warm or cold. *Makes 9 2½-tablespoon servings.*

One serving (gingerbread with sauce)—Calories: 274; Total fat: 7.9 g; Saturated fat: 0.3 g; Cholesterol: 40 mg; Sodium: 222 mg; Carbohydrates: 49.6 g; Fiber: 0.9 g; Sugar: 26.6 g; Protein: 3.9 g

Cherry Nut Spice Cake

This cake is a family hit, whether served plain or frosted with any creamy white icing.

  1½ cups sugar
  ¾ cup butter, softened
  3 eggs
  2 teaspoons gluten-free mayonnaise

2 cups Gluten-Free Flour Mixture (See the Hints chapter.)

1½ teaspoons baking soda

1½ teaspoons gluten-free baking powder

1 teaspoon cinnamon

1 teaspoon ground cloves

Pinch salt

1 cup buttermilk

1 tablespoon apple cider vinegar

1 15-ounce can tart cherries, well drained

½ cup chopped walnuts

Preheat oven to 350°F, and grease a 9″ × 13″ baking pan. In a large bowl, cream the sugar, butter, eggs, and mayonnaise until thick and creamy. Sift together the flour mixture, baking soda, baking powder, cinnamon, cloves, and salt. Stir together the buttermilk and vinegar. Add the dry ingredients to the egg mixture alternately with the sour buttermilk. Beat until well mixed. Fold in the cherries and nuts. Pour the batter into the greased pan, and bake 50 to 60 minutes or till top of cake springs back when lightly touched. *Makes 18 3- by 2-inch servings.*

One serving—Calories: 204; Total fat: 11.5 g; Saturated fat: 0.5 g; Cholesterol: 55 mg; Sodium: 103 mg; Carbohydrates: 22.8 g; Fiber: 0.7 g; Sugar: 11.8 g; Protein: 3.4 g

Walnut Sponge Cake

Cut sponge cakes with a sharp serrated knife in a sawing motion. (This prevents the cake from compressing.)

6 eggs, separated

½ cup cold water

1½ cups sugar

½ teaspoon vanilla

1¼ cups Gluten-Free Flour Mixture (See the Hints chapter.)

½ teaspoon cinnamon

¼ teaspoon salt

¾ teaspoon cream of tartar

¾ cup chopped walnuts

Maple-Nut Filling (Recipe follows.)

Preheat oven to 325°F, and grease a 10-inch tube pan. Beat the egg yolks until thick; add the water and continue to beat. Beat in the sugar gradually. Add the vanilla. Sift together the flour mixture, cinnamon, and salt; fold into the egg yolk mixture. Whip the egg whites with the cream of tartar till stiff peaks form. Fold the egg whites and nuts into the egg yolk mixture. Pour the batter into the greased pan, and bake 1 hour or till a toothpick inserted in the center comes out clean. Cool in the pan 10 minutes, then invert onto a wire rack. When cool, cut the cake in half horizontally. Place the bottom layer on a plate; spread with the Maple-Nut Filling. Replace the top half of the cake. *Makes 12 1½-inch-thick servings.*

One serving—Calories: 189; Total fat: 7.5 g; Saturated fat: 1.3 g; Cholesterol: 106 mg; Sodium: 81 mg; Carbohydrates: 25.5 g; Fiber: 0.9 g; Sugar: 15.1 g; Protein: 5.5 g

Maple-Nut Filling

½ cup whipping cream

2½ tablespoons cornstarch

¾ cup pure maple syrup

2 egg yolks

½ teaspoon salt

2 cups chopped walnuts

Gradually stir the cream into the cornstarch in a saucepan. Stir in the maple syrup, then the egg yolks and salt. Cook over medium heat, stirring constantly, until thick. Remove from heat, and stir in the nuts. *Makes 3 cups.*

One serving—Calories: 234; Total fat: 17.6 g; Saturated fat: 3.8 g; Cholesterol: 49 mg; Sodium: 106 mg; Carbohydrates: 17.8 g; Fiber: 1.3 g; Sugar: 14 g; Protein: 3.7 g

𝒯ropical Cake

When spreading glaze over the top of the cake, allow some to drip down the sides for a decorative effect.

    2 cups sugar
    3 cups Gluten-Free Flour Mixture (See the Hints chapter.)
    ¾ teaspoon salt
    1¼ teaspoons baking soda
    1 teaspoon cinnamon
    1½ cups corn oil
    1 tablespoon gluten-free mayonnaise
    3 eggs, slightly beaten
    1 8-ounce can crushed pineapple, drained
    1½ teaspoons vanilla
    2 cups minced bananas
    Lemon Glaze (Recipe follows.)

Preheat oven to 350°F, and grease a 10-inch tube pan. Sift the sugar, flour mixture, salt, baking soda, and cinnamon into a large bowl. Stir in the corn oil, mayonnaise, eggs, drained pineapple, and vanilla. Stir in the bananas till well blended. Pour the batter into the greased pan, and bake 1 hour 10 minutes or till a toothpick inserted in the center comes out clean. Cool 20 minutes; remove from the pan to cool on a wire rack. While the cake is still warm, spread the top with the Lemon Glaze. *Makes 16 1-inch-thick servings.*

One serving—Calories: 367; Total fat: 22.2 g; Saturated fat: 2.9 g; Cholesterol: 40 mg; Sodium: 129 mg; Carbohydrates: 39.3 g; Fiber: 1.4 g; Sugar: 17.5 g; Protein: 3.7 g

Lemon Glaze

    1 cup sifted confectioners' sugar
    1 tablespoon lemon juice
    1–2 tablespoons water
    ½ teaspoon vanilla

Stir all of the ingredients together until smooth. *Makes 16 1-tablespoon servings.*

One serving—Calories: 30; Total fat: 0 g; Saturated fat: 0 g; Cholesterol: 0 mg; Sodium: 1 mg; Carbohydrates: 7.6 g; Fiber: 0 g; Sugar: 7.2 g; Protein: 0 g

*P*ecan-Filled Coffee Cake

Any leftover coffee cake is wonderful with breakfast!

½ cup butter, softened

2 cups sugar

1 tablespoon gluten-free mayonnaise

1 teaspoon vanilla

1 egg

3 egg yolks

2½ cups Gluten-Free Flour Mixture (See the Hints chapter.)

4 teaspoons gluten-free baking powder

¾ teaspoon salt

1 cup water

Pecan Filling (Recipe follows.)

Preheat oven to 325°F, and generously grease a 10-inch tube pan. Line the bottom only with waxed paper, and grease the waxed paper. Cream the butter, sugar, mayonnaise, vanilla, and whole egg until fluffy. Add the egg yolks one at time, beating well after each. Sift together the flour mixture, baking powder, and salt; add to the egg mixture alternately with the water, blending till smooth. Pour half of the batter into the prepared pan. Drop the

Pecan Filling by spoonfuls onto the batter; pour in the remaining batter. Bake 1 hour 20 minutes or until a toothpick inserted in the center comes out clean. Cool the cake in the pan 25 minutes; remove from the pan to finish cooling on a rack. *Makes 16 1-inch-thick servings.*

Pecan Filling

- 3 egg whites
- ¼ teaspoon salt
- ¼ cup water
- 2 tablespoons Gluten-Free Flour Mixture (See the Hints chapter.)
- ½ cup sugar
- 1¼ teaspoons gluten-free baking powder
- 4 cups ground pecans

Whip egg whites, salt, and water until stiff peaks form. Sift together flour mixture, sugar, and baking powder. Gradually beat dry ingredients into egg mixture until stiff. Fold in pecans. *Makes 4 cups.*

One serving (cake with filling)—Calories: 418; Total fat: 29 g; Saturated fat: 2.3 g; Cholesterol: 68 mg; Sodium: 157 mg; Carbohydrates: 36.8 g; Fiber: 3.5 g; Sugar: 20 g; Protein: 6.2 g

*B*anana Cake

If you are a true lover of bananas, frost with Banana Icing (see Index).

- 3 eggs, separated
- 1½ cups sugar
- ½ cup butter, softened
- 2¾ cups (about 4 small) very ripe bananas, mashed
- 1 tablespoon gluten-free mayonnaise
- 2 teaspoons vanilla

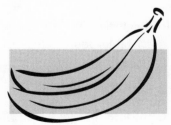

2 cups Gluten-Free Flour Mixture (See the Hints chapter.)

1½ teaspoons gluten-free baking powder

1 teaspoon baking soda

1 teaspoon salt

¼ cup buttermilk

1 cup chopped walnuts

Seafoam Frosting (Recipe follows.)

Preheat oven to 350°F, and grease two 9-inch round cake pans. Beat the egg whites with 4 tablespoons of the sugar until stiff peaks form. In another bowl, cream the butter until soft and fluffy. Add the remaining 1¼ cups of sugar to the butter, and beat well. Add the bananas, mayonnaise, and vanilla; beat for 1 minute. Add the egg yolks to the butter and banana mixture, one at a time, beating after each. Sift together the flour mixture, baking powder, baking soda, and salt; add to the butter and banana mixture alternately with the buttermilk. Stir in the nuts. Fold in the egg whites. Pour the batter into the greased pans, and bake 25 minutes or until a toothpick inserted in the center comes out clean. Cool, and frost with the Seafoam Frosting. *Makes 12 1½-inch-thick servings.*

One serving—Calories: 328; Total fat: 16.6 g; Saturated fat: 1.1 g; Cholesterol: 73 mg; Sodium: 305 mg; Carbohydrates: 40.9 g; Fiber: 2.3 g; Sugar: 15 g; Protein: 5.6 g

Seafoam Frosting

2 egg whites

¾ cup light brown sugar

¼ teaspoon cream of tartar

1 tablespoon water

¼ teaspoon salt

1 teaspoon vanilla

Combine the egg whites, brown sugar, cream of tartar, water, and salt in the top of a double boiler. Cook over rapidly boiling water, beating with a mixer until the mixture stands in peaks. Remove from heat, and stir in the vanilla. Beat until the frosting is of spreading consistency. *Makes 12 2½-tablespoon servings.*

One serving—Calories: 33; Total fat: 0 g; Saturated fat: 0 g; Cholesterol: 0 mg; Sodium: 59 mg; Carbohydrates: 7.6 g; Fiber: 0 g; Sugar: 7.2 g; Protein: 0.6 g

Yam Cake

The taste of this unique cake is very similar to pumpkin muffins or pumpkin pie, but sweeter.

  3 cups sugar
  3 cups Gluten-Free Flour Mixture (See the Hints chapter.)
  2 teaspoons gluten-free baking powder
  1½ teaspoons baking soda
  2½ teaspoons cinnamon
  1½ cups corn oil
  1 tablespoon gluten-free mayonnaise
  1 teaspoon vanilla
  4 eggs
  3 cups peeled, grated yams
  1 cup chopped pecans
  ½ cup orange juice

Preheat oven to 300°F, and grease a 10-inch tube pan. Sift 2 cups of the sugar with the flour mixture, baking powder, baking soda, and cinnamon. Stir in the corn oil, mayonnaise, and vanilla. Add one egg at a time, beating well after each addition. Stir in the yams and pecans. Pour the batter into the greased pan, and bake 1¼ hours or until a toothpick inserted in the center comes out clean. Mix the orange juice with the remaining 1 cup of sugar; pour slowly over the hot cake. *Makes 12 1½-inch-thick servings.*

One serving—Calories: 607; Total fat: 36.5 g; Saturated fat: 4.6 g; Cholesterol: 71 mg; Sodium: 36 mg; Carbohydrates: 64.7 g; Fiber: 3.5 g; Sugar: 31.5 g; Protein: 6.6 g

*W*hite Chocolate Cake

Almost any frosting or filling will blend with the flavors of this cake. Try using a different one each time.

½ cup white chocolate

½ cup hot water

1 cup butter, softened

1½ cups sugar

4 eggs, separated

1 tablespoon gluten-free mayonnaise

1 teaspoon vanilla

2½ cups Gluten-Free Flour Mixture (See the Hints chapter.)

1½ teaspoons baking soda

¼ teaspoon salt

1 cup buttermilk

1 cup chopped pecans

1 cup coconut

Coconut Frosting (Recipe follows.)

Preheat oven to 350°F, and grease three 8-inch round cake pans. Melt the white chocolate in the hot water, then cool. Cream the butter and sugar; beat in the egg yolks, one at a time. Whip in the chocolate mixture, mayonnaise, and vanilla. Sift the flour mixture, baking soda, and salt; add to the butter mixture alternately with the buttermilk. Do not overbeat. With clean, dry beaters, whip the egg whites till stiff; fold into the butter mixture. Fold in the pecans and coconut. Pour into the greased pans; bake 25 minutes or until a toothpick inserted in the center comes out clean. Be careful not to overbake. When the cake is cool, spread the Coconut Frosting between the layers and on top of the cake. *Makes 16 ¾-inch-thick servings.*

One serving—Calories: 549; Total fat: 46.6 g; Saturated fat: 3.4 g; Cholesterol: 144 mg; Sodium: 435 mg; Carbohydrates: 30.9 g; Fiber: 1.8 g; Sugar: 15 g; Protein: 5.1 g

Coconut Frosting

1 cup evaporated milk

1 cup sugar

3 egg yolks

½ cup butter

1 teaspoon vanilla

1 cup chopped pecans

1 cup shredded coconut

Combine the milk, sugar, egg yolks, and butter in a saucepan; cook for 10 minutes over low heat, stirring constantly. Remove from heat; stir in the vanilla. Stir in the nuts and coconut. *Makes 16 ¼-cup servings.*

One serving—Calories: 160; Total fat: 14 g; Saturated fat: 2.3 g; Cholesterol: 55 mg; Sodium: 81 mg; Carbohydrates: 7.4 g; Fiber: 1.1 g; Sugar: 5.9 g; Protein: 2.5 g

Cake Fillings and Toppings

While there are cake fillings and toppings listed throughout this chapter, this section includes additional ones because you can never have enough of a good thing.

Banana Icing

While this icing obviously goes well on a banana cake, it's also yummy on chocolate and white cakes.

1 large banana, mashed

½ teaspoon lemon juice

¼ cup butter, softened

3½ cups sifted confectioners' sugar

In a small bowl, mix the banana and lemon juice together with a fork. In a medium-size mixing bowl, cream the butter with 1 cup of the sugar, then add the banana mixture and enough remaining sugar to make mixture thick enough to spread. *Makes 3¼ cups (about 15 3½-tablespoon servings).*

One serving—Calories: 158; Total fat: 4.3 g; Saturated fat: 0 g; Cholesterol: 11 mg; Sodium: 44 mg; Carbohydrates: 29.9 g; Fiber: 0.2 g; Sugar: 27.1 g; Protein: 0.06 g

Chocolate Nut Filling

If you love coconut, merely substitute it for the nuts.

> 1 cup sugar
>
> 2 egg yolks
>
> 2 ounces (2 squares) gluten-free unsweetened chocolate, grated
>
> 2 tablespoons butter
>
> ⅓ cup heavy cream
>
> ½ cup chopped nuts

In a saucepan, stir the sugar into the egg yolks. Stir in the chocolate, butter, and cream; cook over medium heat, stirring constantly, only until bubbles appear around the edge of the pan. Remove from heat, and beat until thick. Stir in the nuts. Cool before using to fill a cake. *Makes 2½ cups (about 13 3-tablespoon servings).*

One serving—Calories: 87; Total fat: 6.6 g; Saturated fat: 2.1 g; Cholesterol: 29 mg; Sodium: 15 mg; Carbohydrates: 7.3 g; Fiber: 0.6 g; Sugar: 6 g; Protein: 1.1 g

ℒemon Butter Filling

This filling is wonderful between layers of cake or spooned on top of slices of sponge cake or over gluten-free ice cream.

    4 egg yolks
    1 cup sugar
    1 teaspoon cornstarch
    2 tablespoons butter
    1 teaspoon grated lemon zest
    ¼ cup lemon juice

Beat the egg yolks. Mix the sugar and cornstarch thoroughly; add to the yolks. Add the butter, lemon zest, and lemon juice; cook in the top of a double boiler, stirring frequently, until thickened (about 20 minutes). *Makes 2 cups (16 2-tablespoon servings).*

One serving—Calories: 59; Total fat: 2.7 g; Saturated fat: 0.4 g; Cholesterol: 60 mg; Sodium: 18 mg; Carbohydrates: 7.9 g; Fiber: 0 g; Sugar: 7.2 g; Protein: 0.7 g

ℐeven-Minute Frosting

This recipe is an old standby that has been around for generations.

    3 egg whites
    2¼ cups sugar
    1½ tablespoons light corn syrup
    ½ cup water
    1½ teaspoons vanilla
    1 ounce (1 square) gluten-free unsweetened chocolate
    1 teaspoon butter

Place the egg whites, sugar, corn syrup, and water in the top of a double boiler. With a mixer, beat the ingredients 1 minute. Cook over rapidly boiling water, beating constantly, for 7 minutes or until stiff peaks form. Remove from heat. Add the vanilla; continue beating 2 minutes or till the frosting is thick enough to spread. Fill and frost a cake. Melt the chocolate with the butter over barely simmering water. Drizzle the chocolate from the tip of a spoon around the top edge of the cake, letting it drip down the sides of the cake. *Makes 2½ cups (about 13 3-tablespoon servings).*

One serving—Calories: 100; Total fat: 1.4 g; Saturated fat: 0.6 g; Cholesterol: 1 mg; Sodium: 17 mg; Carbohydrates: 20.5 g; Fiber: 0.3 g; Sugar: 18.6 g; Protein: 0.9 g

Chocolate Fudge Frosting

If you need a frosting for brownies, this is it!

> 4 ounces (4 squares) gluten-free unsweetened chocolate
> ½ cup butter
> 2 cups confectioners' sugar
> ½ cup milk
> 2 teaspoons vanilla

Melt the chocolate and butter over low heat until melted; remove from heat. Sift the sugar into a bowl; stir in the milk and vanilla. Stir in the chocolate until smooth. Set the bowl in a pan of ice water; beat with a wooden spoon till thick enough to spread. *Makes 2 cups (about 16 2-tablespoon servings).*

One serving—Calories: 77; Total fat: 5 g; Saturated fat: 1.2 g; Cholesterol: 8 mg; Sodium: 33 mg; Carbohydrates: 8.6 g; Fiber: 0.6 g; Sugar: 3.7 g; Protein: 0.5 g

Chocolate Decorator Icing

This icing is firm enough to use in a pastry tube for lettering on a cake.

> 2 ounces (2 squares) gluten-free unsweetened chocolate
> 2 teaspoons butter

2 cups sifted confectioners' sugar

1–2 tablespoons boiling water

Melt the chocolate and butter in a double boiler over hot water. Remove from heat, and blend in the sugar and 1 tablespoon of the boiling water. Beat until smooth. Add more boiling water, a teaspoon at a time, until the icing is of desired consistency. *Makes 2 cups (16 2-tablespoon servings).*

One serving—Calories: 83; Total fat: 2.4 g; Saturated fat: 0.6 g; Cholesterol: 1 mg; Sodium: 7 mg; Carbohydrates: 16 g; Fiber: 0.5 g; Sugar: 14.5 g; Protein: 0.4 g

Mocha Frosting

The mocha flavoring makes this frosting perfect for most chocolate, white, yellow, or nut cakes.

1 15-ounce can sweetened condensed milk

1 teaspoon gluten-free instant coffee

1 tablespoon warm water

⅛ teaspoon salt

2 ounces (2 squares) gluten-free unsweetened chocolate

½ teaspoon vanilla

Pour the milk into the top of a double boiler. Dissolve the coffee in the water; add to the milk. Add the salt and chocolate. Cook over rapidly boiling water, stirring frequently, until thick.

Remove from heat and cool. Stir in the vanilla. *Makes 2 cups (16 2-tablespoon servings).*

One serving—Calories: 110; Total fat: 4 g; Saturated fat: 1.5 g; Cholesterol: 10 mg; Sodium: 48 mg; Carbohydrates: 17.7 g; Fiber: 0.3 g; Sugar: 7.2 g; Protein: 1.6 g

ℬutterscotch Filling

Try this filling between the layers of any chocolate, yellow or white cake.

- 1 cup light brown sugar
- 3 tablespoons cornstarch
- 1 cup milk
- 2 egg yolks, slightly beaten
- 2 tablespoons butter
- 1 teaspoon vanilla
- ½ cup chopped walnuts

Combine the sugar and cornstarch in a saucepan. Gradually stir in the milk. Cook over medium heat, stirring constantly, until the mixture thickens and boils 1 minute. Remove from heat, and slowly stir at least half of the hot mixture into the egg yolks. Blend the egg yolk mixture into the remaining hot mixture in the saucepan. Boil 1 minute, stirring constantly. Remove from heat, and blend in the butter and vanilla. Cool. Spread the filling on a cake, and sprinkle with the nuts. *Makes 2½ cups (20 2-tablespoon servings).*

One serving—Calories: 72; Total fat: 4 g; Saturated fat: 0.6 g; Cholesterol: 26 mg; Sodium: 19 mg; Carbohydrates: 8.1 g; Fiber: 0.2 g; Sugar: 6.5 g; Protein: 1.1 g

Caramel Icing

The brown sugar makes this icing ideal to spread on apple cakes, brown sugar cakes, and nut cakes.

    2 cups light brown sugar
    1 cup granulated sugar
    1 cup buttermilk
    1 tablespoon butter
    1 teaspoon vanilla

Mix the brown and granulated sugars and the buttermilk in a saucepan. Cook, stirring constantly, to 238°F or until a small amount forms a soft ball when dropped into cold water. Add the butter and vanilla; stir until the butter has melted. Cool to luke-warm without stirring. If the frosting becomes too thick, beat in a few drops of hot water. *Makes 3 cups (24 2-tablespoon servings).*

One serving—Calories: 69; Total fat: 0.8 g; Saturated fat: 0 g; Cholesterol: 1 mg; Sodium: 12 mg; Carbohydrates: 15.5 g; Fiber: 0 g; Sugar: 14.5 g; Protein: 0.3 g

Butterscotch Sauce

Put a spoonful of this sauce in a dish, then set a slice of sponge cake on it, or serve it hot or cold over gluten-free ice cream.

    ⅔ cup light corn syrup
    1½ cups light brown sugar
    Pinch salt
    4 tablespoons butter
    ⅔ cup evaporated milk

Combine the corn syrup, brown sugar, salt, and butter in a saucepan. Boil until the mixture is the consistency of heavy syrup. Remove from heat and cool slightly, about 10 minutes. Stir in the milk. Use immediately or keep the sauce refrigerated. To heat, warm in the top of a double boiler. *Makes 3 cups (24 2-tablespoon servings).*

One serving—Calories: 80; Total fat: 2.4 g; Saturated fat: 0 g; Cholesterol: 6 mg; Sodium: 34 mg; Carbohydrates: 14.4 g; Fiber: 0 g; Sugar: 14 g; Protein: 0.6 g

*D*ecorator Frosting

This frosting, firmer than most frostings, is an excellent choice when using a decorating tube.

½ cup butter, softened

2 cups confectioners' sugar, sifted

¼ teaspoon almond extract

3 tablespoons hot water

Whip together the butter, sugar, almond extract, and water till smooth and easy to spread. Add more water if needed. *Makes 1½ cups (12 2-tablespoon servings).*

One serving—Calories: 75; Total fat: 4 g; Saturated fat: 0 g; Cholesterol: 10 mg; Sodium: 41 mg; Carbohydrates: 10 g; Fiber: 0 g; Sugar: 9.7 g; Protein: 0 g

*O*range Custard Topping

This custard topping is excellent spooned on any light-textured gluten-free white or yellow cake.

2 eggs, beaten

½ cup sugar

⅓ cup orange juice

1 tablespoon grated orange zest

1 cup whipping cream

½ cup chopped almonds, toasted

Cook the eggs, sugar, and orange juice in a double boiler over hot water until thick (about 15 minutes). Remove from heat. Stir in

the orange zest, and let the mixture cool. Whip the cream just until stiff peaks form. Fold the whipped cream and almonds into the orange mixture. Refrigerate covered for 45 minutes or until serving time. *Makes 3 cups (24 2-tablespoon servings).*

One serving—Calories: 64; Total fat: 5.2 g; Saturated fat: 2.5 g; Cholesterol: 32 mg; Sodium: 10 mg; Carbohydrates: 3.5 g; Fiber: 0.2 g; Sugar: 3 g; Protein: 1.1 g

Chocolate Truffle Frosting

This frosting is sinfully rich. The glaze is shiny; do not touch it once it is poured on the cake, or it will lose its shine.

1 cup heavy cream
8 ounces good-quality gluten-free semisweet chocolate, grated

Pour the cream into a microwavable 4-cup measure. Microwave, uncovered, at 100 percent power for 2½ minutes. Add the chocolate, stirring until melted and smooth. Let stand, stirring frequently, until thickened to a good coating consistency. Slowly pour the frosting over the top of a cake to coat it evenly. *Makes 2 cups (16 2-tablespoon servings).*

One serving—Calories: 60; Total fat: 4.9 g; Saturated fat: 3 g; Cholesterol: 11 mg; Sodium: 4 mg; Carbohydrates: 4.6 g; Fiber: 0.4 g; Sugar: 4.2 g; Protein: 0.4 g

2

Cookies

$\mathcal{S}$ ome of the recipes in this chapter call for buttermilk. If you do not have it on hand, you can "sour" whole milk by placing 1 tablespoon of apple cider vinegar or lemon juice in a measuring cup; add milk or cream to make 1 cup. Let the milk stand at room temperature 25 minutes. If you are out of unsweetened chocolate, substitute 3 tablespoons unsweetened cocoa plus 1 tablespoon butter for each square of unsweetened chocolate called for in a recipe.

When a recipe calls for chopped dates, dried apricots, or prunes, the easiest way to handle them is to cut them with a pair of clean scissors that have been dipped into hot water or sprayed with gluten-free nonstick spray.

To prevent cookies from spreading during baking, refrigerate the dough for 1 hour before rolling it out. If cookie dough seems too soft to roll, chill it until firm. If the dough seems slightly dry, work in 1 tablespoon of cream with your hands.

To test if gluten-free cookies are done baking, touch the top of a cookie. When your finger leaves no imprint, the cookies are done.

To recrisp unfrosted cookies, place on an ungreased baking sheet, and bake at 300°F for 3 to 5 minutes. To freshen unfrosted drop cookies, reheat in a covered casserole at 300°F for 8 minutes.

𝒫eanut Butter Kisses

Peanut butter and sweetened condensed milk take the place of flour, resulting in moist cookies.

> 1½ cups sweetened condensed milk
> 3 cups chopped peanuts
> 1½ cups gluten-free creamy peanut butter
> ½ teaspoon vanilla
> ⅛ teaspoon salt
> Peanut Butter Icing (Recipe follows.)

Preheat oven to 375°F. Stir together the condensed milk, peanuts, peanut butter, vanilla, and salt; mix well. Drop by teaspoonfuls onto a greased cookie sheet. Bake 10 minutes. Cool on a wire rack, and frost with the Peanut Butter Icing. *Makes 50 cookies.*

One cookie—Calories: 145; Total fat: 9 g; Saturated fat: 2.5 g; Cholesterol: 18 mg; Sodium: 133 mg; Carbohydrates: 10.3 g; Fiber: 1.4 g; Sugar: 2.3 g; Protein: 4.7 g

Peanut Butter Icing

> 2 tablespoons gluten-free chunky peanut butter
> 1½ cups sifted confectioners' sugar
> 1 tablespoon milk

Stir together all the ingredients until creamy. Add more milk if needed to make a spreading consistency. *Makes 1½ cups (about 50 1½-teaspoon servings).*

One serving—Calories: 18; Total fat: 0.3 g; Saturated fat: 0.3 g; Cholesterol: 0 mg; Sodium: 3 mg; Carbohydrates: 3.7 g; Fiber: 0 g; Sugar: 3.5 g; Protein: 0.2 g

✑pricot Pineapple Strips

On the base of these attractive strips is a fruit layer topped with a pretty coconut meringue.

½ cup butter, softened

½ cup confectioners' sugar

2 egg yolks

2 cups Gluten-Free Flour Mixture (See the Hints chapter.)

½ cup apricot preserves

½ cup pineapple preserves

Coconut Meringue (Recipe follows.)

Preheat oven to 350°F, and lightly grease a 9″ × 13″ baking pan. Whip together the butter, sugar, and egg yolks. Sift the flour mixture, then stir into the butter mixture. Press and flatten the mixture into the bottom of the greased pan. Bake 10 minutes; remove from oven. Stir together the apricot and pineapple preserves; spread over the crust. Spread the Coconut Meringue over the top. Bake 20 minutes or until the meringue is golden brown. Cool slightly, then cut into bars, using a knife dipped in hot water. *Makes 48 bars.*

Coconut Meringue

2 egg whites

½ cup sugar

½ cup coconut

Beat the egg whites until frothy. Gradually add the sugar, and beat till stiff peaks form. Fold in the coconut. *Makes 1¾ cups (about 48 1¾-teaspoon servings).*

One bar (with meringue)—Calories: 67; Total fat: 2.5 g; Saturated fat: 0.3 g; Cholesterol: 14 mg; Sodium: 23 mg; Carbohydrates: 10.6 g; Fiber: 0.2 g; Sugar: 6.6 g; Protein: 0.8 g

*P*ecan Tea Cookies

This is the Greek version of Russian tea cookies. Do not substitute walnuts for the pecans; pecans make a big difference in the taste and richness of this cookie.

½ pound butter, softened
1½ cups confectioners' sugar
1½ teaspoons vanilla
2 cups Gluten-Free Flour Mixture (See the Hints chapter.)
1 cup chopped pecans

Preheat oven to 325°F. Cream the butter; add ½ cup of the sugar and the vanilla, creaming well. Sift the flour mixture; whip into the butter. Stir in the pecans. Pinch off pieces of dough; form into 1-inch balls. Place the cookies on an ungreased cookie sheet; bake 20 minutes or till lightly browned on the bottom. Cover the bottom of a 9″ × 13″ plastic container with ¼ cup confectioners' sugar; place the warm cookies on the sugar. Sift ¼ cup confectioners' sugar on top of the cookies. When the cookies are cool, sift additional ½ cup confectioners' sugar over the cookies. *Makes 48 cookies.*

One cookie—Calories: 84; Total fat: 5.8 g; Saturated fat: 0.1 g; Cholesterol: 10 mg; Sodium: 50 mg; Carbohydrates: 7.7 g; Fiber: 0.4 g; Sugar: 3.9 g; Protein: 0.7 g

*B*anana Cookies

Everyone will be sneaking back to the cookie jar to get another one of these moist, soft cookies.

½ cup butter, softened

1 tablespoon gluten-free mayonnaise

1 cup light brown sugar

2 eggs

2 large ripe bananas, mashed

2¼ cups Gluten-Free Flour Mixture (See the Hints chapter.)

2½ teaspoons gluten-free baking powder

½ teaspoon baking soda

¼ teaspoon salt

½ teaspoon cinnamon

¼ teaspoon ground cloves

½ cup chopped walnuts

Butter Icing (Recipe follows.)

Cream butter, mayonnaise, sugar, and eggs. Whip in bananas. Sift together flour mixture, baking powder, baking soda, salt, cinnamon, and cloves; then blend into creamed mixture. Stir in nuts. Cover and refrigerate dough for 1 hour. Preheat oven to 375°F. Drop dough by teaspoonfuls onto a lightly greased baking sheet. Bake for 8 to 10 minutes or until bottoms are very lightly browned. When cooled, frost with Butter Icing. *Makes 42 cookies.*

One cookie—Calories: 72; Total fat: 3.5 g; Saturated fat: 0.2 g; Cholesterol: 16 mg; Sodium: 40 mg; Carbohydrates: 9.1 g; Fiber: 0.5 g; Sugar: 3 g; Protein: 1.2 g

Butter Icing

2½ tablespoons butter, softened

1½ cups sifted confectioners' sugar

1½ tablespoons light cream

¾ teaspoon vanilla

Whip butter and sugar together until creamy. Stir in cream and vanilla until smooth. *Makes 3¾ cups (about 42 1⅓-tablespoon servings).*

One serving—Calories: 25; Total fat: 0.8 g; Saturated fat: 0.1 g; Cholesterol: 2 mg; Sodium: 7 mg; Carbohydrates: 4.3 g; Fiber: 0 g; Sugar: 4.1 g; Protein: 0 g

Chocolate Chip Date Bars

Everyone will love these! They stay fresh for several days if kept well covered.

1 cup finely chopped dates

1½ cups hot water

1½ teaspoons baking soda

¾ cup butter, softened

½ cup sugar

2 eggs

1 teaspoon vanilla

1½ cups Gluten-Free Flour Mixture (See the Hints chapter.)

¼ teaspoon salt

1 cup chocolate chips

¾ cup chopped walnuts

Preheat oven to 350°F, and grease a 9″ × 13″ baking pan. Mix the dates, hot water, and 1¼ teaspoons of the baking soda. Let cool. Cream the butter, sugar, eggs, and vanilla. Sift together the flour mixture, remaining ¼ teaspoon of baking soda, and the salt; add to the creamed mixture. Stir in the date mixture. Pour the batter into the greased pan. Sprinkle the top with the chocolate chips and nuts. Bake 35 minutes. Cool; cut into bars. *Makes 48 bars.*

One bar—Calories: 77; Total fat: 4.7 g; Saturated fat: 0.7 g; Cholesterol: 16 mg; Sodium: 46 mg; Carbohydrates: 8.9 g; Fiber: 0.5 g; Sugar: 3.3 g; Protein: 0.9 g

✐ate Bars

The orange flavor in the glaze complements the flavor of the dates in the mix.

¼ cup butter, softened

1 cup light brown sugar

2 eggs

1 teaspoon gluten-free mayonnaise

½ teaspoon vanilla

1 cup Gluten-Free Flour Mixture (See the Hints chapter.)

¼ teaspoon salt

Heaping ¼ teaspoon gluten-free baking powder

1 cup chopped dates

½ cup coarsely chopped pecans

Orange Glaze (Recipe follows.)

Preheat oven to 350°F, and grease an 8-inch square pan. Cream the butter till fluffy. Gradually add the sugar. Beat in the eggs, mayonnaise, and vanilla till light. Sift the flour mixture, salt, and baking powder; blend into the butter mixture. Stir in the dates and nuts. Spread in the greased pan, and bake 30 to 35 minutes or till a toothpick inserted in the center comes out clean. Cool; spread with the Orange Glaze. *Makes 16 bars.*

Orange Glaze

> 1 cup sifted confectioners' sugar
>
> 1 tablespoon orange juice
>
> ½ teaspoon vanilla

Stir all ingredients together till smooth. Add more juice if needed to make a smooth glaze. *Makes 16 1-tablespoon servings.*

One bar (with glaze)—Calories: 175; Total fat: 5 g; Saturated fat: 0.3 g; Cholesterol: 34 mg; Sodium: 79 mg; Carbohydrates: 29 g; Fiber: 0.1 g; Sugar: 15 g; Protein: 2.3 g

Chocolate Chip Kisses

Egg whites replace the use of flour in this recipe. This cookie not only freezes well but is low in cholesterol.

> 2 egg whites
>
> ⅛ teaspoon salt
>
> ⅛ teaspoon cream of tartar
>
> ¾ cup sugar
>
> ½ teaspoon vanilla
>
> ⅔ cup mini semisweet chocolate chips
>
> ½ cup chopped walnuts

Preheat oven to 300°F. Beat the egg whites until foamy; add the salt and cream of tartar, and continue beating until stiff. Add the sugar, 2 tablespoons at a time, beating thoroughly after each addition. Add the vanilla, and blend. Fold in the chocolate chips and nuts. Drop by teaspoonfuls onto an ungreased cookie sheet, and bake 22 minutes. *Makes 25 cookies.*

One cookie—Calories: 53; Total fat: 2.3 g; Saturated fat: 0.6 g; Cholesterol: 0 mg; Sodium: 17 mg; Carbohydrates: 5.4 g; Fiber: 0.3 g; Sugar: 4.8 g; Protein: 0.7 g

𝒞rescents

With their coating of chopped almonds, these cookies look bakery-shop perfect.

½ pound almond paste
½ cup sifted confectioners' sugar
1 egg white
1 cup finely chopped almonds

With your hands, mix together the almond paste, sugar, and egg white. Pinch off tablespoons of dough; roll each piece into a ball. Roll each ball in the chopped almonds, and form into a crescent. Place on a lightly greased cookie sheet, and let stand 20 minutes. Preheat oven to 300°F. Bake 20 minutes or until lightly browned. *Makes 30 cookies.*

One cookie—Calories: 61; Total fat: 3.7 g; Saturated fat: 0.3 g; Cholesterol: 0 mg; Sodium: 3 mg; Carbohydrates: 5.9 g; Fiber: 0.7 g; Sugar: 2.1 g; Protein: 1.5 g

𝒲alnut Meringue Bars

Both kids and adults love these!

½ cup butter, softened
2 cups light brown sugar
½ teaspoon salt
2 teaspoons vanilla
2 eggs, separated
1¼ cups Gluten-Free Flour Mixture (See the Hints chapter.)
2 teaspoons gluten-free baking powder
1 cup chopped walnuts
⅔ cup semisweet chocolate chips
2 tablespoons corn oil

Preheat oven to 300°F, and grease an 8″ × 12″ baking pan. Cream the butter and 1 cup of the brown sugar. Add the salt and 1 teaspoon of the vanilla. Beat in the egg yolks. Sift the flour mixture and baking powder; stir into the butter mixture. Spread in the greased pan. Beat the egg whites till stiff peaks form; slowly beat in the remaining 1 cup of brown sugar and 1 teaspoon of vanilla; stir in the walnuts. Spread the meringue over the cookie layer. Bake 35 minutes. Cool. Melt the chocolate chips with the corn oil in the top of a double boiler over simmering water. Drizzle the chocolate over the cookies. Cut into bars, using a sharp knife dipped in hot water. *Makes 32 bars.*

One bar—Calories: 126; Total fat: 7.7 g; Saturated fat: 1.1 g; Cholesterol: 21 mg; Sodium: 72 mg; Carbohydrates: 13.7 g; Fiber: 0.6 g; Sugar: 9.5 g; Protein: 1.6 g

Croatian Walnut Cookies

Ground walnuts replace the flour in these delicious cookies.

    ¾ cup ground walnuts
    2 egg whites
    ⅔ cup sugar
    40 walnut halves

Preheat oven to 350°F. Mix the ground walnuts with the egg whites and sugar. Form the dough into small balls (about the size of 2 teaspoons), and place them on an oiled cookie sheet. Press a walnut half onto the top of each ball. Bake 5 minutes; reduce heat to 325°F, and continue baking 15 to 20 more minutes till edges of cookies are barely golden. *Makes 40 cookies.*

One cookie—Calories: 49; Total fat: 3.9 g; Saturated fat: 0.3 g; Cholesterol: 0 mg; Sodium: 4 mg; Carbohydrates: 3 g; Fiber: 0.3 g; Sugar: 2 g; Protein: 1.1 g

Lemon Crinkles

Crinkles get their personality by forming crack lines on top during baking.

½ cup butter, softened

1 cup light brown sugar

1 egg

1 tablespoon grated lemon zest

1 teaspoon lemon juice

1¾ cups Gluten-Free Flour Mixture (See the Hints chapter.)

¾ teaspoon baking soda

½ teaspoon cream of tartar

¼ teaspoon salt

¼ teaspoon ground ginger

¼ cup granulated sugar

Preheat oven to 350°F. With a mixer, thoroughly beat the butter, brown sugar, and egg. Blend in the lemon zest and juice. Sift together the flour mixture, baking soda, cream of tartar, salt, and ginger; blend into the butter mixture. Roll the dough into 1-inch balls; roll the balls in the granulated sugar. Place on an ungreased baking sheet, and bake 10 minutes. *Makes 36 cookies.*

One cookie—Calories: 58; Total fat: 2.8 g; Saturated fat: 0 g; Cholesterol: 13 mg; Sodium: 61 mg; Carbohydrates: 7.6 g; Fiber: 0.2 g; Sugar: 3.4 g; Protein: 0.7 g

Almond Biscotti

Biscotti are made to be dunked into a hot cup of coffee! Whether you include the aniseed is up to your taste.

2 eggs

⅔ cup sugar

½ teaspoon almond extract

1 teaspoon crushed aniseed (optional)

1 cup Gluten-Free Flour Mixture
    (See the Hints chapter.)

¼ teaspoon gluten-free baking powder

½ cup chopped almonds

Preheat oven to 375°F, and grease a 9″ × 5″ loaf pan. Thoroughly beat the eggs, sugar, and almond extract. Add the aniseed. Sift together the flour mixture and baking powder; blend into the egg mixture. Stir in the nuts. Pour into the greased pan. Bake 20 minutes or until a toothpick inserted in the center comes out clean. (The cake will only come halfway up the sides of the pan.) Cool 10 minutes; remove from pan. Slice into ½-inch-thick slices. Place the slices on a baking sheet, and bake 5 minutes or until the bottoms are light golden. Turn the slices over, and bake another 5 minutes. (Do not overbake.) *Makes 16 biscotti.*

One biscotti—Calories: 63; Total fat: 2.1 g; Saturated fat: 0.3 g; Cholesterol: 27 mg; Sodium: 8 mg; Carbohydrates: 9 g; Fiber: 0.6 g; Sugar: 3.1 g; Protein: 2.2 g

𝒟ream Bars

These bars have a wonderful toffee flavor, a chewy inside, and a crusty top . . . yum!

    ½ cup butter, softened
    ½ cup light brown sugar
    1 cup Gluten-Free Flour Mixture (See the Hints chapter.)
    Almond Topping (Recipe follows.)

Preheat oven to 350°F. Whip the butter and sugar till fluffy. Sift the flour mixture, then whip into the butter mixture. Press the dough into an ungreased 9″ × 13″ baking pan, and flatten it with your hand to cover the bottom of the pan. Bake 10 minutes. Spread with the Almond Topping. Bake an additional 25 minutes or until lightly golden brown. When cooled, cut into bars with a knife dipped into warm water. *Makes 30 bars.*

Almond Topping

    2 eggs, well beaten
    1 cup light brown sugar

1 teaspoon vanilla

2 tablespoons Gluten-Free Flour Mixture (See the Hints chapter.)

1 ¼ teaspoons gluten-free baking powder

½ teaspoon salt

1 cup coconut

1 cup slivered almonds

Whip together the eggs, sugar, and vanilla. Stir in the flour mixture, baking powder, and salt. Stir in the coconut and almonds. *Makes 3½ cups (about 30 1½-tablespoon servings).*

One bar (with topping)—Calories: 102; Total fat: 6.2 g; Saturated fat: 1 g; Cholesterol: 22 mg; Sodium: 76 mg; Carbohydrates: 10.4 g; Fiber: 0.8 g; Sugar: 6.1 g; Protein: 1.7 g

Snickerdoodles

These cookies have been an all-time favorite for generations.

1 cup butter, softened

1 ½ cups plus 2 tablespoons sugar

2 eggs

2¾ cups Gluten-Free Flour Mixture
    (See the Hints chapter.)

1 teaspoon baking soda

½ teaspoon gluten-free baking powder

2 teaspoons cream of tartar

¼ teaspoon salt

2 teaspoons cinnamon

Preheat oven to 400°F. Whip the butter with 1½ cups of the sugar and the eggs. Sift the flour mixture, baking soda, baking powder, cream of tartar, and salt; blend into the butter mixture. In a small bowl, stir together the remaining 2 tablespoons of sugar and the cinnamon. Roll the dough into 1-inch balls; roll each ball in the cinnamon sugar. Place on an ungreased baking sheet; bake 8 minutes or till the bottoms are barely browned. *Makes 72 cookies.*

One cookie—Calories: 51; Total fat: 2.1 g; Saturated fat: 0 g; Cholesterol: 11 mg; Sodium: 30 mg; Carbohydrates: 5.9 g; Fiber: 0.1 g; Sugar: 2.8 g; Protein: 0.6 g

Chocolate Pecan Haystacks

One pan, one spoon—that's all you need to mix together these haystacks.

    1 14-ounce can sweetened condensed milk
    3 ounces (3 squares) gluten-free unsweetened chocolate
    1 teaspoon vanilla
    Few grains salt
    2 cups shredded coconut
    1 cup chopped pecans

Preheat oven to 350°F. In a saucepan, heat the milk and chocolate over low heat until the chocolate melts, stirring frequently. Remove from heat; stir in the vanilla, salt, coconut, and pecans. Drop teaspoonfuls of the mixture on a greased cookie sheet. Bake 10 minutes. *Makes 40 cookies.*

One cookie—Calories: 92; Total fat: 5.9 g; Saturated fat: 2.8 g; Cholesterol: 5 mg; Sodium: 19 mg; Carbohydrates: 9.4 g; Fiber: 0.9 g; Sugar: 0.1 g; Protein: 1.7 g

Pumpkin Cookies

For a special Halloween treat, use melted chocolate to create "jack-o'-lantern faces" on these cookies.

    1½ cups light brown sugar
    ½ cup butter, softened
    1 teaspoon gluten-free mayonnaise
    2 eggs

1½ cups pumpkin

2¾ cups Gluten-Free Flour Mixture (See the Hints chapter.)

1 tablespoon plus 2 teaspoons gluten-free baking powder

1 teaspoon cinnamon

½ teaspoon nutmeg

½ teaspoon salt

¼ teaspoon ground ginger

1 cup raisins

1 cup coarsely chopped pecans

Browned Butter Icing (Recipe follows.)

Preheat oven to 400°F. Cream together the sugar, butter, mayonnaise, and eggs. Mix in the pumpkin. Sift together the flour mixture, baking powder, cinnamon, nutmeg, salt, and ginger; blend into the pumpkin mixture. Stir in the raisins and pecans. Drop by teaspoonfuls onto an ungreased baking sheet. Bake 12 minutes or till very lightly browned. Cool; frost with the Browned Butter Icing. *Makes 72 cookies.*

One cookie—Calories: 59; Total fat: 2.7 g; Saturated fat: 0.2 g; Cholesterol: 9 mg; Sodium: 33 mg; Carbohydrates: 8.2 g; Fiber: 0.6 g; Sugar: 4.4 g; Protein: 0.9 g

Browned Butter Icing

½ cup butter

2 cups sifted confectioners' sugar

1 teaspoon vanilla

2–4 tablespoons hot water

Melt the butter until golden brown. Blend in the sugar and vanilla. Stir in hot water 1 teaspoon at a time until the icing spreads smoothly. *Makes 2 cups (about 72 1⅓-teaspoon servings).*

One serving—Calories: 25; Total fat: 1.3 g; Saturated fat: 0 g; Cholesterol: 3 mg; Sodium: 14 mg; Carbohydrates: 3.3 g; Fiber: 0 g; Sugar: 3.2 g; Protein: 0 g

Peanut Butter and Jelly Cookies

For variety, roll these cookies in granulated sugar and, in place of the jelly, set a gluten-free chocolate kiss in the center before baking.

½ cup butter, softened
½ cup gluten-free creamy peanut butter
½ cup granulated sugar
½ cup light brown sugar
1 egg
1¼ cups Gluten-Free Flour Mixture (See the Hints chapter.)
¾ teaspoon gluten-free baking powder
¾ teaspoon baking soda
½ teaspoon salt
1 egg white
1½ cups finely chopped peanuts
½ cup jelly or preserves, any kind

Whip the butter, peanut butter, granulated and brown sugars, and egg until fluffy. Sift the flour mixture, baking powder, baking soda, and salt; add to the butter mixture. Chill the dough 1 hour. Preheat oven to 375°F. Shape the dough into 1-inch balls. Whip the egg white with 1 tablespoon of water. Roll each cookie ball in the egg white, then roll in the chopped peanuts. Place on a baking sheet, and press a thumb gently in the center of each cookie. Fill the depression with ¼ teaspoon of jelly or preserves. Bake 10 minutes or till the bottoms of the cookies are light golden. *Makes 42 cookies.*

One cookie—Calories: 100; Total fat: 5.7 g; Saturated fat: 0.5 g; Cholesterol: 11 mg; Sodium: 126 mg; Carbohydrates: 10.2 g; Fiber: 0.5 g; Sugar: 5.9 g; Protein: 2.5 g

Greek Honey Dainties

Quickly dip each cookie into the honey syrup with a fork. (If a cookie is left too long in the syrup, it will fall apart.)

½ cup corn oil

½ cup butter, softened

1 teaspoon gluten-free mayonnaise

1 cup plus 6 tablespoons sugar

Juice of ½ orange

Juice of ½ lemon

½ teaspoon vanilla

2 cups Gluten-Free Flour Mixture (See the Hints chapter.)

½ teaspoon baking soda

¾ teaspoon gluten-free baking powder

¼ teaspoon xanthan gum

Dash salt

2 cups ground walnuts

2 tablespoons cinnamon

Honey Cinnamon Syrup (Recipe follows.)

Preheat oven to 350°F. Cream the corn oil, butter, and mayonnaise and 1 cup of the sugar till fluffy. Add the orange and lemon juices and the vanilla; beat well. Sift together the flour mixture, baking soda, baking powder, xanthan gum, and salt. Add to the creamed mixture gradually, beating well. Pinch off heaping tablespoons of the dough, and roll into balls; form each ball into an elongated egg shape. Place on a greased cookie sheet, and bake 15 minutes or till light golden. In a bowl, combine the walnuts, remaining 6 tablespoons of sugar, and cinnamon. Dip each cooled cookie into the Honey Cinnamon Syrup, and roll in the nut mixture. Set on a rack to cool. *Makes 55 cookies.*

Honey Cinnamon Syrup

2 cups sugar

2 cinnamon sticks

1 cup honey

1 slice fresh orange

1½ cups water

Boil all the ingredients together 5 minutes, stirring occasionally. *Makes 4¼ cups (about 55 1⅓-tablespoon servings).*

One cookie (with syrup)—Calories: 115; Total fat: 5.7 g; Saturated fat: 0.4 g; Cholesterol: 4 mg; Sodium: 19 mg; Carbohydrates: 15.9 g; Fiber: 0.3 g; Sugar: 11.8 g; Protein: 0.9 g

Chocolate Peanut Butter Balls

Chocolate will burn very easily if melted over *boiling* water. Melt the chocolate over hot, barely simmering water.

   1 cup gluten-free creamy peanut butter

   1½ cups gluten-free cornflakes

   2 cups semisweet chocolate chips

   1 cup confectioners' sugar

   2 tablespoons butter, melted

Mix the peanut butter, cornflakes, 1 cup of the chocolate chips, and the sugar and butter. Roll into 1-inch small balls. Melt the remaining 1 cup chocolate chips in the top of a double boiler over hot (not boiling) water. Dip each ball into the chocolate to coat the top. Set the undipped side on waxed paper, and leave undisturbed for an hour until the chocolate coating has set. *Makes 42 cookies.*

One cookie—Calories: 87; Total fat: 5.2 g; Saturated fat: 1.7 g; Cholesterol: 1 mg; Sodium: 38 mg; Carbohydrates: 9.8 g; Fiber: 0.5 g; Sugar: 5.5 g; Protein: 1.7 g

Toffee Squares

In place of walnuts, try using almonds, pecans, or more exotic nuts, like Brazil, macadamia, or pistachio nuts.

   1 cup butter, softened

   1 cup light brown sugar

   1 egg yolk

1 teaspoon vanilla

2 cups Gluten-Free Flour Mixture (See the Hints chapter.)

½ teaspoon salt

1 cup semisweet chocolate chips

½ cup finely chopped walnuts

Preheat oven to 350°F. Cream the butter and sugar until fluffy. Add the egg yolk, beating well. Add the vanilla. Sift together the flour mixture and salt, then add to the creamed mixture, mixing thoroughly. Spread in an ungreased 10″ x 15″ baking pan; bake 25 minutes. Sprinkle with the chocolate chips. Bake an additional 1 to 2 minutes to soften the chocolate; spread the chocolate evenly over the top. Sprinkle with the nuts. Cut into bars. *Makes 48 bars.*

One bar—Calories: 87; Total fat: 6 g; Saturated fat: 0.7 g; Cholesterol: 14 mg; Sodium: 65 mg; Carbohydrates: 8.5 g; Fiber: 0.4 g; Sugar: 4.6 g; Protein: 0.9 g

Holiday Fruit Drops

The pie filling not only provides the cherry taste and color but adds moisture to this wonderful cookie.

1 cup butter

2 cups light brown sugar

2 eggs

½ cup buttermilk

3½ cups Gluten-Free Flour Mixture
   (See the Hints chapter.)

2 teaspoons baking soda

1 teaspoon salt

1½ cups broken pecans

1 16-ounce can gluten-free cherry pie filling

2 cups chopped dates

96 pecan halves

Thoroughly blend the butter, sugar, and eggs. Stir in the butter-milk. Sift the flour mixture, baking soda, and salt; whip into the butter mixture. Stir in the broken pecans, pie filling, and dates. Refrigerate 1 hour. Preheat oven to 400°F. Drop the dough by tea-spoonfuls onto a lightly greased baking sheet. Place a pecan half on top of each cookie. Bake 8 minutes or until no imprint remains when a cookie is lightly touched. *Makes 96 cookies.*

One cookie—Calories: 79; Total fat: 4.3 g; Saturated fat: 0.2 g; Cholesterol: 9 mg; Sodium: 48 mg; Carbohydrates: 9.7 g; Fiber: 0.6 g; Sugar: 2.7 g; Protein: 0.9 g

*B*utterscotch Brownies

Butterscotch Brownies will stay soft and chewy for several days if kept in a tightly covered container.

    1 cup light brown sugar
    ¼ cup corn oil
    1 egg
    ½ teaspoon vanilla
    ¾ cup Gluten-Free Flour Mixture (See the Hints chapter.)
    ½ teaspoon salt
    1½ teaspoons gluten-free baking powder
    ½ cup coarsely chopped walnuts or Brazil nuts

Preheat oven to 350°F, and generously grease an 8-inch square pan. Stir the sugar into the corn oil until blended. Stir in the egg and vanilla. Sift together the flour mixture, salt, and baking pow-der; stir into the corn oil mixture. Stir in the nuts. Spread in the greased pan, and bake 25 minutes. Do not overbake. Cut into bars while still warm, using a knife dipped in hot water. *Makes 18 brownies.*

One brownie—Calories: 96; Total fat: 5.5 g; Saturated fat: 0.6 g; Cholesterol: 12 mg; Sodium: 70 mg; Carbohydrates: 10.8 g; Fiber: 0.4 g; Sugar: 6.7 g; Protein: 0.6 g

✒wiss Stars

These star-shaped cookies will puff up just a bit during baking.

3 tablespoons butter, softened

1½ cups sugar

2 eggs

1 egg, separated

2 teaspoons lemon juice

1 teaspoon vanilla

3 cups Gluten-Free Flour Mixture (See the Hints chapter.)

2½ teaspoons gluten-free baking powder

1½ teaspoons cinnamon

¼ teaspoon salt

¼ teaspoon nutmeg

½ cup finely chopped walnuts

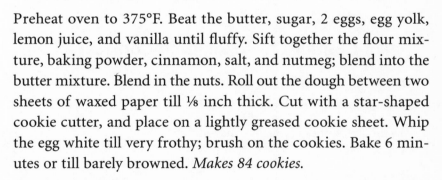

Preheat oven to 375°F. Beat the butter, sugar, 2 eggs, egg yolk, lemon juice, and vanilla until fluffy. Sift together the flour mixture, baking powder, cinnamon, salt, and nutmeg; blend into the butter mixture. Blend in the nuts. Roll out the dough between two sheets of waxed paper till ⅛ inch thick. Cut with a star-shaped cookie cutter, and place on a lightly greased cookie sheet. Whip the egg white till very frothy; brush on the cookies. Bake 6 minutes or till barely browned. *Makes 84 cookies.*

One cookie—Calories: 37; Total fat: 1.3 g; Saturated fat: 0.2 g; Cholesterol: 16 mg; Sodium: 18 mg; Carbohydrates: 5.4 g; Fiber: 0.2 g; Sugar: 2.2 g; Protein: 0.8 g

✒emon Squares

The filling will puff up during baking, then flatten as the bars cool.

1 cup Gluten-Free Flour Mixture (See the Hints chapter.)

¼ cup confectioners' sugar

½ cup butter, softened

2 eggs

1 cup granulated sugar

¾ teaspoon gluten-free baking powder

¼ teaspoon salt

2 tablespoons lemon juice

Preheat oven to 350°F, and lightly grease an 8-inch square pan. Sift together the flour mixture and confectioners' sugar. Whip the butter till fluffy, then blend in the combined flour mixture and sugar. Press evenly in the greased pan. Bake 20 minutes. Beat together the eggs, granulated sugar, baking powder, salt, and lemon juice; pour over the crust, and bake 20 minutes more. Cut into squares when cooled. *Makes 16 squares.*

One square—Calories: 125; Total fat: 6.6 g; Saturated fat: 0.2 g; Cholesterol: 42 mg; Sodium: 106 mg; Carbohydrates: 15.1 g; Fiber: 0.2 g; Sugar: 3.1 g; Protein: 1.6 g

*P*eanut Butter Chocolate Chip Cookies

These cookies contain only four ingredients, none of which are flour. If you like raisins, add 1 cup to the mix.

1 cup gluten-free chunky peanut butter

1 cup sugar

2 eggs

2 cups semisweet chocolate chips

Preheat oven to 350°F. Mix the peanut butter, sugar, and eggs with a wooden spoon. Stir in the chocolate chips. Drop by teaspoonfuls onto an ungreased baking sheet. Bake 10 minutes or till the bottoms of the cookies are barely browned. Cool 2 minutes on the cookie sheet; remove to a rack to finish cooling. *Makes 40 cookies.*

One cookie—Calories: 84; Total fat: 5.2 g; Saturated fat: 1.9 g; Cholesterol: 11 mg; Sodium: 22 mg; Carbohydrates: 9.1 g; Fiber: 0.8 g; Sugar: 8 g; Protein: 2 g

Cocoa Chip Drops

Remove these cookies from the oven as soon as the bottoms start to brown. If the tops brown, the cookies will be overdone.

½ cup butter, softened

1 cup sugar

1 teaspoon gluten-free mayonnaise

1 egg

¾ cup buttermilk

1 teaspoon vanilla

½ cup unsweetened cocoa

1¾ cups Gluten-Free Flour Mixture (See the Hints chapter.)

¾ teaspoon baking soda

½ teaspoon salt

1 cup semisweet chocolate chips

Cocoa Frosting (Recipe follows.)

Cream the butter, sugar, mayonnaise, and egg till fluffy. Stir in the buttermilk and vanilla. Sift the cocoa, flour mixture, baking soda, and salt; blend into butter mixture. Stir in the chocolate chips. Chill the dough 1 hour. Preheat oven to 400°F. Drop the chilled dough by teaspoonfuls onto a lightly greased baking sheet; bake 8 minutes or till no imprint remains when a cookie is lightly touched. Cool on a wire rack; drizzle with the Cocoa Frosting. *Makes 48 cookies.*

One cookie—Calories: 63; Total fat: 3.4 g; Saturated fat: 0.7 g; Cholesterol: 9 mg; Sodium: 50 mg; Carbohydrates: 8.6 g; Fiber: 0.6 g; Sugar: 4.6 g; Protein: 1 g

Cocoa Frosting

2 tablespoons butter

3 tablespoons unsweetened cocoa

1½ tablespoons hot water

1 tablespoon heavy cream

1 cup sifted confectioners' sugar

Melt the butter. Stir in the cocoa, then the hot water and cream. Beat in the sugar until the icing spreads easily. *Makes 1½ cups (about 48 1¼-teaspoon servings).*

One serving—Calories: 16; Total fat: 0.7 g; Saturated fat: 0.1 g; Cholesterol: 2 mg; Sodium: 5 mg; Carbohydrates: 2.7 g; Fiber: 0.1 g; Sugar: 2.4 g; Protein: 0.1 g

ℛaspberry-Filled Bars

For variety, try replacing the raspberry jam with an equal amount of orange marmalade, pineapple preserves, or seedless blackberry preserves.

    1 cup butter, softened
    1 cup sugar
    2 egg yolks
    2 cups Gluten-Free Flour Mixture (See the Hints chapter.)
    1 cup chopped pecans
    ⅔ cup raspberry jam

Preheat oven to 325°F, and very lightly spray an 8-inch square pan with gluten-free nonstick spray. Cream the butter; add the sugar gradually, and cream till fluffy. Add the egg yolks, and blend well. Sift the flour mixture; add to the butter mixture, and mix thoroughly. Fold in the pecans. With your fingers, pat half of the dough evenly onto the bottom of the pan. Spread the jam over the bottom crust. Crumble the remaining crust evenly over the top, then pat down. Bake 1 hour or until lightly browned. Cool; cut into bars. *Makes 16 bars.*

One bar—Calories: 197; Total fat: 12 g; Saturated fat: 0.6 g; Cholesterol: 42 mg; Sodium: 61 mg; Carbohydrates: 21.2 g; Fiber: 1.2 g; Sugar: 9.5 g; Protein: 2.5 g

Pineapple Cookies

These cookies stay perfectly round as formed. For a slightly flatter cookie, dip the moistened bottom of a drinking glass into granulated sugar, then press each cookie down a bit to flatten before baking.

    1 cup shortening
    1½ cups sugar
    1½ teaspoons gluten-free mayonnaise
    1 egg
    1 8¾-ounce can crushed pineapple
    3½ cups Gluten-Free Flour Mixture (See the Hints chapter.)
    1½ teaspoons baking soda
    ½ teaspoon salt
    ¼ teaspoon nutmeg
    1 cup shredded coconut
    Pineapple Frosting (Recipe follows.)

Thoroughly mix the shortening, sugar, mayonnaise, and egg. Stir in the pineapple with its juice. Sift together the flour mixture, baking soda, salt, and nutmeg; blend into the shortening mixture. Stir in the coconut. Chill at least 1 hour. Preheat oven to 375°F. Drop the dough by teaspoonfuls onto a lightly greased baking sheet. Bake 8 minutes or till no imprint remains when a cookie is lightly touched. Cool on a wire rack; frost with the Pineapple Frosting. *Makes 60 cookies.*

One cookie—Calories: 74; Total fat: 4 g; Saturated fat: 1.6 g; Cholesterol: 5 mg; Sodium: 22 mg; Carbohydrates: 30.8 g; Fiber: 0.4 g; Sugar: 3.4 g; Protein: 0.9 g

Pineapple Frosting

    3 tablespoons butter, softened
    2 cups sifted confectioners' sugar
    2 tablespoons pineapple juice
    1 teaspoon vanilla

Whip the butter and sugar together. Blend in the pineapple juice and vanilla until smooth. *Makes 2 cups (about 60 1½-teaspoon servings).*

One serving—Calories: 21; Total fat: 0.6 g; Saturated fat: 0 g; Cholesterol: 2 mg; Sodium: 6 mg; Carbohydrates: 4 g; Fiber: 0 g; Sugar: 3.9 g; Protein: 0 g

Rocky Road Fudge Bars

These layered bar cookies are impressive enough to serve to company. Store in the refrigerator for up to 2 days until ready to serve.

    ½ cup butter
    1 ounce (1 square) gluten-free unsweetened chocolate
    1 cup sugar
    1 cup Gluten-Free Flour Mixture (See the Hints chapter.)
    1½ teaspoons gluten-free baking powder
    1 cup chopped walnuts
    1¼ teaspoons vanilla
    3 eggs, slightly beaten
    Chocolate Cheese Filling (Recipe follows.)
    2 cups gluten-free miniature marshmallows
    Rocky Road Frosting (Recipe follows.)

Preheat oven to 350°F, and grease a 9″ × 13″ baking pan. In a large saucepan over low heat, melt the butter and chocolate. Sift together the sugar, flour mixture, and baking powder; stir into the butter and chocolate. Stir in the walnuts, vanilla, and eggs;

mix well. Spread the dough in the greased pan. Spread the Chocolate Cheese Filling over the dough. Bake 25 to 35 minutes or until a toothpick inserted in the center comes out clean. Sprinkle with the marshmallows; bake 2 minutes longer. Immediately pour the Rocky Road Frosting over the marshmallows, and swirl together. Cool; cut into bars. *Makes 48 bars.*

Chocolate Cheese Filling

> 6 ounces gluten-free cream cheese, softened
> ½ cup sugar
> 2 tablespoons Gluten-Free Flour Mixture (See the Hints chapter.)
> ¼ cup butter, softened
> 1 egg
> ½ teaspoon vanilla
> ¼ cup chopped walnuts
> 1 cup semisweet chocolate chips

Combine the cream cheese, sugar, flour mixture, butter, egg, and vanilla; beat 1 minute at medium speed until smooth and fluffy. Stir in the nuts. Spread over the cookie base; sprinkle with the chocolate chips. *Makes 2½ cups.*

Rocky Road Frosting

> ¼ cup butter
> 1 ounce (1 square) gluten-free unsweetened chocolate
> 2 ounces gluten-free cream cheese, softened
> ¼ cup milk
> 3 cups sifted confectioners' sugar
> 1 teaspoon vanilla

In a large saucepan over low heat, melt the butter, chocolate, and cream cheese with the milk. Remove from heat; stir in the sugar and vanilla, mixing until smooth. *Makes 2½ cups (about 48 2½-teaspoon servings).*

One bar (with filling and frosting)—Calories: 171; Total fat: 11 g; Saturated fat: 3.8 g; Cholesterol: 35 mg; Sodium: 72 mg; Carbohydrates: 17.8 g; Fiber: 0.7 g; Sugar: 14.4 g; Protein: 2 g

Coconut Bar Cookies

These bar cookies stay moist for several days if kept well covered with foil.

> ½ cup butter, softened
> ½ teaspoon salt
> ½ cup light brown sugar
> 1 cup Gluten-Free Flour Mixture (See the Hints chapter.)
> Coconut Topping (Recipe follows.)

Preheat oven to 350°F. Cream the butter, salt, and sugar well. Sift the flour mixture; blend into the butter mixture. Press the dough onto the bottom of an ungreased 9-inch square baking dish; bake 15 minutes. While the cookies are still warm, carefully spread the Coconut Topping over the cookies. Bake 15 minutes more or till lightly browned. Cool; cut into bars. *Makes 16 bars.*

Coconut Topping

> 2 tablespoons Gluten-Free Flour Mixture (See the Hints chapter.)
> ½ teaspoon gluten-free baking powder
> Pinch salt
> 1 cup light brown sugar
> 2 eggs, slightly beaten
> 1 teaspoon vanilla
> 1½ cups shredded coconut
> 1 cup chopped walnuts

Sift together the flour mixture, baking powder, and salt. Stir in the brown sugar, eggs, vanilla, coconut, and nuts, one ingredient at a time, till well blended. *Makes 4 cups (about 16 4-tablespoon servings).*

One bar (with topping)—Calories: 237; Total fat: 14 g; Saturated fat: 2.9 g; Cholesterol: 42 mg; Sodium: 144 mg; Carbohydrates: 19.6 g; Fiber: 1.4 g; Sugar: 11.3 g; Protein: 3 g

Peanut Butter Flakes

Make this ahead, wrap well, and freeze up to a month so there will always be treats available for the kids.

> 3 cups sugar
> 1½ cups light corn syrup
> 3 cups gluten-free peanut butter
> 1 small 10.6-ounce box gluten-free cornflakes

Cook the sugar and syrup in a saucepan over medium heat until bubbly. Remove from heat; stir in the peanut butter and cornflakes. Press into a greased 9″ × 13″ pan. Cool; cut into bars. *Makes 48 bars.*

One bar—Calories: 186; Total fat: 8 g; Saturated fat: 1 g; Cholesterol: 0 mg; Sodium: 158 mg; Carbohydrates: 25 g; Fiber: 1.2 g; Sugar: 9.1 g; Protein: 5.2 g

Spritz Cookies

To make festive holiday spritz cookies, tint the dough with food coloring.

> 1 cup butter, softened
> ¾ cup sugar
> 1 teaspoon almond extract
> 1 egg

1 egg yolk
2½ cups Gluten-Free Flour Mixture (See the Hints chapter.)
½ teaspoon gluten-free baking powder
⅛ teaspoon salt
Butter Rum Glaze (Recipe follows.)

Preheat oven to 400°F. Cream the butter, sugar, and almond extract. Whip in the egg and yolk. Sift together the flour mixture, baking powder, and salt; slowly add to the butter mixture till well blended. Put the dough in a cookie press, and press out cookies onto an ungreased baking sheet. Bake 8 minutes or till set but not brown. Let the cookies set on the cookie sheet 1 minute before removing to a wire rack. Finish cooling; spread with the Butter Rum Glaze. *Makes 72 cookies.*

Butter Rum Glaze

⅓ cup butter
1½ cups sifted confectioners' sugar
3 tablespoons gluten-free light rum

Melt the butter in a saucepan over medium-low heat until the butter begins to brown. Remove from heat, and stir in the sugar and rum until well blended. Add a few drops of hot water if needed to make the glaze a spreading consistency. *Makes 1½ cups (about 72 1-teaspoon servings).*

One cookie (with glaze)—Calories: 57; Total fat: 3.5 g; Saturated fat: 0 g; Cholesterol: 14 mg; Sodium: 39 mg; Carbohydrates: 6 g; Fiber: 0.1 g; Sugar: 2.9 g; Protein: 0.5 g

Orange Sugar Cookies

To decorate these moist cookies for Halloween, let the frosting set, then draw "faces" with melted chocolate.

¾ cup sugar

½ cup butter, melted

2 eggs, beaten

1 teaspoon gluten-free mayonnaise

1 tablespoon orange juice

2 tablespoons grated orange zest

2 cups Gluten-Free Flour Mixture (See the Hints chapter.)

½ teaspoon salt

1 teaspoon cream of tartar

¾ teaspoon baking soda

Orange Frosting (Recipe follows.)

Preheat oven to 375°F. Stir together the sugar and melted butter. Whip in the eggs, mayonnaise, juice, and zest. Sift together the flour mixture, salt, cream of tartar, and baking soda; add to the butter mixture, blending well. Drop by teaspoonfuls onto a greased cookie sheet. Bake 10 minutes or till barely golden. Cool on a wire rack; frost with the Orange Frosting. *Makes 40 cookies.*

One cookie—Calories: 54; Total fat: 2.7 g; Saturated fat: 0.1 g; Cholesterol: 17 mg; Sodium: 58 mg; Carbohydrates: 6.7 g; Fiber: 0.2 g; Sugar: 2.4 g; Protein: 0.9 g

Orange Frosting

¼ cup butter, softened

1 teaspoon grated orange zest

⅛ teaspoon salt

2½ cups confectioners' sugar

2 tablespoons orange juice

1 teaspoon lemon juice

Cream the butter until fluffy. Add the zest and salt. Gradually add the sugar, then the orange and lemon juices, and whip to blend well. Add additional orange juice if needed to make the mixture of spreading consistency. *Makes 2½ cups (about 40 1-tablespoon servings).*

One serving—Calories: 41; Total fat: 1.2 g; Saturated fat: 0 g; Cholesterol: 3 mg; Sodium: 20 mg; Carbohydrates: 7.5 g; Fiber: 0 g; Sugar: 7.3 g; Protein: 0 g

White Chocolate Bars

To toast the almonds, spread them on a cookie sheet; bake at 325°F for 6 minutes or until light golden brown, stirring frequently.

½ cup butter

2 cups (12 ounces) gluten-free white vanilla chips

2 eggs

½ cup sugar

1 cup Gluten-Free Flour Mixture (See the Hints chapter.)

½ teaspoon salt

1 teaspoon almond extract

½ cup raspberry jelly

¼ cup sliced almonds, toasted

Preheat oven to 325°F, and grease an 8-inch square pan. Melt the butter in a small saucepan over medium heat. Remove from heat, and add 1 cup of the vanilla chips; let the mixture stand—*do not stir*. In a large bowl, beat the eggs until foamy. Gradually add the sugar, beating on high, until thickened and paler yellow. Stir in the vanilla chip mixture. Sift together the flour mixture and salt; add to the egg mixture. Stir in the almond extract at low speed just till combined. Spread half of the dough (about 1 cup) into the greased pan. Bake 15 minutes. Melt the jelly in a saucepan over low heat; spread over the partially baked crust. Gently drop teaspoonfuls of the remaining batter over the jelly. (It's OK if some jelly shows through.) Sprinkle with the almonds. Bake an additional 25 minutes or until a toothpick inserted in the center comes out clean. Cool completely; cut into bars. *Makes 16 bars.*

One bar—Calories: 250; Total fat: 14.2 g; Saturated fat: 4.4 g; Cholesterol: 46 mg; Sodium: 161 mg; Carbohydrates: 28.7 g; Fiber: 0.4 g; Sugar: 22.7 g; Protein: 3.1 g

ℒots-of-Chips Cookies

Everyone loves these cookies because they are crowded with tons of goodies in every bite!

½ cup butter, softened

½ cup light brown sugar

½ cup granulated sugar

1 egg

1 teaspoon vanilla

1¼ cups Gluten-Free Flour Mixture (See the Hints chapter.)

1 teaspoon gluten-free baking powder

¼ teaspoon salt

¾ cup semisweet chocolate chips

¾ cup M & M's candies

¼ cup raisins

¼ cup chopped pistachios

Preheat oven to 350°F. Cream the butter and the brown and granulated sugars till fluffy. Add the egg and vanilla, and beat well. Sift the flour mixture, baking powder, and salt; blend into the butter mixture. Gently fold in the chocolate chips, M & M's, raisins, and pistachios. Drop tablespoonfuls of dough onto a lightly greased cookie sheet, and bake about 8 minutes or until barely browned. (The length of baking time will vary depending on the size of the cookies.) Do not overbake. *Makes 32 cookies.*

One cookie—Calories: 75; Total fat: 3.9 g; Saturated fat: 0.9 g; Cholesterol: 14 mg; Sodium: 51 mg; Carbohydrates: 9.3 g; Fiber: 0.4 g; Sugar: 5.5 g; Protein: 0.9 g

Chocoholic Brownies

These brownies will satisfy the cravings of all chocoholics! For even *more* decadence, frost with chocolate icing.

> 2 ounces (2 squares) gluten-free unsweetened chocolate
> ½ cup butter
> 1 cup granulated sugar
> 2 eggs
> ½ teaspoon gluten-free mayonnaise
> 1 teaspoon vanilla
> ½ cup Gluten-Free Flour Mixture (See the Hints chapter.)
> ½ teaspoon gluten-free baking powder
> ½ cup chopped walnuts
> ½ cup mini semisweet chocolate chips
> 2 tablespoons confectioners' sugar

Preheat oven to 350°F, and generously grease a 9-inch square pan. Melt the chocolate and butter over low heat in a saucepan. Remove from heat, and transfer to a large bowl. Stir in the granulated sugar, then add the eggs one at a time, stirring well after each addition. Add the mayonnaise and vanilla, and blend well. Sift together the flour mixture and baking powder; stir into the chocolate mixture. Stir in the nuts and chocolate chips. Spread in the greased pan, and bake 35 minutes or till set. Do not overbake, or the brownies will be dry. Cool completely; sift the confectioners' sugar over the top. *Makes 16 brownies.*

One brownie—Calories: 173; Total fat: 12.6 g; Saturated fat: 2.5 g; Cholesterol: 42 mg; Sodium: 71 mg; Carbohydrates: 15.1 g; Fiber: 1.2 g; Sugar: 10.5 g; Protein: 2.3 g

Chocolate Peanut Squares

Keep these cookies refrigerated for up to 2 days until ready to serve.

1 cup butter

6 ounces (6 squares) gluten-free semisweet chocolate

1½ cups crushed gluten-free chocolate puffed-rice cereal

1 cup flaked coconut

½ cup chopped unsalted peanuts

1 pound gluten-free cream cheese, softened

1 cup sugar

1 teaspoon vanilla

In a large bowl, microwave ¾ cup of the butter and 2 ounces of the chocolate on High 1 to 2 minutes until melted when stirred, stirring every 30 seconds. Stir in the cereal crumbs, coconut, and peanuts. Press onto the bottom of a 9″ × 13″ baking pan, and chill 30 minutes. Whip the cream cheese with the sugar and vanilla until well blended. Spread over the crust, and chill 30 minutes. Microwave the remaining ¼ cup of butter and 4 ounces of chocolate on High 1 to 2 minutes until melted, stirring every 30 seconds. Spread over the cream cheese layer. Chill for 2 hours or until chocolate is set; cut into squares. *Makes 48 squares.*

One square—Calories: 119; Total fat: 8.3 g; Saturated fat: 2.8 g; Cholesterol: 17 mg; Sodium: 82 mg; Carbohydrates: 7.6 g; Fiber: 0.4 g; Sugar: 3.2 g; Protein: 1 g

*K*azillion-Calorie Cookies

This cookie gives a whole new meaning to the term *sugar rush*— but it's worth every bite!

2 cups crushed gluten-free chocolate puffed-rice cereal

¼ cup sifted confectioners' sugar

½ cup melted butter

1 14-ounce can sweetened condensed milk

2 cups flaked coconut

1 teaspoon vanilla

10 1.55-ounce gluten-free chocolate bars

Preheat oven to 350°F, and grease a 9″ × 13″ baking pan. Mix the cereal crumbs with the sugar and butter till well blended. Place in the bottom of the greased pan, and smooth with a spoon to cover the bottom of the pan evenly. Bake 10 minutes. Mix the milk with the coconut and vanilla; spread over the hot crust. Bake 15 more minutes. Immediately lay the chocolate bars over the top. With the back of a spoon, smooth the chocolate over the base. Cool; cut into bars. *Makes 48 bars.*

One bar—Calories: 105; Total fat: 6.5 g; Saturated fat: 4.1 g; Cholesterol: 9 mg; Sodium: 44 mg; Carbohydrates: 11.2 g; Fiber: 0.6 g; Sugar: 1.4 g; Protein: 1.3 g

Chocolate Gobs

This cookie is the next best thing to an Oreo!

 2 cups Gluten-Free Flour Mixture (See the Hints chapter.)
 ¾ teaspoon gluten-free baking powder
 1¾ teaspoons baking soda
 ¾ teaspoon salt
 ½ cup unsweetened cocoa
 ½ cup butter, softened
 1 cup sugar
 2 eggs
 1 cup milk
 ½ cup finely ground walnuts
 Gob Filling (Recipe follows.)

Preheat oven to 400°F. Sift together the flour mixture, baking powder, baking soda, salt, and cocoa. Set aside. Whip the butter until fluffy. Add the sugar, then the eggs, then the milk, blending well after each. Beat in the dry ingredients. Stir in the nuts. Drop by teaspoonfuls onto a greased cookie sheet. Bake 7 minutes. Cool; spread half of the cookies with 1 tablespoon of the Gob Filling each. Top each frosted half with an unfrosted cookie. *Makes 48 filled cookies.*

Gob Filling

½ cup butter, softened

2 cups sifted confectioners' sugar

1 cup gluten-free marshmallow creme

1 teaspoon vanilla

3 teaspoons milk

Cream the butter and sugar. Beat in the marshmallow creme, vanilla, and milk until smooth and well blended, adding more milk if needed to make filling spreadable. *Makes 3 cups.*

One filled cookie—Calories: 114; Total fat: 5.4 g; Saturated fat: 3.4 g; Cholesterol: 19 mg; Sodium: 83 mg; Carbohydrates: 15.6 g; Fiber: 0.8 g; Sugar: 9.4 g; Protein: 1.3 g

ℐustrian Cheese Bars

Guests will rave about these elegant squares, and no one will suspect they are gluten-free.

1½ cups Gluten-Free Flour Mixture
(See the Hints chapter.)

1 cup light brown sugar

½ teaspoon cinnamon

⅔ cup butter, softened

Austrian Topping (Recipe follows.)

1 cup semisweet chocolate chips

¾ cup chopped pecans, lightly toasted

Preheat oven to 350°F. Sift the flour mixture into a bowl. Add the brown sugar, cinnamon, and butter; beat at medium speed 2 minutes or until crumbled and well blended. Press into an ungreased 9″ × 13″ baking pan, and bake 12 minutes. Pour the Austrian Topping over the partially baked crust. Bake 15 minutes more or until the topping is almost set. After removing the crust with the Austrian Topping from the oven, immediately sprinkle the chocolate chips over the top. Bake 1 minute to melt the chocolate, then gently spread the chocolate over the top till smooth. Sprinkle with the pecans, lightly pressing them into the glaze. Refrigerate 1 hour to set the topping. Cut into bars. Store in the refrigerator. *Makes 48 bars.*

Austrian Topping

8 ounces gluten-free cream cheese, softened

¾ cup sugar

2 tablespoons Gluten-Free Flour Mixture (See the Hints chapter.)

2 eggs

1 cup (6 ounces) semisweet chocolate chips

In a small bowl, beat the cream cheese with the sugar, flour mixture, and eggs until smooth, about 2 minutes. Stir in the chocolate chips. *Makes 3¼ cups (slightly more than 48 1-tablespoon servings).*

One bar (with topping)—Calories: 118; Total fat: 7.8 g; Saturated fat: 2.5 g; Cholesterol: 21 mg; Sodium: 45 mg; Carbohydrates: 12.4 g; Fiber: 0.7 g; Sugar: 8.6 g; Protein: 1.4 g

ℛum Cookies

For variety and color, try rolling some of these cookies in cocoa, coconut, or nuts instead of the confectioners' sugar. This recipe calls for gluten-free crushed cookies; especially good ones to use are Crescents, Lemon Crinkles, Almond Biscotti, Snickerdoodles,

Spritz, or Swiss Stars. Each one will give these Rum Cookies a unique flavor.

> 1 cup finely crushed gluten-free cookies
> 1 ¼ cups confectioners' sugar
> 2 tablespoons unsweetened cocoa
> 1 cup chopped nuts (walnuts, macadamia nuts, almonds, or
>   Brazil nuts)
> 2 tablespoons light corn syrup
> ½ cup gluten-free light rum

Mix the cookie crumbs with 1 cup of the sugar, cocoa, and nuts. In a small bowl, mix the corn syrup with the rum; pour slowly over the dry ingredients. Mix well. Shape tablespoonfuls into small balls, and roll in the remaining ¼ cup of confectioners' sugar. *Makes 32 cookies.*

One cookie (Snickerdoodle with walnuts)—Calories: 62; Total fat: 2.8 g; Saturated fat: 0.3 g; Cholesterol: 1 mg; Sodium: 6 mg; Carbohydrates: 7.1 g; Fiber: 0.4 g; Sugar: 5.1 g; Protein: 0.7 g

Chocolate Cinnamon Bars

There's no need to frost these bar cookies. They have their own topping baked right on top.

> 2 cups Gluten-Free Flour Mixture (See the Hints chapter.)
> 1 cup sugar
> 2 teaspoons gluten-free baking powder
> 3 teaspoons cinnamon
> 1 cup butter, melted
> 1 teaspoon gluten-free mayonnaise
> 2 whole eggs
> 1 egg, separated
> Chocolate Topping (Recipe follows.)

Preheat oven to 350°F, and grease a 10″ × 15″ baking pan. Sift together into a large bowl the flour mixture, sugar, baking powder, and cinnamon. Add the butter, mayonnaise, 2 eggs, and egg yolk; stir together until well blended. Spread evenly in the greased pan. Beat the egg white slightly, and brush it over the cookie dough. Sprinkle with the Chocolate Topping. Bake 25 minutes. Cool; cut into squares. *Makes 64 bars.*

Chocolate Topping

⅓ cup sugar

1 teaspoon cinnamon

1 cup semisweet chocolate chips

½ cup chopped walnuts

Stir all of the ingredients together. *Makes 1¾ cups (about 64 1⅓-teaspoon servings).*

One bar (with topping)—Calories: 71; Total fat: 4.6 g; Saturated fat: 0.6 g; Cholesterol: 17 mg; Sodium: 35 mg; Carbohydrates: 6.9 g; Fiber: 0.3 g; Sugar: 3.9 g; Protein: 0.9 g

ℐlmond Nests

After you remove these cookies from the oven, let them rest on the baking pan about 10 minutes before moving them to a cooling rack.

¼ cup water

½ cup granulated sugar

2 cups semisweet chocolate chips

½ pound blanched almonds, finely ground

3 egg whites

2 cups confectioners' sugar

Preheat oven to 300°F. Cook the water and granulated sugar in a medium-size saucepan over medium heat until the syrup spins a thread (240°F on a candy thermometer). Finely chop or grate the chocolate chips. Stir the chocolate and almonds into the sugar water. Beat the egg whites until very stiff peaks form; gradually add the confectioners' sugar, whipping until well combined. Fold in the chocolate mixture. Put half-teaspoonfuls of dough on greased cookie sheets; bake about 25 minutes or until dry. *Makes about 80 cookies.*

One cookie—Calories: 53; Total fat: 2.8 g; Saturated fat: 0.8 g; Cholesterol: 0 mg; Sodium: 3 mg; Carbohydrates: 6.9 g; Fiber: 0.5 g; Sugar: 6.1 g; Protein: 0.9 g

No-Bake Cornflake Macaroons

The secret to rounded macaroons is to keep spoon and fingers moistened with warm water while forming them.

¾ cup sugar

⅓ cup evaporated milk

2 tablespoons butter

1 teaspoon vanilla

1½ cups crushed gluten-free cornflakes

1 cup shredded coconut

½ cup chopped walnuts

Mix sugar, milk, and butter in a medium-size saucepan. Cook over medium-high heat, stirring constantly, till mixture comes to a boil. Cook 2 minutes more, then remove pan from heat. Stir in remaining ingredients. Drop by teaspoonfuls onto waxed paper. Let cookies stand about 1 hour until set. *Makes 24 cookies.*

One cookie—Calories: 61; Total fat: 4 g; Saturated fat: 1.3 g; Cholesterol: 4 mg; Sodium: 23 mg; Carbohydrates: 6 g; Fiber: 0.6 g; Sugar: 5 g; Protein: 0.8 g

Fruit Desserts

As well as making desserts moist and colorful, fruits may also be used as eye-catching garnishes. Slice a strawberry almost to the top, leaving the green stem intact, then spread the slices slightly to form a fan. Use a small star-shaped cookie cutter to cut stars from kiwi slices. Dip thin slices of banana in melted chocolate, let them air-dry, then cluster them on the center of a cake to form a flower. When decorating with fruits, the possibilities are limited only by your imagination.

White Chocolate Fruit Torte

Using a variety of fruits makes this torte more colorful and tasty. Try combining sliced strawberries, blueberries, sliced peaches (fresh or canned), and sliced kiwi.

> ¾ cup butter, softened
> ½ cup confectioners' sugar
> 1½ cups Gluten-Free Flour Mixture (See the Hints chapter.)

Vanilla Filling (Recipe follows.)
2 cups assorted sliced fresh fruits
Fruit Topping (Recipe follows.)

Preheat oven to 300°F, and lightly grease a 12-inch pizza pan. Whip together the butter and sugar until fluffy. Sift the flour mixture; add to the butter mixture, and blend well. Press onto the bottom and slightly up the sides of the greased pan. Bake 20 minutes or till lightly browned. Cool completely. Spread with the Vanilla Filling; arrange the fruits on top in an attractive pattern. Spread the Fruit Topping over the fruit. Refrigerate 1 hour or until ready to serve. *Makes 12 1¾-inch-thick servings.*

Vanilla Filling

1⅔ cups gluten-free white vanilla chips
¼ cup whipping cream
8 ounces gluten-free cream cheese, softened

In a microwave-safe bowl, microwave the chips and cream at 100 percent power 1 to 2 minutes till the chips are melted and the mixture is smooth when stirred. With a mixer, beat in the cream cheese. *Makes 3 cups.*

Fruit Topping

6 tablespoons sugar
1½ tablespoons cornstarch
⅔ cup pineapple juice
¾ teaspoon lemon juice

In a small saucepan, combine the sugar and cornstarch; stir in the juices. Cook over medium heat, stirring constantly, until thickened. Remove from heat and cool. *Makes 1¾ cups (about 12 7-teaspoon servings).*

One serving (torte with filling and topping)—Calories: 224; Total fat: 21.3 g;
Saturated fat: 8.3 g; Cholesterol: 44 mg; Sodium: 139 mg; Carbohydrates: 40.2 g;
Fiber: 1.3 g; Sugar: 25.5 g; Protein: 4 g

$\mathscr{G}$rilled Bananas Flambé

Having friends over for a barbecue? These bananas are fun to make while everyone is standing around the grill, but may also be made on the stove.

4 medium bananas
4 tablespoons butter
½ cup light brown sugar
¼ teaspoon cinnamon
¼ cup lime juice
¼ cup gluten-free light rum

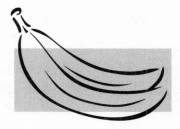

Cover the heated grill with foil. Grill the unpeeled bananas about 8 minutes or till just barely tender and darkened. Remove from grill. In an ovenproof skillet, melt the butter on the grill over medium heat. Add the brown sugar and cinnamon. Heat till bubbly, stirring frequently. Stir in the lime juice, then remove pan from grill. Slit the bananas lengthwise (do not remove the peel). Arrange the bananas in the skillet, skin side down, and place the skillet on the grill. Cook, uncovered, 6 to 8 minutes till the sauce is thickened, spooning the sauce over the bananas frequently. Remove the skillet from the grill. In a small saucepan on the grill, heat the rum over low heat just till hot. Carefully light with a match, and pour the flaming rum over the bananas in the skillet. When the flame subsides, serve the bananas with the sauce spooned over the top. *Makes 8 ½-banana servings.*

One serving—Calories: 173; Total fat: 6.5 g; Saturated fat: 0 g; Cholesterol: 10 mg;
Sodium: 40 mg; Carbohydrates: 24.4 g; Fiber: 1.5 g; Sugar: 10.2 g; Protein: 0.3 g

Cherry Torte

When you take this dessert out of the oven, you will be disappointed at how it looks. Cover your eyes, and get out your fork—you will love the taste! This is great topped with a scoop of gluten-free vanilla ice cream.

> ½ cup butter, softened
> 5 tablespoons confectioners' sugar
> 1 cup Gluten-Free Flour Mixture (See the Hints chapter.)
> Cherry Torte Topping (Recipe follows.)
> Sweetened whipped cream (optional)

Preheat oven to 350°F, and lightly grease a 9-inch square pan. Whip the butter and sugar until fluffy. Sift the flour mixture; blend into the butter mixture. Pat the dough into the greased pan. Bake 15 minutes. Spread the Cherry Torte Topping over the crust. Bake an additional 30 minutes. Cool; cut into squares, and top with whipped cream, if desired. *Makes 9 3-inch squares.*

Cherry Torte Topping

> 1½ cups sugar
> 2 eggs, beaten
> ¼ teaspoon salt
> 1 teaspoon vanilla
> ¼ cup Gluten-Free Flour Mixture (See the Hints chapter.)
> ¾ teaspoon gluten-free baking powder
> ¾ cup coarsely chopped walnuts or almonds
> 1 16-ounce can tart pitted cherries, drained

Whip together the sugar, eggs, salt, and vanilla. Sift together the flour mixture and baking powder; stir into the egg mixture. Stir in the nuts and cherries. *Makes 3½ cups (about 9 6-tablespoon servings).*

One serving (with topping)—Calories: 338; Total fat: 18.3 g; Saturated fat: 0.9 g; Cholesterol: 74 mg; Sodium: 188 mg; Carbohydrates: 40.6 g; Fiber: 1.3 g; Sugar: 26.5 g; Protein: 4.8 g

ℬrandied Fruit Pot

Prepare this 1 week ahead of time to allow fruits time to ferment. As you use it up, keep adding additional fruits.

2 cups peeled and sectioned oranges

2 cups chopped fresh pineapple

2 cups pared and chopped
    fresh pears

2 cups peeled and chopped
    fresh peaches

2½ cups granulated sugar

2½ cups light brown sugar

2 cinnamon sticks

1 pint gluten-free apricot brandy

In a large bowl, combine the fruits and sugars. Let stand 3 hours, stirring several times. Tie the cinnamon in a cheesecloth bag, and add to fruit, along with the brandy. Cover loosely. Let stand 1 week at room temperature, stirring once a day.

To keep the starter going, add 1 cup of sugar and 2 cups of chopped fruit to replace every 2 cups of fruit and syrup removed. If you remove only fruit and begin to have too much syrup, add fruit only and no sugar. If the brandy mixture will not be used for several weeks, refrigerate it; then remove from refrigerator and let it reach room temperature (about 2 hours) before serving. *Makes 20 ½-cup servings.*

One serving—Calories: 99; Total fat: 0.2 g; Saturated fat: 0 g; Cholesterol: 0 mg; Sodium: 2 mg; Carbohydrates: 23.6 g; Fiber: 1 g; Sugar: 16 g; Protein: 0.3 g

𝒟ifferent Kind of Fruitcake

Try replacing the bread crumbs in this recipe with an equal amount of soft gluten-free cookie crumbs.

> 1 4½-ounce can whole blanched almonds
> 14 ounces gluten-free cream cheese, softened
> ½ cup milk
> ½ cup confectioners' sugar
> 1 cup seedless green grapes, cut in half
> ½ cup coarsely chopped pecans
> ⅓ cup pine nuts
> 1 cup soft gluten-free bread crumbs
> 1 tablespoon grated lemon zest
> 10 large strawberries, stems removed and sliced in half
> 1 peach, peeled and sliced

One day before serving, finely grind the almonds in a blender. In a bowl, whip the cream cheese with 5 tablespoons of the milk till smooth. Beat in ½ cup of the ground almonds and the confectioners' sugar. Stir in the grapes, pecans, and pine nuts. In a small bowl, with a fork, mix the bread crumbs with the remaining ground almonds and the lemon zest. Add 1 tablespoon of the milk; toss with the fork until the mixture begins to stick together. Line the bottom and sides of an 8½″ × 4½″ loaf pan with waxed paper, letting the paper extend 3 inches above the edges of the pan. Press half of the crumb mixture onto the bottom of the pan. Spread one-third of the cheese mixture over the crumbs; arrange one-half of the strawberries and peach slices on the cheese. Gently press the fruit halfway into the cheese mixture. (The fruit should not touch the edges of the pan.) Repeat the cheese and fruit layers. Top with the remaining cheese mixture, and smooth the top. Sprinkle the remaining crumbs evenly over the top. Fold the waxed paper extensions over the cake; press down firmly, and refrigerate 6 hours or overnight. To serve, unmold onto a serving plate, and carefully remove the waxed paper. Slice with a sharp knife that has been rinsed in very hot water. *Makes 10 ¾-inch-thick servings.*

One serving—Calories: 345; Total fat: 27.5 g; Saturated fat: 11.2 g; Cholesterol: 51 mg; Sodium: 201 mg; Carbohydrates: 20.1 g; Fiber: 3.2 g; Sugar: 11.9 g; Protein: 8.4 g

*M*elon Dip

Insert toothpicks into the melon balls so guests may dip their own melon balls into the cheese dip.

- 1 ripe honeydew melon
- 16 ounces gluten-free cream cheese, softened
- 7 tablespoons milk
- ½ teaspoon salt
- 2 tablespoons confectioners' sugar
- 2 teaspoons powdered ginger *or* 1 tablespoon cut-up crystallized ginger

Cut the honeydew in half crosswise; remove the seeds. With a melon baller, scoop balls from both halves. Cut a scalloped, attractive pattern along the top of each shell. Drain the shells well. Fill one of the shells with all of the melon balls (cover with foil and refrigerate if not serving immediately). Whip together the cream cheese, milk, salt, sugar, and ginger until smooth and fluffy; spoon into the remaining melon shell. (Cover and refrigerate if not serving immediately.) To serve, place the melon shells side by side on large platter. *Makes 8 ¼-cup servings of dip.*

One serving—Calories: 158; Total fat: 10.3 g; Saturated fat: 7.1 g; Cholesterol: 36 mg; Sodium: 120 mg; Carbohydrates: 15.1 g; Fiber: 0.7 g; Sugar: 3.5 g; Protein: 3.1 g

Strawberry Refrigerator Dessert

Whenever you are cutting a dessert that has meringue, it helps to first dip your knife in hot water.

> 2 cups Gluten-Free Flour Mixture (See the Hints chapter.)
> ¾ cup plus 3 tablespoons sugar
> ½ teaspoon plus ⅛ teaspoon salt
> ¾ cup butter
> 3 tablespoons cornstarch
> 20 ounces frozen strawberries, thawed
> ¼ cup honey
> 4 egg whites
> ⅛ teaspoon cream of tartar
> ½ teaspoon almond extract

Preheat oven to 350°F, and lightly grease a 9″ × 13″ baking pan. Sift together the flour mixture, ¾ cup of the sugar, and ½ teaspoon of the salt. Thoroughly cut in the butter. Press in the bottom of the greased pan. Bake 10 minutes or till lightly browned. Cool the crust, and reduce the oven temperature to 325°F. Combine the cornstarch and 2 tablespoons of the sugar in a saucepan. Add the berries with their juice and the honey; cook, stirring constantly, until the mixture comes to a boil, thickens, and is clear.

Cool slightly. Pour over the crust. Whip the egg whites, cream of tartar, the remaining ⅛ teaspoon of salt, and the almond extract till foamy. Very slowly add 1 tablespoon of the sugar, beating well, till stiff peaks form. Spread over the fruit filling. Bake 20 minutes or till lightly browned. *Makes 15 3- by 2½-inch servings.*

One serving—Calories: 205; Total fat: 9.6 g; Saturated fat: 0 g; Cholesterol: 16 mg; Sodium: 166 mg; Carbohydrates: 28 g; Fiber: 1.3 g; Sugar: 11.3 g; Protein: 2.7 g

℘each Melba Cakes

It is such a pleasant surprise when guests discover their little cakes have a filling!

> Batter for Sweet Cream Cake, without filling (See Index.)
> 1 15-ounce can sliced peaches, well drained
> ¼ cup raspberry jam, at room temperature
> 1 tablespoon gluten-free white wine
> 1 cup whipping cream
> 3 tablespoons confectioners' sugar

Bake the Sweet Cream Cake in 10 small greased custard cups at 350°F for 15 minutes or until toothpick inserted in the center comes out clean. Cool cakes in cups for 5 minutes, then remove cakes and cool on wire racks; gently hollow out the inside of each cake, leaving at least a ¼-inch shell. (Save the crumbled cake centers to sprinkle over ice cream or mix with sweetened whipped cream another day.) Fill the cake shells with the peaches. Stir together the jam and wine; spoon over the peaches. Whip the cream and sugar till stiff, then spread over the filled cakes. *Makes 10 cakes.*

One cake—Calories: 364; Total fat: 17.3 g; Saturated fat: 10 g; Cholesterol: 121 mg; Sodium: 120 mg; Carbohydrates: 44.4 g; Fiber: 1.3 g; Sugar: 28.7 g; Protein: 4.8 g

Chocolate-Dipped Strawberries

These delicacies are delicious served alone, but they are also stunning when used to decorate other desserts.

> 2 pints fresh strawberries, rinsed
> 1 cup semisweet chocolate chips
> 2 tablespoons butter

Drain the strawberries on paper towels until dry. In the top of a double boiler, over hot water (not boiling), stir the chocolate and butter until melted and smooth. Keep warm. Insert a toothpick in the stem of each strawberry. Dip the tapered end of each berry into the chocolate; lift out quickly, and let the excess run off into the pan. Twirl slightly, then place the berry on waxed paper. Remove the toothpicks, and allow the berries to dry till the chocolate is set, about 1 hour. May be refrigerated several hours before serving. *Makes 16 2-berry servings.*

One serving—Calories: 77; Total fat: 4.8 g; Saturated fat: 1.9 g; Cholesterol: 4 mg; Sodium: 17 mg; Carbohydrates: 8.2 g; Fiber: 1.6 g; Sugar: 6 g; Protein: 0.7 g

Frozen Banana Pops

These are great to keep on hand for kids!

> 1 cup semisweet chocolate chips
> 1 tablespoon butter
> 1½ cups chopped dry-roasted peanuts
> 6 Popsicle sticks
> 6 bananas, peeled

Melt the chocolate chips and butter in the top of a double boiler over hot (not boiling) water. Place the peanuts on a plate. Insert a Popsicle stick in the bottom of each banana. Cover a 9″ × 13″ pan with waxed paper. Dip each banana in chocolate, using a spoon to scoop up chocolate to cover the banana completely. Roll the banana in nuts, then lay it in the pan covered with waxed paper. Repeat with the remaining bananas. Cover the bananas with foil, and freeze for at least 4 hours. *Makes 6 banana pops.*

One banana pop—Calories: 317; Total fat: 14.6 g; Saturated fat: 5.5 g; Cholesterol: 5 mg; Sodium: 126 mg; Carbohydrates: 48.7 g; Fiber: 5 g; Sugar: 16.9 g; Protein: 4 g

ℬaked Pineapple in Shell

Hollowing out a pineapple shell is easier if you use a grapefruit knife.

1 large, ripe pineapple
1 tablespoon gluten-free light rum
10 No-Bake Cornflake Macaroons (See Index.)
½ cup apricot preserves
1 quart gluten-free vanilla ice cream

Preheat oven to 400°F. Cut a 2-inch-thick slice from the top of the pineapple. Remove the fruit from the shell. Reserve the shell. Remove the core from the fruit, and discard. Cut the pineapple into 1-inch pieces. Place in a bowl, and toss with the rum. Let set 20 minutes. Crumble the macaroons over the pineapple, and add the preserves. Gently mix. Spoon into the pineapple shell, mounding in the center. Cover the top with foil, and stand the pineapple in a shallow pan. Bake 30 minutes. Serve right from the shell over scoops of ice cream. *Makes 16 ⅓-cup servings of fruit.*

One serving—Calories: 180; Total fat: 7.1 g; Saturated fat: 5 g; Cholesterol: 30 mg; Sodium: 80 mg; Carbohydrates: 27.1 g; Fiber: 0.4 g; Sugar: 23 g; Protein: 2.1 g

ℋot Spiced Fruit

This fruit dessert is also good served over gluten-free ice cream.

1 16-ounce can pineapple tidbits
2 16-ounce cans sliced peaches

2 16-ounce cans apricot halves

¼ teaspoon cloves

½ teaspoon cinnamon

¼ teaspoon nutmeg

2 tablespoons light brown sugar

2 tablespoons light corn syrup

2 tablespoons pure maple syrup

1 Sweet Cream Cake, without filling (See Index.)

Drain the fruits, reserving ¼ cup of each of the pineapple, peach, and apricot juices. Combine the reserved fruit juices, pineapple, peaches, apricots, cloves, cinnamon, nutmeg, brown sugar, corn syrup, and maple syrup in a saucepan; simmer 10 minutes, stirring occasionally. Spoon the hot spiced fruit over 12 slices of Sweet Cream Cake that have been cut in half. *Makes 24 ½-cup servings of fruit and slices of cake.*

One serving—Calories: 246; Total fat: 8.7 g; Saturated fat: 5 g; Cholesterol: 63 mg; Sodium: 83 mg; Carbohydrates: 39.5 g; Fiber: 1.6 g; Sugar: 24.9 g; Protein: 3.7 g

Stewed Apples

Stewed Apples are so versatile. Serve them plain. Serve them over gluten-free ice cream. Even serve them beside a roast.

3 tablespoons butter

6 Rome Beauty apples, pared and sliced

½ cup gluten-free white wine

½ cup water

½ cup granulated sugar

½ cup light brown sugar

2 cinnamon sticks

1 tablespoon lemon juice

1 tablespoon grated lemon zest

Melt the butter in a large skillet. Add the apples, and sauté 5 minutes. In a saucepan, simmer the wine, water, granulated and brown sugars, cinnamon sticks, lemon juice, and lemon zest for 5 minutes. Pour over the apples, and simmer, uncovered, until the apples are tender but not mushy, about 10 minutes. *Makes 12 ½-cup servings.*

One serving—Calories: 109; Total fat: 3.2 g; Saturated fat: 0.1 g; Cholesterol: 8 mg; Sodium: 93 mg; Carbohydrates: 21 g; Fiber: 1.8 g; Sugar: 18.2 g; Protein: 1.7 g

*P*ineapple Mallow Delight

Cutting larger marshmallows (instead of using miniature ones) lets them absorb more of the flavor of the pineapple.

1 10½-ounce package large gluten-free marshmallows
1 20-ounce can crushed juice-packed pineapple
1 cup shredded coconut
1 pint heavy cream
2 tablespoons confectioners' sugar
2 large bananas

Cut the marshmallows into quarters, and place them in a bowl. Drain the pineapple, reserving the juice. Add the juice to the marshmallows; stir, then cover and chill 6 hours or overnight.

One hour before serving, add the pineapple and coconut. Whip the cream with the sugar until stiff, and fold into the marshmallow mixture. Slice the bananas, and fold in. Chill until serving time. *Makes 10 1-cup servings.*

One serving—Calories: 248; Total fat: 13.9 g; Saturated fat: 8 g; Cholesterol: 34 mg; Sodium: 24 mg; Carbohydrates: 36.9 g; Fiber: 1.5 g; Sugar: 29.6 g; Protein: 1.4 g

Nectarine Blueberry Crisp

All ages love this dessert. Try topping it off with a dollop of whipped cream or a scoop of gluten-free ice cream.

  2 cups fresh blueberries

  3 cups peeled, sliced nectarines

  ½ teaspoon cinnamon

  3 tablespoons plus ¾ cup sugar

  1 cup Gluten-Free Flour Mixture (See the Hints chapter.)

  1 teaspoon gluten-free baking powder

  ½ teaspoon salt

  1 egg, slightly beaten

  ¼ cup diced pecans

  5 tablespoons melted butter

Preheat oven to 375°F. Place the blueberries and nectarine slices in a 2-quart baking dish. Stir together the cinnamon and 3 tablespoons of the sugar, then sprinkle over the fruit. Sift together the flour mixture, the remaining ¾ cup of sugar, and the baking powder and salt. Stir in the egg. Stir in the pecans. Crumble this topping over the fruit. Drizzle the melted butter over the topping, and bake 35 to 40 minutes until the topping is browned. *Makes 10 ⅔-cup servings.*

One serving—Calories: 215; Total fat: 9 g; Saturated fat: 0.4 g; Cholesterol: 36 mg; Sodium: 187 mg; Carbohydrates: 32.6 g; Fiber: 2.5 g; Sugar: 19.7 g; Protein: 3 g

✺trawberries Flambé

This makes an impressive dessert for guests when you prepare it at the table in a chafing dish.

    Zest of 1 lemon
    Juice and zest of 2 oranges
    8 cubes sugar
    1 quart strawberries, cut in half lengthwise
    ½ cup gluten-free brandy
    1 quart gluten-free vanilla ice cream

Put the lemon zest, orange juice, orange zest, and sugar in a saucepan; cook slowly for 5 minutes, pressing the peels with a spoon to get all the flavor possible. Remove the peels, and discard them. Stir in the berries. Spoon the hot syrup gently over the berries until they are well coated. Add the brandy, and light it with a match. Serve over scoops of ice cream. *Makes 6 ⅔-cup servings.*

One serving—Calories: 299; Total fat: 9.9 g; Saturated fat: 6.7 g; Cholesterol: 40 mg; Sodium: 118 mg; Carbohydrates: 47.1 g; Fiber: 2.8 g; Sugar: 31 g; Protein: 3.8 g

4

Ice-Cream Desserts

While there are many commercial ice creams that are gluten-free, some companies have started adding wheat to their products to help prevent ice crystals from forming on the surface. Read labels whenever purchasing ice cream. If calories, fat, and cholesterol consumption are a concern, consider using gluten-free frozen yogurt in place of ice cream in these recipes.

Chocolate Strawberry Mousse Cups

A small pastry brush makes it easier to spread the chocolate inside the pastry cups.

> 6 ounces (6 squares) gluten-free semisweet chocolate
> 1 tablespoon butter
> 1 10-ounce package frozen strawberries, thawed
> 1½ envelopes gluten-free unflavored gelatin
> ⅓ cup sugar
> 1 cup whipping cream
> 12 fresh strawberries

Melt the chocolate and butter in the top of a double boiler over hot (not boiling) water. Remove from heat, but keep over warm water. Spread a thin layer of chocolate over the insides of 12 pleated miniature foil cupcake liners. Refrigerate 1 hour or until firm. Gently peel off the foil from the chocolate cups; keep the cups refrigerated until ready to fill. Puree the strawberries with their juice in a blender. Transfer to a saucepan. Sprinkle the gelatin and 2 tablespoons of the sugar over the strawberries. Place over low heat, and stir to dissolve the gelatin and sugar. Transfer to a bowl, and place over ice water, stirring often, until the mixture begins to thicken. Beat the cream with the remaining 3⅓ tablespoons of sugar until stiff. Fold into the strawberry mixture. Pipe the strawberry and cream mixture through a decorating tube into each chocolate cup. Top each with a fresh strawberry. Refrigerate until ready to serve. *Makes 12 ⅓-cup servings.*

One serving—Calories: 156; Total fat: 10.6 g; Saturated fat: 6.5 g; Cholesterol: 23 mg; Sodium: 19 mg; Carbohydrates: 14 g; Fiber: 2 g; Sugar: 10.4 g; Protein: 0.6 g

𝒫eanut Balls

Instead of rolling the ice-cream balls in chopped nuts, you may want to roll them in shredded coconut.

> 1 quart firm gluten-free chocolate ice cream
> 3 cups chopped salted peanuts
> 2 ounces gluten-free unsweetened chocolate
> ¼ teaspoon salt
> 1 cup dark corn syrup
> 1 teaspoon vanilla
> ½ cup boiling water

Working quickly with an ice-cream scoop, shape eight firm balls from the ice cream. Roll each ball in the chopped nuts, and set it on a cookie sheet lined with waxed paper. Cover and freeze for 2 hours or until firm. Melt the chocolate in a double boiler over boiling water. Add the salt and corn syrup, and stir until thick. Stir in the vanilla. Add the boiling water, and stir. (Add additional boiling water, 1 tablespoon at a time, until the sauce reaches the desired thickness.) To serve, spoon warm sauce into each dessert bowl, and top with an ice-cream ball. *Makes 8 ½-cup servings.*

One serving—Calories: 364; Total fat: 15.8 g; Saturated fat: 8 g; Cholesterol: 25 mg; Sodium: 129 mg; Carbohydrates: 57.2 g; Fiber: 3.1 g; Sugar: 19 g; Protein: 6.7 g

Coffee Ice-Cream Pie

The sauce for this pie may be made ahead, covered, and refrigerated for up to 1 week. Just reheat to serve.

1 egg white
¼ teaspoon salt
¼ cup granulated sugar
2 cups chopped walnuts
1 pint gluten-free coffee ice cream,
    slightly softened
3 tablespoons butter
1 cup light brown sugar
½ cup whipping cream
1 teaspoon vanilla

Preheat oven to 400°F, and grease a 9-inch pie plate. Beat the egg white and salt until frothy. Add the granulated sugar, gradually beating until stiff. Fold in ½ cup of the walnuts. With the back of a spoon, press the mixture on the bottom and sides of the greased pie plate. Bake 10 minutes or till lightly browned. Cool, then chill in the freezer for 20 minutes. When chilled, spoon the ice cream into the shell; cover and freeze till firm, about 2 hours. To make the sauce, melt the butter. Stir in the brown sugar; heat slowly, stirring constantly, for 10 minutes. Stir in the whipping cream;

cook over low heat 1 minute, stirring. Remove from heat; stir in 1½ cups of the walnuts and vanilla. Spoon warm sauce over slices of ice-cream pie. *Makes 8 1-inch-thick servings with ⅔ cup sauce.*

One serving—Calories: 435; Total fat: 33.2 g; Saturated fat: 7.8 g; Cholesterol: 45 mg; Sodium: 161 mg; Carbohydrates: 32.9 g; Fiber: 2 g; Sugar: 28.9 g; Protein: 6.8 g

Maple Rum Sundaes

For company, you may wish to freeze the ice cream in a piecrust, then drizzle the sauce over each piece of pie.

½ gallon gluten-free vanilla ice cream

6 tablespoons gluten-free light rum

1 cup pure maple syrup

½ cup whipping cream

1 teaspoon vanilla

½ cup chopped pecans

Soften the ice cream till mushy; stir in 4 tablespoons of the rum; mix well. Refreeze the ice cream. Stir together the maple syrup and whipping cream in a saucepan. Boil to soft ball stage (238°F); boil 1 additional minute. Remove from heat; stir in the vanilla, the remaining 2 tablespoons of rum, and the pecans. To serve, spoon the sauce (warm or at room temperature) over scoops of ice cream. *Makes 12 ⅔-cup servings with 3 tablespoons sauce.*

One serving—Calories: 236; Total fat: 10.8 g; Saturated fat: 5.6 g; Cholesterol: 30 mg; Sodium: 59 mg; Carbohydrates: 29.7 g; Fiber: 0.2 g; Sugar: 29.2 g; Protein: 1.8 g

Tricolor Mousse

Whipping cream doubles in volume when whipped, so ½ pint cream becomes 2 cups whipped cream.

3 cups whipping cream

1 10-ounce package frozen strawberries, thawed

1 14-ounce can apricot halves, drained

¼ teaspoon almond extract

1 10-ounce package frozen raspberries, thawed

12 fresh strawberries

Whip whipping cream at high speed until stiff peaks form. In a blender, puree the strawberries. Fold into 2 cups whipped cream. Spread this mixture into a 10-inch tube pan. Place in freezer until firm, about 1 hour. Puree the apricots in blender. Fold in the almond extract, then fold into 2 cups whipped cream. Spread the apricot mixture over the strawberry layer. Return to the freezer until firm, about 1 hour. Puree the raspberries and their juice in a blender; fold into 2 cups whipped cream. Spread the raspberry mixture over the apricot layer. Freeze until firm, about 1½ hours. When set, wrap well in foil and freeze up to 2 weeks. To serve, unwrap the pan, and dip the pan quickly in warm (not hot) water; unmold onto a serving plate. To serve, place fresh strawberries around base of mousse. *Makes 12 1½-inch-thick servings.*

One serving—Calories: 101; Total fat: 6.7 g; Saturated fat: 4.1 g; Cholesterol: 25 mg; Sodium: 10 mg; Carbohydrates: 10.7 g; Fiber: 2.1 g; Sugar: 0.5 g; Protein: 0.8 g

𝒥ce-Cream Cones

If you prefer, quickly mold the hot, fried cones into lightly greased muffin cups, and let them air-dry.

5 tablespoons sugar

½ cup Gluten-Free Flour Mixture
  (See the Hints chapter.)

⅛ teaspoon salt

2 tablespoons cornstarch

2 egg whites, slightly beaten

½ teaspoon vanilla

2½ tablespoons water

Sift together the sugar, flour mixture, salt, and cornstarch. Stir in the egg whites, then the vanilla, then the water. Lightly grease a small skillet. Pour in 3 tablespoons of the batter, and spread it in a circle. Cook over low heat till lightly browned, about 4 minutes. (If you cook the cones too quickly, they will not harden properly.) Turn and cook till the second side is browned. Remove from pan, and quickly roll into a cone shape. Secure the cone with a toothpick, and let it air-dry. Repeat with the remaining batter. Remove the toothpicks when cones are dry. *Makes 9 cones.*

One cone—Calories: 49; Total fat: 0 g; Saturated fat: 0 g; Cholesterol: 0 mg; Sodium: 45 mg; Carbohydrates: 8.2 g; Fiber: 0.2 g; Sugar: 1.8 g; Protein: 1.4 g

Ice-Cream Brownie Torte

Expecting company? Avoid last-minute haste by making this frozen brownie torte several days ahead.

¼ cup unsweetened cocoa

3 tablespoons water

1 large egg

1 teaspoon vanilla

½ cup butter, softened

1 cup sugar

1⅓ cups Gluten-Free Flour Mixture (See the Hints chapter.)

3 pints gluten-free coffee ice cream

2 cups sweetened whipped cream

1 ounce (1 square) gluten-free semisweet chocolate, grated

Preheat oven to 375°F. Using an 8-inch round cake pan as a guide, cut seven 8-inch circles from waxed paper. Whisk the cocoa, water, egg, and vanilla in a bowl till smooth. With a mixer, beat the butter and sugar till fluffy. Beat in the cocoa mixture (the batter may look curdled, but it's OK). Sift the flour mixture; whip into the butter mixture at low speed till blended. Moisten a cookie sheet with water (to keep the waxed paper from shifting). Set two rounds of waxed paper on the baking sheet. Spread ⅓ cup of batter on each round, almost to the edges. Bake 8 minutes till the surface looks dry but is slightly springy to the touch (do not overbake). Cover a wire rack with waxed paper, and cool the cake rounds, with their waxed paper, on the rack. Continue baking the remaining rounds, two at a time.

Line an 8-inch springform pan with plastic wrap, letting enough wrap extend above the sides of the pan to cover the top when filled. Peel the waxed paper off the cooled brownie layers. Place one layer in the bottom of the springform pan. Spread evenly with 1 cup of the ice cream. Repeat with five more layers of brownie and ice cream. Top with the last brownie. Fold the plastic wrap over the top, and freeze 8 hours. Remove the sides of the pan, and peel the plastic wrap from the sides. Lift the cake from the plastic wrap onto a serving plate. Spoon the sweetened whipped cream in the center of the top layer, and sprinkle with the grated chocolate. Refrigerate about 20 minutes before serving. *Makes 10 1⅓-inch-thick servings.*

One serving—Calories: 471; Total fat: 28.6 g; Saturated fat: 12.5 g; Cholesterol: 109 mg; Sodium: 180 mg; Carbohydrates: 38.5 g; Fiber: 1.4 g; Sugar: 26.1 g; Protein: 6.7 g

Meringue Glacé au Chocolat

You've never had an ice-cream sandwich like this before! This is also excellent made with gluten-free coffee ice cream.

    4 egg whites, at room temperature
    ⅛ teaspoon cream of tartar
    1 cup granulated sugar
    1 teaspoon apple cider vinegar

½ cup minced blanched almonds

2 ounces (2 squares) gluten-free unsweetened chocolate, grated

1 quart gluten-free chocolate ice cream

4 ounces (4 squares) gluten-free sweet cooking chocolate

1 tablespoon butter

3 tablespoons light corn syrup

2 tablespoons milk

1 tablespoon gluten-free light rum

1½ cups whipping cream

¼ cup confectioners' sugar

Preheat oven to 275°F. Line a large baking sheet with foil; mark off two 10″ × 6″ rectangles on the foil. Beat the egg whites and cream of tartar on high speed till foamy. Beat in the granulated sugar, 1 tablespoon at a time, and vinegar until stiff peaks begin to form. Fold in the almonds and unsweetened chocolate. Spread half of the meringue within each marked rectangle on the baking sheet, smoothing the tops. Bake 45 minutes till the layers are firm. Turn off oven; leave meringues in oven for 30 minutes. Cool on a wire rack. Peel off the foil. Let the ice cream soften slightly. Spread the ice cream carefully in an even layer on one meringue layer. Top with the second meringue. Wrap and freeze for at least 2 hours.

Combine the sweet chocolate, butter, corn syrup, and milk in a saucepan. Stir over low heat until the chocolate is melted and the sauce is smooth. Remove from heat, and stir in the rum. Beat the cream with the confectioners' sugar until stiff. Spoon the chocolate sauce over the top meringue to form a thin layer. Frost the sides with part of the whipped cream. Pipe the remaining whipped cream over the top of the meringue to form a lattice pattern over the chocolate. Place in the freezer for at least 1 hour. *Makes 12 2″ × 2½″ servings.*

One serving—Calories: 384; Total fat: 25.7 g; Saturated fat: 14 g; Cholesterol: 61 mg; Sodium: 88 mg; Carbohydrates: 38.1 g; Fiber: 1.8 g; Sugar: 25.8 g; Protein: 6 g

$\mathscr{P}$umpkin Squares

For company, you may wish to top off this dessert with a dollop of sweetened whipped cream to which you've added a hint of cinnamon.

    1 cup canned pumpkin
    ½ cup light brown sugar
    ¼ teaspoon salt
    ½ teaspoon cinnamon
    ½ teaspoon ground ginger
    ¼ teaspoon nutmeg
    1 quart gluten-free vanilla ice cream, slightly softened
    Crumb mixture for 1 Cornflake Nut Crust (See Index.)

Whip together the pumpkin, sugar, salt, cinnamon, ginger, and nutmeg until well blended. Stir in the ice cream. Reserve 2 tablespoons of the crumb mixture for the Cornflake Crust. Press the remaining crumbs firmly and evenly into the bottom of an ungreased 9-inch square pan. Pour the pumpkin mixture on top of the crust; sprinkle with the reserved crumbs. Freeze until firm (about 4 hours). Remove from the freezer 15 minutes before serving. *Makes 9 3-inch-square servings.*

One serving—Calories: 408; Total fat: 23.4 g; Saturated fat: 9.3 g; Cholesterol: 71 mg; Sodium: 380 mg; Carbohydrates: 45.4 g; Fiber: 1.3 g; Sugar: 40.1 g; Protein: 4.1 g

$\mathscr{C}$hocolate Ice Cream Linzer Torte

Start making this dessert one or two days before you plan to serve it. To cut, dip a knife in hot water.

    5 egg whites, at room temperature
    ½ cup granulated sugar
    1¼ cups sifted confectioners' sugar
    1 tablespoon cornstarch

¼ cup unsweetened cocoa

1⅔ cups ground almonds, toasted

1 12-ounce jar raspberry preserves

1 quart gluten-free chocolate ice cream, slightly softened

2 cups whipping cream

3 cups fresh raspberries

Preheat oven to 275°F. Cut three 9-inch circles from plain brown paper; place on cookie sheets. Beat the egg whites till soft peaks form. Slowly beat in the granulated sugar, 1 tablespoon at a time, until the meringue is stiff. Sift 1 cup of the confectioners' sugar with the cornstarch and cocoa; gradually beat into the meringue. Fold in ⅔ cup of the almonds. Spread the meringue evenly over the paper circles to the edge of each circle; smooth tops. Bake 45 minutes. Turn off the oven; let the meringues cool 30 minutes in the oven. Carefully remove the cooled meringues from the brown paper, being careful not to break or crack them.

Place a meringue on a plate; spread with one-third of the preserves. Spread with half of the ice cream, smoothing the sides. Freeze this layer 30 minutes. Top with a second layer of meringue, one-third of the preserves, and the remainder of the ice cream. Top with the third meringue; press down gently to secure the layers. Freeze 3 hours till firm. Whip the cream with the remaining ¼ cup of confectioners' sugar till stiff; frost the top and sides of the torte. Press the remaining 1 cup of ground almonds into the sides of the torte. Arrange the raspberries on top in the center; spoon the remaining one-third of the preserves over the berries. Cover; freeze 1 hour or till ready to serve. *Makes 12 1¼-inch-thick servings.*

One serving—Calories: 492; Total fat: 26.8 g; Saturated fat: 13.4 g; Cholesterol: 73 mg; Sodium: 77 mg; Carbohydrates: 61 g; Fiber: 4.9 g; Sugar: 51.6 g; Protein: 7.7 g

ℒayered Confetti Bombe

Ice-cream bombes are easier to slice if you use a heavy knife that has been dipped in hot water.

    1 cup coarsely chopped pecans
    2 pints gluten-free vanilla ice cream, slightly softened
    1 cup mini semisweet chocolate chips
    2 pints gluten-free chocolate ice cream, slightly softened
    1 cup drained mandarin oranges, chopped
    1 pint gluten-free orange sherbet, slightly softened
    1 10-ounce package frozen strawberries, thawed, drained,
        and chopped
    1 pint gluten-free strawberry ice cream, slightly softened

Stir the pecans into the vanilla ice cream. With the back of a spoon, spread the vanilla ice cream along the bottom and sides of a chilled 3-quart bowl or mold to form a shell, leaving the center hollow. Freeze for 1½ hours or until firm. Stir the chocolate chips into the chocolate ice cream. Spread the chocolate ice cream over the vanilla layer, leaving center hollow. Freeze for 1½ hours or till firm. Fold the mandarin oranges into the sherbet. Spread the sherbet over the chocolate layer, packing it in firmly, leaving the center hollow. Freeze for 1½ hours or till firm. Fold the strawberries into the strawberry ice cream. Fill in the center of the bombe with the strawberry ice cream, smoothing the top. Cover and freeze for 2 hours. Carefully dip the bowl into lukewarm water 5 to 10 seconds. Loosen the top edge with a knife, and unmold onto a serving platter; freeze until serving time. Cut into wedges. *Makes 6 1-cup servings.*

One serving—Calories: 282; Total fat: 14 g; Saturated fat: 6 g; Cholesterol: 20 mg; Sodium: 66 mg; Carbohydrates: 40.7 g; Fiber: 2 g; Sugar: 32.9 g; Protein: 3.3 g

*L*emon Alaska

Lemon and raspberry are two tastes that blend perfectly in this dessert. Lemon Alaska is baked on a wooden bread board, which distributes heat evenly and helps prevent the ice cream from melting while the meringue browns.

> 1 9-inch layer unfrosted Lemonade Cake (See Index.)
> 1 quart gluten-free lemon sherbet
> 6 egg whites
> ½ teaspoon cream of tartar
> 1 cup sugar
> Raspberry Sauce (Recipe follows.)

Cover and freeze the cake for 2 hours. Line a 1½-quart bowl with foil. Pack the sherbet into the bowl; cover and freeze for 1 hour. Cover a baking sheet with foil. Place the cake on the foil; invert the bowl of sherbet on top of the cake, and remove the bowl and foil. Continue freezing the cake and sherbet on the baking sheet until meringue is made. Place an oven rack in the lowest position in the oven, and preheat oven to 475°F. Whip the egg whites and cream of tartar till foamy. Gradually add the sugar; whip until very stiff. Completely cover the cake and sherbet with the meringue, sealing it to the foil. Place baking sheet on a bread board and place them in the oven to bake for 2 to 3 minutes until the meringue is light brown. Trim the foil to the edge of the meringue; transfer the cake to a serving plate. Serve immediately or freeze up to two days until ready to serve. Remove from freezer 10 minutes before serving to make cutting easier. Drizzle each slice with Raspberry Sauce. *Makes 8 2-inch-thick servings.*

One serving—Calories: 339; Total fat: 7.7 g; Saturated fat: 2.4 g; Cholesterol: 71 mg; Sodium: 244 mg; Carbohydrates: 62.1 g; Fiber: 0.2 g; Sugar: 56.9 g; Protein: 6.5 g

Raspberry Sauce

- 1 10-ounce package frozen raspberries, thawed
- 1 teaspoon sugar
- 1¼ teaspoons cornstarch
- 1 tablespoon water

In a saucepan, heat the raspberries (with their syrup) and sugar to boiling. Stir together the cornstarch and water in a separate bowl; add to the raspberries. Heat to boiling, stirring constantly. Boil and stir for 1 minute or till thickened, then cool. *Makes 1¼ cups (8 2½-tablespoon servings).*

One serving—Calories: 39; Total fat: 0.1 g; Saturated fat: 0 g; Cholesterol: 0 mg; Sodium: 1 mg; Carbohydrates: 9.9 g; Fiber: 1.6 g; Sugar: 0.3 g; Protein: 0.2 g

ℱudge Crepe Sundaes

These sundaes take a little advance preparation, but the effort will be rewarded with raves.

- Batter for Make-Ahead Filled Crepes (See Index.)
- 1 tablespoon plus ⅓ cup unsweetened cocoa
- 1 teaspoon plus 1 cup sugar
- 1 quart gluten-free chocolate ice cream
- ½ cup butter
- 1 teaspoon gluten-free instant-coffee powder
- ⅛ teaspoon salt

2 tablespoons gluten-free light rum

1 cup whipping cream

1 teaspoon vanilla

Prepare the crepes as directed in the recipe for Make-Ahead Filled Crepes, adding 1 tablespoon of the cocoa and 1 teaspoon of the sugar to the batter. (Do not make the filling for the crepes.) Form small ice-cream balls with a melon baller. Set on a cookie sheet; cover and freeze. Melt the butter in a saucepan. Blend in the remaining 1 cup of sugar and ⅓ cup of cocoa, the coffee, salt, and rum. Stir in the cream. Simmer 5 minutes, stirring frequently. Remove from heat, and stir in the vanilla. To serve, top each crepe with 3 ice-cream balls; fold the crepe over the ice cream to cover. Spoon the fudge sauce over the top. *Makes 12 ice-cream crepes with 3 tablespoons sauce per serving.*

One serving—Calories: 344; Total fat: 21.1 g; Saturated fat: 8.2 g; Cholesterol: 115 mg; Sodium: 224 mg; Carbohydrates: 35.2 g; Fiber: 1.3 g; Sugar: 23.8 g; Protein: 6.5 g

ℱruited Sherbet

Topped with a sprig of fresh mint, this light sherbet is the perfect finishing touch for a luncheon.

1 banana, mashed

½ cup orange juice

¼ cup lemon juice

¾ cup sugar

⅛ teaspoon salt

1 cup ice-cold evaporated milk

Whip together the banana, orange juice, 2 tablespoons of the lemon juice, the sugar, and salt. Pour into a 5-cup bowl; freeze for 3 hours. Whip the milk until fluffy; add the remaining 2 tablespoons of lemon juice. Continue beating till stiff. Fold into the fruit mixture. Freeze without stirring for 3 hours until firm. *Makes 4 1-cup servings.*

One serving—Calories: 106; Total fat: 2.5 g; Saturated fat: 1.5 g; Cholesterol: 6 mg; Sodium: 74 mg; Carbohydrates: 24.9 g; Fiber: 0.7 g; Sugar: 18.8 g; Protein: 1.7 g

Crunchy Squares

Vary this dessert by using a different flavor of gluten-free ice cream each time you make it.

> 2 cups crushed gluten-free cornflakes
> 1 1/3 cups shredded coconut
> 1/2 cup chopped pecans
> 1/2 cup light brown sugar
> 1/3 cup butter, melted
> 1/2 gallon gluten-free ice cream, slightly softened
> 1/2 cup gluten-free chocolate syrup

Mix together the cereal, coconut, nuts, sugar, and butter. Press two-thirds of the mixture evenly into a lightly greased 9″ × 13″ baking pan. Pack half of the ice cream over the cereal layer; drizzle half of the chocolate syrup over the ice cream. Repeat the layers with the remainder of the ice cream and syrup. Marble in the chocolate sauce by swirling a knife through the ice cream; smooth the top to make it level. Sprinkle with the remaining cereal mixture. Freeze until firm (at least 12 hours). *Makes 18 3- by 2-inch servings.*

One serving—Calories: 216; Total fat: 10.3 g; Saturated fat: 3.5 g; Cholesterol: 16 mg; Sodium: 155 mg; Carbohydrates: 29.6 g; Fiber: 1.2 g; Sugar: 21.5 g; Protein: 3.2 g

ℱruit and Rum Sundaes

This sauce keeps well in the refrigerator; just reheat to use.

- ¼ cup raisins
- ¼ cup light brown sugar
- ¼ cup orange juice
- ¼ cup butter
- 1 20-ounce can peach slices, drained
- ¼ cup gluten-free light rum
- ¼ cup coarsely chopped walnuts
- 1 quart gluten-free vanilla ice cream

In a small saucepan, cook the raisins, brown sugar, orange juice, and butter, stirring, for 5 minutes till hot and bubbly. Cut each peach slice into thirds; stir into the raisin mixture, and simmer 3 minutes. Stir in the rum and walnuts. Spoon the sauce over scoops of the ice cream. *Makes 8 ½-cup servings with ¼ cup sauce.*

One serving—Calories: 323; Total fat: 21 g; Saturated fat: 12.3 g; Cholesterol: 38 mg; Sodium: 127 mg; Carbohydrates: 29.2 g; Fiber: 1.7 g; Sugar: 26.5 g; Protein: 4.3 g

ℐtalian Spumoni Dessert

For a different taste sensation, omit the rum, and add 2 table-spoons of crème de cacao.

- 1 pint gluten-free chocolate ice cream, slightly softened
- ½ teaspoon cinnamon
- 2 tablespoons gluten-free light rum
- ½ cup minced candied pineapple

½ cup minced candied cherries

¾ cup slivered almonds

1 pint gluten-free vanilla ice cream, slightly softened

2 tablespoons gluten-free apricot brandy

Combine the chocolate ice cream with the cinnamon, rum, and half of the pineapple, cherries, and almonds. Place the chocolate mixture in the bottom of a 9″ × 5″ loaf pan. Freeze for 1½ hours until firm. Mix the vanilla ice cream, brandy, and remaining half of the pineapple, cherries, and almonds. Cover chocolate layer with the vanilla mixture. Freeze 1½ hours until firm. *Makes 9 1-inch-thick servings.*

One serving—Calories: 284; Total fat: 13.9 g; Saturated fat: 4.8 g; Cholesterol: 24 mg; Sodium: 61 mg; Carbohydrates: 25.6 g; Fiber: 1.4 g; Sugar: 16.4 g; Protein: 4.3 g

*K*ids' Parfaits

These are great to have on hand in the freezer to give to kids for a treat on a hot afternoon.

2½ cups gluten-free cornflakes, coarsely crushed

1 cup shredded coconut

1 cup light brown sugar

1 cup chopped almonds

¼ cup butter

½ gallon gluten-free vanilla ice cream, slightly softened

Crumble together in a bowl the cornflakes, coconut, sugar, and almonds. Melt the butter, and pour over the cereal mixture. Stir well to blend. Fill 20 5-ounce plastic cups half full with the ice cream. Spoon in the cornflake mixture. Fill the remainder of each cup with the remaining ice cream. Freeze at least 1½ hours. *Makes 20 parfaits.*

One parfait—Calories: 220; Total fat: 12.8 g; Saturated fat: 6.3 g; Cholesterol: 30 mg; Sodium: 126 mg; Carbohydrates: 23.9 g; Fiber: 0.6 g; Sugar: 20.1 g; Protein: 3.1 g

$\mathscr{C}$hocolate Nut Cups

For a special effect, cover the top of the ice cream with toasted shredded coconut.

½ cup chopped walnuts
2 cups shredded coconut
⅔ cup semisweet chocolate chips, melted
1 quart gluten-free chocolate ice cream

Stir together the nuts, coconut, and chocolate to coat evenly. Spray six muffin tins with gluten-free nonstick spray. Spoon the chocolate mixture into the tins to form shells. Place in the refrigerator for 1 hour to harden. To serve, fill the shells with the ice cream. *Makes 6 shells with ⅔ cup ice cream.*

One serving—Calories: 436; Total fat: 29.9 g; Saturated fat: 18.6 g; Cholesterol: 33 mg; Sodium: 81 mg; Carbohydrates: 43.6 g; Fiber: 4.1 g; Sugar: 36.2 g; Protein: 7.1 g

$\mathscr{M}$ocha Sundae Pie

Mocha Sundae Pie is equally good when made with gluten-free chocolate or vanilla ice cream.

2 ounces (2 squares) gluten-free semisweet chocolate
1 tablespoon butter
½ cup sugar
¼ cup evaporated milk
1 Chocolate Crumb Crust (See Index.)
1 quart gluten-free coffee ice cream, slightly softened
¼ cup chopped pecans

Melt the chocolate and butter in the top of a double boiler. Stir in the sugar and milk. Simmer over low heat, stirring constantly, until thick. Remove from heat, cool, then refrigerate for ½ hour. Fill the crust with the ice cream. Spread the chocolate sauce over the top. Sprinkle with the pecans. Freeze for 6 hours or up to 1 month. *Makes 8 1¾-inch-thick servings.*

One serving—Calories: 383; Total fat: 26 g; Saturated fat: 4.9 g; Cholesterol: 34 mg; Sodium: 208 mg; Carbohydrates: 38.5 g; Fiber: 1.1 g; Sugar: 34.9 g; Protein: 4.6 g

Cocoa Rum Parfaits

This parfait is also excellent with gluten-free mint chocolate-chip ice cream or gluten-free coffee ice cream.

¼ cup unsweetened cocoa

⅓ cup hot water

½ tablespoon butter

¼ cup honey

¼ cup light corn syrup

¼ teaspoon vanilla

2 tablespoons gluten-free light rum

1 quart gluten-free vanilla ice cream

1½ cups sweetened whipped cream

1 1.55-ounce gluten-free milk chocolate candy bar, grated

In a saucepan, stir together the cocoa, water, butter, honey, and corn syrup. Bring to a boil; immediately remove from heat. Stir in the vanilla and rum. Fill six parfait glasses half full with the ice cream; pour 2 tablespoons of the sauce in each parfait glass. Repeat the layers. Freeze until firm, about 3 hours. Just before serving, top the parfaits with the whipped cream, and sprinkle with the grated chocolate. *Makes 6 parfaits.*

One parfait—Calories: 384; Total fat: 18.7 g; Saturated fat: 11.8 g; Cholesterol: 65 mg; Sodium: 65 mg; Carbohydrates: 52.4 g; Fiber: 1.4 g; Sugar: 34.9 g; Protein: 4.2 g

5

Low–Calorie Desserts

$\mathcal{T}$he cakes, cookies, puddings, and other recipes in this chapter contain no artificial sweeteners. In many cases, processed sugars have been replaced with the natural sugars of fruits; skim or low-fat milk replaces whole milk and creams. None of these substitutions have sacrificed taste or texture. Enjoy!

Cakes

*P*ineapple Upside-Down Cake

You can vary the fruits in this recipe by replacing the pineapple with drained canned peaches, apricots, or cherries; or canned apples for pies; or sliced bananas.

>   3 tablespoons gluten-free margarine
>   3 tablespoons light brown sugar
>   2 tablespoons light corn syrup

1 8-ounce can crushed pineapple (in juice), drained,
   reserving juice

1 cup Gluten-Free Flour Mixture (See the Hints chapter.)

1 ¼ teaspoons gluten-free baking powder

2 egg whites

1 egg

¾ cup granulated sugar

1 teaspoon vanilla

1 tablespoon gluten-free mayonnaise

½ cup skim milk

Spray a 9-inch round cake pan with gluten-free nonstick spray. Place 1 tablespoon of the margarine in the pan; place the pan in a cold oven. Heat oven to 350°F for 5 minutes. Remove the pan from the oven. Stir in the brown sugar and corn syrup. Spread the pineapple on top of the brown sugar mixture. Sift the flour mixture and baking powder into a small bowl. Beat the egg whites and egg at high speed for 4 minutes or till light and fluffy. Gradually add the granulated sugar; add 1 tablespoon of the reserved pineapple juice, the vanilla, and the mayonnaise. Add the flour mixture and baking powder, beating at low speed, just until combined. In a small saucepan, heat the milk and remaining 2 tablespoons of margarine just until the margarine melts. Stir into the batter just till combined; pour the batter over the pineapple in the cake pan. Bake at 350°F for 30 minutes or till a toothpick inserted in the center comes out clean. Cool on a wire rack 5 minutes; invert the cake onto a serving platter. *Makes 8 2-inch-thick servings.*

One serving—Calories: 194; Total fat: 4.5 g; Saturated fat: 1.1 g; Cholesterol: 27 mg; Sodium: 103 mg; Carbohydrates: 34.7 g; Fiber: 0.7 g; Sugar: 15 g; Protein: 3.8 g

$\mathscr{B}$lack Forest Cake

Be prepared to use a lot of bowls and pans. The effort will be worth it!

6 tablespoons unsweetened cocoa

6 tablespoons Gluten-Free Flour Mixture (See the Hints chapter.)

1 cup plus 2 tablespoons granulated sugar

⅛ teaspoon salt

9 egg whites

1 teaspoon cream of tartar

2 teaspoons gluten-free mayonnaise

1½ teaspoons vanilla

1 16-ounce can pitted tart cherries, drained, reserving ½ cup juice

2 tablespoons water

1 teaspoon gluten-free unflavored gelatin

4 teaspoons light brown sugar

2 teaspoons cornstarch

½ teaspoon grated lemon zest

⅓ cup whipping cream

4 teaspoons confectioners' sugar

⅓ cup ice-cold evaporated skim milk

1 teaspoon lemon juice

Preheat oven to 375°F, and line the bottoms of two 8-inch round cake pans with waxed paper. Sift together the cocoa, flour mixture, 1 cup of the granulated sugar, and the salt. In a large bowl, beat the egg whites till foamy; add the cream of tartar and the remaining 2 tablespoons of granulated sugar, 1 tablespoon at a time. Beat till soft peaks form (not too stiff). Whip in the mayonnaise and 1 teaspoon of the vanilla; continue to beat 1 minute longer. Fold in the cocoa mixture, one-third at a time; pour the batter into the cake pans. Bake 20 minutes or until the cake begins to pull away from the sides of the pans and a toothpick inserted in the center comes out clean. Cool on wire racks, upside down in the pans. When cool, loosen the sides, and turn the cake out onto the wire racks; remove the waxed paper.

Place the cherries in a bowl; set aside 4 to decorate the cake. Pour the water into a small saucepan; sprinkle the gelatin on top. Let stand 5 minutes to soften. Set on very low heat and cook, stirring, till the gelatin dissolves, about 4 minutes. Set the gelatin aside. In another saucepan, combine the brown sugar, cornstarch, and lemon zest; slowly whisk in the reserved cherry juice. Bring to a boil, stirring constantly; boil 1 minute over medium heat. Remove from heat; stir in cherries. In a bowl, whip the cream till soft peaks form. Whip in the confectioners' sugar and the remaining ½ teaspoon of vanilla; beat until stiff peaks form. In a small bowl, combine the evaporated milk and lemon juice; beat with clean beaters at high speed until very stiff; fold in the cooled gelatin mixture, then fold in the whipped cream.

Place one cake layer upside down on a cake plate. Top with the cherry mixture, spreading it to the edge. Gently spread 1 cup of the whipped cream mixture over the cherries. Place the second cake layer on top. Using a pastry bag fitted with a star tip, pipe the remaining whipped cream into rosettes around the edge of the cake. Decorate the center with the reserved cherries. Refrigerate from 1 to 8 hours until serving time. *Makes 12 1¼-inch-thick servings.*

One serving—Calories: 129; Total fat: 3 g; Saturated fat: 1.7 g; Cholesterol: 9 mg; Sodium: 80 mg; Carbohydrates: 23 g; Fiber: 1.1 g; Sugar: 17.5 g; Protein: 4.2 g

Chocolate Angel Food Cake

No cholesterol! If you want a real treat, replace the cinnamon with 1 tablespoon of crème de cacao.

1 cup Gluten-Free Flour Mixture (See the Hints chapter.)

1¼ cups granulated sugar

⅓ cup unsweetened cocoa

¾ teaspoon cinnamon

½ teaspoon salt

12 egg whites

1½ teaspoons cream of tartar

2 teaspoons vanilla

2 teaspoons gluten-free mayonnaise

2 tablespoons sifted confectioners' sugar

Preheat oven to 325°F, and very lightly spray the bottom of a 10-inch tube pan with gluten-free cooking spray. Sift the flour mixture, ¾ cup of the granulated sugar, and the cocoa, cinnamon, and salt into a large bowl. Beat the egg whites till foamy. Add the cream of tartar, and beat until soft peaks form. Gradually add ¼ cup of the granulated sugar, 1 tablespoon at a time, and continue beating until stiff peaks form. Beat in the vanilla and mayonnaise. Sprinkle the remaining ¼ cup of granulated sugar over the top of the egg whites, and fold in gently. Fold the whipped mixture into the flour mixture. Spoon the batter into the pan, and bake 45 minutes or till a toothpick inserted in the center comes out clean. Invert the pan, and let cool. Transfer the cooled cake to a serving platter, and dust with the confectioners' sugar. *Makes 14 1¼-inch-thick servings.*

One serving—Calories: 97; Total fat: 0.4 g; Saturated fat: 0.2 g; Cholesterol: 0 mg; Sodium: 138 mg; Carbohydrates: 19.5 g; Fiber: 1 g; Sugar: 11.7 g; Protein: 4.2 g

Almost Fat-Free Chocolate Cake

This cake is ready to put in the oven in less than 10 minutes, and no mixer is needed. It's hard to believe that this moist, rich cake is fat free and so delicious that it needs no frosting. If you wish, sprinkle top lightly with sifted confectioners' sugar before serving.

1¼ cups Gluten-Free Flour Mixture (See the Hints chapter.)

1 cup sugar

½ cup unsweetened cocoa

¼ cup cornstarch

¾ teaspoon baking soda

½ teaspoon salt

4 egg whites

2 teaspoons gluten-free mayonnaise

1 cup water

½ cup light corn syrup

Preheat oven to 350°F, and spray a 9-inch square pan with gluten-free nonstick spray. Sift the flour mixture, sugar, cocoa, cornstarch, baking soda, and salt into a bowl. In another bowl, whisk together the egg whites, mayonnaise, water, and corn syrup. Stir in dry ingredients. Pour into the greased pan, and bake 30 minutes or until the cake springs back when lightly touched. Cool on a wire rack. *Makes 9 3-inch-square servings.*

One serving—Calories: 196; Total fat: 1 g; Saturated fat: 0.4 g; Cholesterol: 0 mg; Sodium: 187 mg; Carbohydrates: 45.4 g: Fiber: 2.1 g; Sugar: 13.5 g; Protein: 4.1 g

Apple Cake from Finland

Baking the apples on top of the cake batter helps to keep this cake moist.

2 tablespoons plus ¾ cup sugar

½ teaspoon cinnamon

¼ teaspoon nutmeg

4 eggs, separated

2 teaspoons gluten-free mayonnaise

1 teaspoon almond extract

⅔ cup Gluten-Free Flour Mixture
(See the Hints chapter.)

1 teaspoon gluten-free baking powder

¼ teaspoon salt

2 medium McIntosh apples

Honey Topping (Recipe follows.)

Preheat oven to 375°F, and spray a 10″ × 15″ jelly roll pan with gluten-free nonstick spray. Combine 2 tablespoons of the sugar and the cinnamon and nutmeg in a small bowl; set aside. Beat the egg yolks until thick. Gradually beat in ½ cup of the sugar, then the mayonnaise and almond extract. With clean, dry beaters, whip the egg whites until foamy. Gradually beat in the remaining ¼ cup of sugar, 1 tablespoon at a time. Beat until soft peaks form. Fold the egg whites into the yolk mixture. Sift together the flour mixture, baking powder, and salt. Sift half of the dry ingredients over the egg mixture, and gently fold in. Repeat with the remaining dry ingredients. Pour the batter into the greased pan. Peel, core, and thinly slice the apples. Arrange the apple slices over the cake batter. Sprinkle the reserved spiced sugar over the apples. Bake 12 to 15 minutes till the top of the cake springs back when lightly touched. Cool slightly. While still warm, cut the cake into 24 serving pieces. Serve the cake warm with a dollop of the Honey Topping on each piece. *Makes 24 2½-inch-square servings.*

Honey Topping

¾ cup gluten-free plain low-fat yogurt

2 tablespoons honey

¼ teaspoon almond extract

Stir together all the ingredients. *Makes 14 tablespoons (about 24 1¾-teaspoon servings).*

One serving (with topping)—Calories: 58; Total fat: 1 g; Saturated fat: 0.3 g; Cholesterol: 36 mg; Sodium: 44 mg; Carbohydrates: 10.6 g; Fiber: 0.4 g; Sugar: 7 g; Protein: 1.8 g

ℳacaroon Cupcakes

These cupcakes are perfect for taking to picnics. They may be lightly dusted with sifted confectioners' sugar or frosted with Caramel Icing (see Index).

6 tablespoons gluten-free margarine, softened

⅔ cup sugar

2 large eggs, separated

1 teaspoon almond extract

½ teaspoon vanilla

1¼ cups Gluten-Free Flour Mixture
  (See the Hints chapter.)

2 teaspoons gluten-free baking powder

½ cup 1% milk

¾ cup shredded coconut

Preheat oven to 350°F, and line muffin tins with paper muffin cups. Cream the margarine; gradually add ½ cup of the sugar, and beat till fluffy. Add the egg yolks, almond extract, and vanilla; beat well. With clean, dry beaters, whip the egg whites till soft peaks form. Gradually add the remaining 2⅔ tablespoons of sugar; beat till stiff. Sift the flour mixture and baking powder; add to the sugar mixture. Beat in the milk. Fold in the coconut. Fold in the egg whites. Spoon the batter into the muffin cups, filling each two-thirds full. Bake 20 minutes or until a toothpick inserted in the center comes out clean. *Makes 18 cupcakes.*

One cupcake—Calories: 93; Total fat: 4.6 g; Saturated fat: 1.9 g; Cholesterol: 24 mg; Sodium: 59 mg; Carbohydrates: 11.2 g; Fiber: 0.6 g; Sugar: 4.6 g; Protein: 1.8 g

Cookies

*C*ake Brownies

Imagine . . . delicious chocolate brownies with 0.1 milligram of cholesterol. Amazing!

    ¼ cup gluten-free margarine
    ⅔ cup granulated sugar
    ¼ cup unsweetened cocoa
    1 egg white, slightly beaten
    2 teaspoons gluten-free mayonnaise
    1 teaspoon vanilla
    ¾ cup Gluten-Free Flour Mixture (See the Hints chapter.)
    ½ teaspoon gluten-free baking powder
    ¼ teaspoon baking soda
    ½ cup skim milk
    ½ cup chopped walnuts
    1 teaspoon confectioners' sugar
    Chocolate Icing (Recipe follows.)

Preheat oven to 350°F, and spray a 9-inch square pan with gluten-free nonstick spray. Melt the margarine in a medium saucepan. Remove from heat; stir in the granulated sugar and cocoa. Whip in the egg white, mayonnaise, and vanilla just till combined. Sift together the flour mixture, baking powder, and baking soda. Stir the dry ingredients and milk into the sugar mixture till well mixed. Stir in the nuts; spread the batter in the greased pan. Bake 16 to 18 minutes or till a toothpick inserted in the center comes out clean. Cool on a wire rack. When cool, sift the confectioners' sugar over the top, and drizzle with the Chocolate Icing. Let stand 30 minutes to set icing. *Makes 16 brownies.*

One brownie—Calories: 100; Total fat: 5.9 g; Saturated fat: 0.9 g; Cholesterol: 0.1 mg; Sodium: 35 mg; Carbohydrates: 10.9 g; Fiber: 0.9 g; Sugar: 5.4 g; Protein: 2.1 g

Chocolate Icing

½ cup sifted confectioners' sugar

1 tablespoon unsweetened cocoa

¼ teaspoon vanilla

1–2 tablespoons skim milk

Stir together the sugar, cocoa, vanilla, and enough milk to make the icing a drizzling consistency. *Makes ½ cup (about 16 1½ teaspoon servings).*

One serving—Calories: 16; Total fat: 0.1 g; Saturated fat: 0 g; Cholesterol: 0 mg; Sodium: 1 mg; Carbohydrates: 4 g; Fiber: 0.1 g; Sugar: 3.7 g; Protein: 0.1 g

Fudgy Brownies

These fudgy brownies taste every bit as good as their high-calorie counterparts.

¼ cup unsweetened cocoa

⅓ cup warm water

¼ cup corn oil

⅓ cup granulated sugar

⅓ cup light brown sugar

2 egg whites

1 egg

1 teaspoon vanilla

¾ cup Gluten-Free Flour Mixture (See the Hints chapter.)

½ teaspoon gluten-free baking powder

¼ teaspoon salt

½ cup chopped walnuts

Preheat oven to 350°F. Spray an 8-inch square pan with gluten-free nonstick spray. In a bowl, sift the cocoa into the water; let stand 5 minutes. Stir in the corn oil and the granulated and brown sugars. Slightly beat the egg whites, egg, and vanilla; stir into the cocoa mixture. Sift the flour mixture, baking powder, and salt. Add the dry ingredients to the cocoa mixture; stir 2 minutes. Fold in the nuts. Pour into the greased pan; bake 20 minutes or till a toothpick inserted in the center comes out clean. Cool in the pan. *Makes 16 brownies.*

One brownie—Calories: 100; Total fat: 6.1 g; Saturated fat: 0.8 g; Cholesterol: 13 mg; Sodium: 49 mg; Carbohydrates: 10.3 g; Fiber: 0.8 g; Sugar: 4.8 g; Protein: 2.1 g

*P*umpkin Bars

Be careful not to overbake these bar cookies. They will stay moist and fresh if covered and refrigerated.

1 cup Gluten-Free Flour Mixture (See the Hints chapter.)

²/₃ cup sugar

1 ¼ teaspoons gluten-free baking powder

1 teaspoon cinnamon

⅛ teaspoon salt

½ teaspoon baking soda

⅛ teaspoon ground cloves

1 tablespoon gluten-free mayonnaise

1 cup pumpkin

3 egg whites, slightly beaten

¼ cup plus 1 tablespoon corn oil

¼ cup water

Orange Cream Frosting (Recipe follows.)

Preheat oven to 350°F, and spray an 8″ × 12″ pan with gluten-free nonstick spray. Sift together the flour mixture, sugar, baking powder, cinnamon, salt, baking soda, and cloves. Stir in the mayonnaise, pumpkin, egg whites, corn oil, and water till thoroughly combined. Spread in the oiled pan. Bake 20 minutes or till a toothpick inserted in the center comes out clean. Cool in the pan on a wire rack. When cool, frost with the Orange Cream Frosting, and cut into bars. Cover the bars, and store in the refrigerator up to 2 days. *Makes 24 bars.*

Orange Cream Frosting

> ¼ cup gluten-free cream cheese, softened
> 1¾ cups sifted confectioners' sugar
> 1 teaspoon vanilla
> ¼ teaspoon grated orange zest

Whip together the cream cheese, 1 cup of the confectioners' sugar, the vanilla, and the orange zest till fluffy. Gradually beat in the remaining ¾ cup of sugar. *Makes 2 cups (about 24 4-teaspoon servings).*

One bar (with frosting)—Calories: 88; Total fat: 3.5 g; Saturated fat: 0.7 g; Cholesterol: 2 mg; Sodium: 38 mg; Carbohydrates: 13.5 g; Fiber: 0.4 g; Sugar: 9.2 g; Protein: 1.3 g

Apricot Cranberry Bars

These bar cookies are perfect for packing into lunch boxes or serving with a small dish of gluten-free ice cream.

> 4 ounces gluten-free cream cheese, softened
> ⅓ cup corn oil
> ½ cup light brown sugar
> ¼ teaspoon nutmeg
> ¼ teaspoon salt
> 1½ cups Gluten-Free Flour Mixture (See the Hints chapter.)
> Cranberry Filling (Recipe follows.)
> 3 tablespoons granulated sugar

Preheat oven to 375°F, and lightly grease a 9-inch square pan. Whip the cream cheese, corn oil, brown sugar, nutmeg, and salt until smooth. Sift the flour mixture; add to the cheese mixture, beating at low speed until just combined. Reserve ½ cup of the dough. Press the remainder into the greased pan, and bake 15 minutes. Spoon the Cranberry Filling over the cookie base, spreading evenly. With a fork, work the granulated sugar into the reserved dough to make a crumbly topping. Sprinkle the topping evenly over the filling. Bake 20 minutes or until the topping is golden. Let the cookies cool in the pan, then cut into small bars. *Makes 18 bars.*

Cranberry Filling

> 2 cups cranberries (fresh or frozen)
> ½ cup chopped dried apricots
> ¼ cup honey
> ¼ cup sugar
> ½ teaspoon allspice
> ½ teaspoon cinnamon
> 2 teaspoons grated orange zest
> ¼ cup orange juice

In a saucepan, combine all the ingredients, and bring to a boil. Cook, stirring frequently, for 8 minutes or until thickened. *Makes 2¾ cups.*

One bar (with filling)—Calories: 146; Total fat: 6 g; Saturated fat: 2 g; Cholesterol: 8 mg; Sodium: 58 mg; Carbohydrates: 22.3 g; Fiber: 1.1 g; Sugar: 12.3 g; Protein: 1.6 g

Chocolate Chip Cookies

This recipe uses half the fat and less chocolate than conventional recipes. Using mini chocolate chips gives the illusion of more chocolate.

> ½ cup granulated sugar
> ¼ cup light brown sugar
> 1 teaspoon vanilla

1 egg white, slightly beaten

1 cup Gluten-Free Flour Mixture

(See the Hints chapter.)

¾ teaspoon baking soda

¼ teaspoon salt

¾ cup mini semisweet chocolate chips

Preheat oven to 375°F. Mix the granulated and brown sugars, vanilla, and egg white in a large bowl. Sift the flour mixture, baking soda, and salt; stir into the sugar mixture. Stir in the chocolate chips. Drop by teaspoonfuls onto an ungreased baking sheet. Bake 8 minutes or till very lightly golden. Cool slightly; remove from cookie sheet. *Makes 30 cookies.*

One cookie—Calories: 54; Total fat: 1.6 g; Saturated fat: 1 g; Cholesterol: 0 mg; Sodium: 22 mg; Carbohydrates: 9.5 g; Fiber: 0.2 g; Sugar: 5.8 g; Protein: 0.6 g

Fruit Desserts

Raspberry Torte

If you don't mind adding a few extra calories, stir ½ cup of mini semisweet chocolate chips into the meringue before baking.

¼ cup finely ground almonds

7 tablespoons sugar

1 tablespoon cornstarch

4 egg whites

⅛ teaspoon salt

⅛ teaspoon cream of tartar

¼ teaspoon almond extract

¼ cup all-fruit raspberry jam

Line a baking sheet with heavy brown paper. Using an 8-inch cake pan for a pattern, draw two 8-inch circles on the paper; set aside. Preheat oven to 275°F. Mix the nuts, 1 tablespoon of the sugar, and the cornstarch; set aside. Beat the egg whites with the salt till foamy. Add the cream of tartar; beat 1 minute. Slowly add the remaining 6 tablespoons of sugar; whip until stiff. Beat in the almond extract; fold in the nut mixture. Put the meringue into a pastry bag with a large plain tip; pipe to fill in the two circles on the paper; smooth the tops. Bake the meringues about 35 minutes or until they are almost crisp but still a little sticky. Set on a wire rack to cool. When cool, invert the meringues, and carefully peel off the paper. Place one meringue, flat side up, on a serving plate. Spread with jam, then top with the remaining meringue. Cut into 8 wedges. *Makes 8 1¾-inch-thick servings.*

One serving—Calories: 106; Total fat: 3.7 g; Saturated fat: 0.2 g; Cholesterol: 0 mg; Sodium: 65 mg; Carbohydrates: 15.3 g; Fiber: 0.7 g; Sugar: 12.6 g; Protein: 3.2 g

Winter Fruit Compote

The apricot nectar in the sauce gives this fruit a fabulous taste.

- ½ cup frozen blueberries, thawed and drained
- 1 16-ounce can apricot halves, drained
- 1 16-ounce can peach slices, drained
- 1 cup seedless grapes
- 1 Delicious apple, peeled and sliced
- ½ teaspoon vanilla
- 2 tablespoons honey
- 1 6-ounce can (¾ cup) apricot nectar

In a large bowl, combine the blueberries, apricots, peaches, grapes, and apple. In a separate bowl, stir together the vanilla, honey, and apricot nectar; pour over the fruit. Stir gently to combine. Cover and chill at least 1 hour. Stir just before serving. *Makes 6 ¾-cup servings.*

One serving—Calories: 143; Total fat: 0.4 g; Saturated fat: 0 g; Cholesterol: 0 mg; Sodium: 9 mg; Carbohydrates: 36.8 g; Fiber: 3.3 g; Sugar: 25.3 g; Protein: 1.3 g

ℱresh Fruit Tart

Delicious choices of fruits to top this tart include halved strawberries, sliced kiwi, sliced peaches, seedless grapes, blueberries, and melon balls.

2 eggs, separated

⅓ cup sugar

1 teaspoon gluten-free mayonnaise

½ teaspoon grated lemon zest

1 teaspoon lemon juice

5 tablespoons Gluten-Free Flour Mixture (See the Hints chapter.)

¾ teaspoon gluten-free baking powder

⅛ teaspoon salt

Orange Zest Filling (Recipe follows.)

4 cups fresh fruit

Orange Zest Glaze (Recipe follows.)

Preheat oven to 375°F, and spray an 8″ × 12″ baking pan with gluten-free nonstick spray. Beat the egg yolks until thick. Gradually beat in ¼ cup of the sugar and the mayonnaise; beat in the lemon zest and juice. In a separate bowl, whip the egg whites until foamy with clean, dry beaters. Slowly whip in the remaining 1⅓ teaspoons of sugar, 1 teaspoon at a time, till soft peaks form. Fold the egg white mixture into the egg yolk mixture. Sift the flour mixture, baking powder, and salt; fold into the egg mixture. Spoon the batter into the greased pan. Bake 12 to 15 minutes until lightly browned. Cool the tart base in the pan at least 1 hour; remove from pan, and place on a platter. Pour the Orange Zest

Filling over the tart base, and smooth the top. Cover with plastic wrap; chill 2 hours to set. Arrange the fruit attractively over the cooled filling, then spoon the Orange Zest Glaze over the fruit. *Makes 12 2¾- by 2⅓-inch servings.*

Orange Zest Filling

> 3 tablespoons sugar
>
> 2 tablespoons cornstarch
>
> 1 cup 1% milk
>
> 1 egg, beaten
>
> 3 tablespoons orange juice
>
> 1 teaspoon grated orange zest

In a saucepan, stir together the sugar and cornstarch. Gradually stir in the milk until blended. Add the egg, stirring until completely combined. Place over medium heat, and bring to a boil, stirring constantly with a wire whisk. Whisk in the juice and zest, stirring constantly until the custard is smooth and thickened. *Makes 1¾ cups.*

Orange Zest Glaze

> ⅓ cup sugar
>
> 1 tablespoon plus 2 teaspoons cornstarch
>
> 1 cup orange juice
>
> ½ teaspoon grated orange zest

In a small saucepan, stir together the sugar and cornstarch. Gradually stir in the orange juice and zest. Bring to a boil, stirring constantly, and boil 1 minute. Cool to room temperature, stirring occasionally; glaze the cake. *Makes 1⅓ cups (about 12 5-teaspoon servings).*

One serving (with 1 cup strawberries, 1 cup kiwi, 1 cup fresh sliced peaches, 1 cup blueberries, filling, and glaze)—Calories: 105; Total fat: 1.5 g; Saturated fat: 0.5 g; Cholesterol: 53 mg; Sodium: 61 mg; Carbohydrates: 19.7 g; Fiber: 0.9 g; Sugar: 13 g; Protein: 3 g

ℱlaming Pineapple

This light dessert is perfect after a heavy meal. Serving this dish makes an impressive finale to a small dinner party.

½ teaspoon grated orange zest

¼ cup orange juice

2 teaspoons cornstarch

1 20-ounce can crushed pineapple, packed in juice

½ teaspoon ground ginger

3 tablespoons gluten-free light rum

1 pint gluten-free vanilla frozen yogurt

In a skillet, stir together the orange zest, orange juice, cornstarch, pineapple (with juice), and ginger. Simmer, stirring constantly, until slightly thickened and bubbly. In a small saucepan, heat the rum over low heat just till warm. Carefully ignite the rum, and pour it over the pineapple mixture. Serve immediately by spooning the sauce over scoops of the frozen yogurt. *Makes 6 ¼-cup servings.*

One serving—Calories: 91; Total fat: 1.5 g; Saturated fat: 0.8 g; Cholesterol: 0 mg; Sodium: 23 mg; Carbohydrates: 16.7 g; Fiber: 0.5 g; Sugar: 10 g; Protein: 1.2 g

Frozen Desserts

ℬanana Rum Sundaes

This is a microwave recipe, but it may also be made in a pan on the stove. Begin by bringing the first five ingredients to a boil; lower heat; add bananas; simmer until heated through. Add rum and continue to follow recipe directions.

¼ cup apple juice

4 teaspoons light brown sugar

1 teaspoon gluten-free margarine

Dash nutmeg

Dash cinnamon

2 large bananas, peeled and sliced

1 tablespoon gluten-free light rum

1 cup gluten-free vanilla frozen yogurt

In a microwave-safe casserole, combine the juice, sugar, margarine, nutmeg, and cinnamon. Microwave 1 minute, uncovered, on High. Add the bananas, and toss to coat well. Cook 2 minutes on High till the bananas are heated through, stirring after 1 minute. Pour the rum over the bananas. Carefully ignite. When the flame extinguishes, serve the banana sauce over scoops of the frozen yogurt. *Makes 4 ¼-cup servings with ⅓ cup sauce.*

One serving—Calories: 119; Total fat: 2.7 g; Saturated fat: 1.5 g; Cholesterol: 1 mg; Sodium: 22 mg; Carbohydrates: 26.4 g; Fiber: 1.5 g; Sugar: 3.4 g; Protein: 1.9 g

Mint Julep Sorbet

This dessert is so pretty served in wide crystal champagne glasses—and there's no cholesterol and almost no fat!

2 cups bite-sized chunks honeydew melon

2 cups loosely packed fresh mint leaves

1½ cups plus 1 tablespoon sugar

1 cup boiling water

½ cup freshly squeezed lemon juice

¼ cup gluten-free light rum

2 pints fresh strawberries

Fresh mint leaves for garnish

Freeze the melon chunks in a single layer on a cookie sheet 1 hour or until hard. Place an 8-inch square metal pan in the freezer. Put the mint leaves and 1½ cups of the sugar in a bowl; add the boiling water, and steep 30 minutes. Pour through a fine strainer, and discard the leaves. Stir in the lemon juice and rum. Refrigerate for

1 hour. Hull the strawberries, and cut the larger berries in half. Add the remaining 1 tablespoon of sugar to the strawberries, and mix. Cover and refrigerate 1 hour. Process the frozen melon chunks and the mint water in a blender until smooth. (The mixture will be slushy.) Scrape into the chilled pan, and freeze 1 hour or until firm enough to scoop. To serve, spoon the strawberries into goblets or champagne glasses; top with scoops of the mint sorbet, and garnish with mint leaves. *Makes 8 1-cup servings.*

One serving—Calories: 147; Total fat: 0.4 g; Saturated fat: 0 g; Cholesterol: 0 mg; Sodium: 6 mg; Carbohydrates: 33 g; Fiber: 2.2 g; Sugar: 21.7 g; Protein: 0.7 g

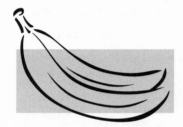

ℬanana Pops

Children love this fun-to-eat snack, so keep plenty on hand in the freezer.

- 4 medium bananas
- 8 Popsicle sticks
- ½ cup gluten-free cornflakes
- 2 tablespoons toasted shredded coconut
- 2 tablespoons finely chopped peanuts
- ½ teaspoon gluten-free apple pie spice
- 4 teaspoons pure maple syrup

Peel the bananas; halve each banana crosswise. Insert a wooden Popsicle stick into the cut end of each banana half. Place on a baking sheet, and freeze 1 hour till the bananas are firm. Coarsely crush the cereal; mix on a sheet of waxed paper with the coconut, peanuts, and apple pie spice. Brush the frozen bananas with the syrup; roll each banana in the cereal mixture to coat it well. Wrap each pop in plastic wrap; return to freezer for 2 hours. *Makes 8 pops.*

One pop—Calories: 98; Total fat: 1.7 g; Saturated fat: 0.5 g; Cholesterol: 0 mg; Sodium: 64 mg; Carbohydrates: 18.2 g; Fiber: 1.7 g; Sugar: 0.8 g; Protein: 1.3 g

ℐineapple Creamsicles

Keep a supply of these high-calcium creamsicles in the freezer for snacking.

> 2 8-ounce cartons gluten-free strawberry or banana
>   low-fat frozen yogurt, slightly softened
> 1 8-ounce can crushed pineapple,
>   packed in juice, undrained
> 6 Popsicle sticks

With a food processor or mixer, combine the yogurt and pineapple until smooth. Fill 5-ounce paper cups three-quarters full, and insert a wooden stick into each. Freeze for 3 hours until firm. Remove each creamsicle from its cup to serve. *Makes 6 pops.*

One pop—Calories: 102; Total fat: 0.7 g; Saturated fat: 0.4 g; Cholesterol: 7 mg; Sodium: 42 mg; Carbohydrates: 21.5 g; Fiber: 0.6 g; Sugar: 19 g; Protein: 3 g

Puddings

ℐumpkin Custard

If you have the time, bake your own fresh pumpkin, remove seeds and stringy pulp, then mash the smooth pulp for a very distinctive taste sensation.

> 2 egg whites
> 1 cup canned or baked and mashed pumpkin
> ¾ cup evaporated skim milk

3 tablespoons granulated sugar

1 teaspoon light brown sugar

½ teaspoon cinnamon

⅛ teaspoon ground ginger

⅛ teaspoon allspice

Dash salt

Preheat oven to 325°F. Place four 6-ounce custard cups in a shallow baking pan. Spray the cups with gluten-free nonstick spray. Whip the egg whites until foamy. Stir in the pumpkin, evaporated milk, granulated and brown sugars, cinnamon, ginger, allspice, and salt. Pour the pumpkin mixture into the custard cups. Pour boiling water around the cups in the baking pan to a depth of 1 inch. Bake 35 to 40 minutes or until a knife inserted near the center comes out clean. Remove the custard cups from the water. Serve warm or chilled. *Makes 4 ½-cup servings.*

One serving—Calories: 89; Total fat: 0.2 g; Saturated fat: 0.1 g; Cholesterol: 2 mg; Sodium: 86 mg; Carbohydrates: 16.1 g; Fiber: 1.7 g; Sugar: 13.4 g; Protein: 6 g

ℬread Pudding with Rum Sauce

Use the most porous gluten-free bread you can find for this recipe.

1½ cups 1% milk

½ cup light brown sugar

⅓ cup granulated sugar

3 egg whites

1 egg

1¼ teaspoons vanilla

¼ teaspoon cinnamon

1 12-ounce can evaporated skim milk

14 slices (½ inch thick each) gluten-free bread, cut into
   ½-inch cubes

½ cup raisins

Rum Sauce (Recipe follows.)

Spray a 7″ × 10″ baking dish with gluten-free nonstick spray. Whisk together the 1% milk, brown and granulated sugars, egg whites, egg, vanilla, cinnamon, and evaporated milk. Add the bread and raisins, and toss gently. Let the mixture stand 1 hour. Preheat oven to 350°F. Spoon the mixture into the greased baking dish, and bake 35 minutes or until the pudding is set. Serve warm with the Rum Sauce. *Makes 10 3½- by 2-inch servings.*

Rum Sauce

½ cup sugar

2 tablespoons gluten-free margarine

1 tablespoon cornstarch

1 cup 1% milk

3 tablespoons gluten-free light rum

Heat the sugar and margarine in a saucepan until the margarine melts. Stir in the cornstarch, and simmer over low heat 1 minute, stirring constantly with a wire whisk. Gradually add the milk, and simmer 4 minutes or until the sauce is thickened, stirring constantly with a wire whisk. Remove from heat, and stir in the rum. *Makes 1¾ cups (about 10 2½-tablespoon servings).*

One serving (with sauce)—Calories: 248; Total fat: 3.7 g; Saturated fat: 1.1 g; Cholesterol: 25 mg; Sodium: 250 mg; Carbohydrates: 40.2 g; Fiber: 1.4 g; Sugar: 29.7 g; Protein: 9 g

6

Pies

$\mathcal{A}$ few tricks will help you make gluten-free piecrusts that are as mouthwatering as crusts made with wheat flour. When making a crumb crust, don't spread the crumbs on the rim of the pie plate—they will just crumble off when you cut the pie.

There are several ways to enhance a piecrust. For a shiny top crust, brush the crust lightly with milk before baking. For a sugary crust, brush the pastry with a little water to moisten, then sprinkle on a little sugar. For a glazed crust, slightly beat 1 egg yolk with a little water, and brush it on the top crust.

When you are making tart shells, the plastic lid of a 1-pound coffee can is the perfect size for cutting rounds of pastry dough.

Piecrusts

Use these piecrusts to make the pie recipes later in this chapter, or create your own gluten-free fillings.

Flaky Piecrust

Although this crust will not be as brown as traditional wheat flour crusts, it is flaky and tastes terrific. If you need a single-crust shell, make this recipe, divide the dough in half, and roll out two crusts, fitting each into a greased pie plate. Cover and freeze the extra one for future use. To customize the flavor, you can add one of the following: ½ cup of shredded cheddar cheese, 3 teaspoons of grated orange or lemon zest, 2 teaspoons of cinnamon, or 4 tablespoons of finely chopped nuts.

> 2¼ cups Gluten-Free Flour Mixture (See the Hints chapter.)
>
> ½ teaspoon sugar
>
> 1 tablespoon cornstarch
>
> ¼ teaspoon salt
>
> ¾ cup butter
>
> ¼ cup ice water

Sift the flour mixture, sugar, cornstarch, and salt; cut in the butter till it is the size of peas. Mix in the water with a fork. Roll half of the dough ⅛ inch thick between two sheets of waxed paper sprinkled with additional Gluten-Free Flour Mixture. Fit into a greased 9-inch pie plate. Spoon filling into crust. Roll out remaining half of dough into a 10-inch circle and lay over filling. Cut a few vent holes or slits in the top crust. Crimp edges to seal. Bake as filling recipe directs. Or for baked pie shells, roll dough as directed above and place in two greased 9-inch pie plates. Prick each shell all over with a fork, and bake 15 minutes at 425°F. *Makes 8 2-inch-thick servings.*

One serving—Calories: 274; Total fat: 18 g; Saturated fat: 0 g; Cholesterol: 45 mg; Sodium: 250 mg; Carbohydrates: 25.8 g; Fiber: 1.1 g; Sugar: 1.3 g; Protein: 3.4 g

*N*o-Roll Flaky Piecrust

This crust is perfect for single-crust baked pies.

    1 cup Gluten-Free Flour Mixture (See the Hints chapter.)
    1 tablespoon sugar
    ¼ cup butter
    1 egg yolk, slightly beaten
    3 tablespoons ice-cold water

Preheat oven to 450°F. Sift together the flour mixture and sugar. Cut in the butter with a fork or two knives. Add the egg yolk and water; mix thoroughly. Press the dough onto the bottom and up the sides of a greased 9-inch pie plate. Pour in desired filling, and bake 10 minutes; reduce heat to 350°F, and continue baking 40 minutes or until the filling is cooked. *Makes 8 2-inch-thick servings.*

One serving—Calories: 114; Total fat: 6.6 g; Saturated fat: 0.2 g; Cholesterol: 42 mg; Sodium: 61 mg; Carbohydrates: 11.9 g; Fiber: 0.5 g; Sugar: 1.4 g; Protein: 1.9 g

*T*oasted Coconut Piecrust

No sugar is needed; toasting releases the natural oils and sugars in the coconut, giving a distinctive "nutty" taste. This crust is perfect for fillings that require refrigeration instead of baking.

    3 tablespoons butter
    1½ cups shredded coconut

Melt the butter in a skillet. Add the coconut; stir over medium heat until the coconut is golden. Press the mixture firmly onto the bottom and sides of a lightly oiled 9-inch pie plate. Let stand at room temperature till cool. *Makes 8 2-inch-thick servings.*

One serving—Calories: 92; Total fat: 8.2 g; Saturated fat: 4.5 g; Cholesterol: 11 mg; Sodium: 48 mg; Carbohydrates: 2.2 g; Fiber: 1.3 g; Sugar: 0 g; Protein: 0.6 g

*U*nbaked Coconut Crust

Using unbaked coconut results in a marvelously moist piecrust for refrigerated pie fillings.

> 1 ½ cups shredded coconut
> ½ cup confectioners' sugar
> 3 tablespoons butter, melted

Combine the coconut with the sugar. Gradually stir in the melted butter. Press the mixture evenly over the bottom and sides of a lightly oiled 9-inch pie plate. Refrigerate until firm. *Makes 8 2-inch-thick servings.*

One serving—Calories: 122; Total fat: 9.5 g; Saturated fat: 4.5 g; Cholesterol: 11 mg; Sodium: 49 mg; Carbohydrates: 9.7 g; Fiber: 1.3 g; Sugar: 7.2 g; Protein: 0.6 g

*C*runchy Piecrust

Dipping your spoon into hot water will make it easier to form this crust. Coconut may be used in place of the nuts. Fill crust with a no-bake filling.

> 1 cup Gluten-Free Flour Mixture (See the Hints chapter.)
> ¼ cup light brown sugar
> ½ cup butter
> ½ cup chopped walnuts

Preheat oven to 400°F. Sift the flour mixture; stir in the brown sugar. Cut in the butter with a fork. Add the nuts; blend the mixture with your hands to combine the ingredients well. Spread on a cookie sheet, and break up any clumps with a fork. Bake 15 minutes. Stir to mix. While still warm, use the back of a spoon to press the mixture into a 9-inch pie plate. Cool before filling. *Makes 8 2-inch-thick servings.*

One serving—Calories: 219; Total fat: 16.9 g; Saturated fat: 0.4 g; Cholesterol: 30 mg; Sodium: 120 mg; Carbohydrates: 15.8 g; Fiber: 1 g; Sugar: 4.3 g; Protein: 2.6 g

$\mathscr{B}$utterscotch Crust

Do not bake or refrigerate this crust, or it will become too hard to slice.

- ½ cup light brown sugar
- ¾ tablespoon light corn syrup
- 3 tablespoons milk
- 1½ tablespoons butter
- 2 cups gluten-free cornflakes (not crushed)

Stir together the brown sugar, corn syrup, milk, and butter in a large saucepan; cook over medium heat to soft ball stage (238°F). Butter a mixing bowl; pour in the syrup. Add the cornflakes, and mix quickly. With the back of a spoon, pack the mixture onto the bottom and sides of a well-buttered 9-inch pie plate. Dip the spoon in hot water to keep the mixture from sticking. Let stand until cool. *Makes 8 2-inch-thick servings.*

One serving—Calories: 84; Total fat: 2.2 g; Saturated fat: 0.1 g; Cholesterol: 6 mg; Sodium: 97 mg; Carbohydrates: 14.4 g; Fiber: 0.3 g; Sugar: 8.3 g; Protein: 0.8 g

$\mathscr{M}$eringue Crust

To make individual meringue shells, form small shells on a baking sheet, and bake as directed in this recipe. For a brown sugar meringue crust, substitute brown sugar for the granulated sugar.

- 4 egg whites
- ⅛ teaspoon salt
- ¼ teaspoon cream of tartar

1 ¼ cups granulated sugar

½ teaspoon vanilla

¼ teaspoon apple cider vinegar

Preheat oven to 300°F, and grease a 9-inch pie plate. Beat the egg whites with salt and cream of tartar till stiff peaks form. Add the sugar, 1 tablespoon at a time, beating well after each addition. Add the vanilla and vinegar, and whip till blended well. Put in the pie plate, using the back of a spoon to build the meringue up on the sides. Bake 1 hour or till firm to the touch but not browned. Cool the shell several hours before filling with a refrigerated filling. *Makes 8 2-inch-thick servings.*

One serving—Calories: 83; Total fat: 0 g; Saturated fat: 0 g; Cholesterol: 0 mg; Sodium: 66 mg; Carbohydrates: 18.9 g; Fiber: 0 g; Sugar: 18.1 g; Protein: 1.7 g

Toasted Nut Crust

For easier slicing, carefully loosen the piecrust around the sides with a small knife as soon as you remove it from the oven.

1 ½ cups finely chopped pecans

¼ cup sugar

⅛ teaspoon salt

1 egg white

Preheat oven to 375°F, and grease a 9-inch pie plate. Mix the pecans with the sugar and salt. Whip the egg white until soft peaks form, then fold the egg white into the nut mixture. Press firmly on the bottom and sides of the greased pie plate. Bake 12 minutes or till light brown. Let stand 15 minutes before filling. *Makes 8 2-inch-thick servings.*

One serving—Calories: 171; Total fat: 16 g; Saturated fat: 1.4 g; Cholesterol: 0 mg; Sodium: 44 mg; Carbohydrates: 6.9 g; Fiber: 0.7 g; Sugar: 4.5 g; Protein: 2.5 g

ℰookie Crust

Cookies that are good to use in this crust are Snickerdoodles, Crescents, Lemon Crinkles, Almond Biscotti, Swiss Stars, and Spritz Cookies (see Index).

1⅓ cups gluten-free crisp cookies, finely crushed
¼ cup butter, softened

Preheat oven to 350°F. With a fork, mix the cookie crumbs with the butter. Press the mixture onto the bottom and sides of an ungreased 9-inch pie plate. Bake 8 minutes. *Makes 8 2-inch-thick servings.*

One serving (made with Lemon Crinkles)—Calories: 82; Total fat: 7 g; Saturated fat: 0.2 g; Cholesterol: 20 mg; Sodium: 75 mg; Carbohydrates: 2.9 g; Fiber: 0 g; Sugar: 2.2 g; Protein: 0.3 g

ℰornflake Nut Crust

Walnuts and cornflakes combine to make a crunchy crust.

1 cup finely crushed gluten-free cornflakes
¼ teaspoon salt
¼ cup butter, softened
½ cup finely chopped walnuts
1 tablespoon honey

Preheat oven to 375°F, and lightly spray a 9-inch pie plate with gluten-free nonstick spray. Mix together all ingredients with a fork. With the back of a spoon, press the mixture into the pie plate. Bake 5 to 7 minutes or till lightly browned. Cool before adding a filling. *Makes 8 2-inch-thick servings.*

One serving—Calories: 123; Total fat: 10.9 g; Saturated fat: 0.4 g; Cholesterol: 15 mg; Sodium: 171 mg; Carbohydrates: 6.3 g; Fiber: 0.6 g; Sugar: 2.6 g; Protein: 1.4 g

Chocolate Coconut Crust

Don't butter the pie plate of a crust that is set in the refrigerator. The butter will harden, making the crust hard to cut.

2 ounces (2 squares) gluten-free unsweetened chocolate

2 tablespoons butter

2 tablespoons hot water

⅔ cup sifted confectioners' sugar

1½ cups shredded coconut

Melt the chocolate and butter in the top of a double boiler. Stir the water and sugar together, then stir the sugar water into the chocolate mixture. Stir in the coconut, and mix till blended. Press the mixture onto the sides and bottom of a 9-inch pie plate. Chill the crust 1 hour till firm. *Makes 8 2-inch-thick servings.*

One serving—Calories: 138; Total fat: 11.9 g; Saturated fat: 6.8 g; Cholesterol: 8 mg; Sodium: 34 mg; Carbohydrates: 9.8 g; Fiber: 2.4 g; Sugar: 5.4 g; Protein: 1.3 g

Chocolate Crumb Crust

To finely crush the puffed-rice cereal, grind it in a blender or food processor.

1¼ cups finely crushed gluten-free puffed-rice cereal

4 tablespoons sugar

1½ tablespoons unsweetened cocoa

½ cup butter, melted

Preheat oven to 350°F, and butter a 9-inch pie plate. In a bowl, stir together the cereal crumbs, sugar, and cocoa. With a fork, stir in the butter. Press the mixture into the pie plate, and bake 6 minutes. Cool before filling. *Makes 8 2-inch-thick servings.*

One serving—Calories: 130; Total fat: 12.1 g; Saturated fat: 0 g; Cholesterol: 30 mg; Sodium: 120 mg; Carbohydrates: 6.2 g; Fiber: 0.3 g; Sugar: 3.6 g; Protein: 0.3 g

Pies and Pie Fillings

You will not find the traditional apple or cherry pie here. Each of these fillings is unique, from the finger-licking down-home Corn Bread Pie to the ultimate decadent indulgence of Brandy Alexander Pie. The nutrition counts for the following pies include the counts for the crusts.

Walnut Flan

When caramelizing sugar, shake the pan frequently to keep the sugar from scorching.

¾ cup butter, softened
3 cups plus 2 tablespoons sugar
2½ cups Gluten-Free Flour Mixture (See the Hints chapter.)
Pinch salt
2 eggs, slightly beaten
1 pint whipping cream
4½ cups walnut halves
1 tablespoon cold water

Preheat oven to 400°F, and lightly grease a 10-inch flan pan with removable bottom. Cream the butter and ½ cup plus 2 tablespoons of the sugar till fluffy. Sift together the flour mixture and salt; beat into the butter. Whip in 1 egg; mix thoroughly. Press the dough into a ball. Between two pieces of waxed paper sprinkled with additional Gluten-Free Flour Mixture, roll out half the dough to a 12-inch circle. Press the dough lightly into the greased pan. Trim by rolling a rolling pin over the top edge. Bake 20 minutes.

In a heavy saucepan, cook the remaining 2½ cups of sugar over low heat till melted and caramelized. Slowly add the cream, stirring constantly. Continue cooking until the sugar melts again. Remove from heat. Stir in the walnuts; let cool. Pour the caramel mixture into the baked pie shell. Roll the second half of the pastry to an 11-inch circle. Place over the filling. Trim excess pastry from edges by pressing lightly with your fingers. Beat together the remaining egg and the water; brush on the surface of the pastry. Score the top of the pastry lightly with the tines of a fork, and prick several times for steam to vent. Bake at 400°F for 20 minutes or till golden. *Makes 12 1½-inch-thick servings.*

One serving—Calories: 626; Total fat: 42.4 g; Saturated fat: 4.8 g; Cholesterol: 75 mg; Sodium: 137 mg; Carbohydrates: 57.8 g; Fiber: 3.6 g; Sugar: 34.5 g; Protein: 9.9 g

ℋot Fudge Sundae Pie

When serving this pie for company, drizzle raspberry sauce on each dessert plate, and set each piece of pie on the sauce.

½ cup butter

2 ounces (2 squares) gluten-free semisweet chocolate

1 cup sugar

2 eggs, lightly beaten

¼ cup Gluten-Free Flour Mixture (See the Hints chapter.)

½ teaspoon salt

1 teaspoon vanilla

1 pint gluten-free vanilla ice cream

1 cup gluten-free chocolate syrup

Preheat oven to 375°F, and grease a 9-inch pie plate. Melt the butter and chocolate in the top of a double boiler over simmering water. Remove from heat, and stir in the sugar. Cool slightly. Stir in the eggs, flour mixture, salt, and vanilla. Pour into the greased pie plate. Bake 35 minutes or till set. Cool slightly; serve each slice warm with a scoop of the ice cream and 2 tablespoons of the chocolate sauce. *Makes 8 2-inch-thick servings.*

One serving—Calories: 351; Total fat: 19 g; Saturated fat: 4.1 g; Cholesterol: 98 mg; Sodium: 360 mg; Carbohydrates: 42.9 g; Fiber: 1 g; Sugar: 37.1 g; Protein: 3.5 g

Peanut Butter Chocolate Pie

This pie is to die for! Every calorie is worth it!

    1 cup semisweet chocolate chips
    1 cup plus 2 tablespoons butter
    2–3 teaspoons water
    ½ cup confectioners' sugar
    1 baked single-crust Flaky Piecrust (See Index.)
    1 cup light brown sugar
    ½ pint whipping cream
    ½ teaspoon vanilla
    1 cup gluten-free creamy peanut butter
    2–3 teaspoons milk
    1½ teaspoons light corn syrup
    ¼ cup chopped unsalted peanuts

In a small pan, melt ½ cup of the chocolate chips with 1 tablespoon of the butter and 2 teaspoons of water, stirring constantly until smooth. Stir in ¼ cup of the confectioners' sugar, and blend until smooth. Add additional water if necessary to make the mixture a thick spreading consistency. Spread the mixture over the bottom and up the sides of the piecrust. Refrigerate 45 minutes to set.

In a saucepan, combine 1 cup of the butter and the brown sugar. Cook over medium heat until the butter is melted and the mixture is smooth, stirring frequently. Refrigerate 10 minutes. In a small bowl, whip the cream with the vanilla and the remaining ¼ cup of confectioners' sugar till stiff. Set aside. In a large bowl, beat the peanut butter with the brown sugar mixture at low speed until blended. Beat 1 minute at medium speed. Add two-thirds of the whipped cream mixture, and beat at low speed till the mixture is smooth and creamy. Pour over the chocolate layer in the pie plate, and refrigerate for 1 hour.

In a small pan over low heat, melt the remaining ½ cup of chocolate chips with the remaining 1 tablespoon of butter, 2 teaspoons of milk, and the corn syrup, stirring constantly until the mixture is smooth. Add additional milk if necessary to make the mixture a spreading consistency. Spoon the chocolate sauce around the edge of the pie; pile the remaining whipped cream mixture in the center of the pie. Sprinkle the peanuts over the whipped cream. Refrigerate from 1 to 24 hours till ready to serve. *Makes 8 2-inch-thick servings.*

One serving—Calories: 714; Total fat: 54.7 g; Saturated fat: 8.4 g; Cholesterol: 98 mg; Sodium: 456 mg; Carbohydrates: 50.5 g; Fiber: 3.7 g; Sugar: 38.1 g; Protein: 12.7 g

Pear Pie

This pie features a cream filling with a luscious caramelized taste.

Pastry for Crunchy Piecrust (See Index.)

2 tablespoons Gluten-Free Flour Mixture (See the Hints chapter.)

½ cup light brown sugar

1½ tablespoons cornstarch

¼ teaspoon salt

2 1-pound cans pear halves, packed in syrup

¾ cup milk

2 eggs, slightly beaten

2 tablespoons butter

½ teaspoon vanilla

¾ cup whipping cream

¼ cup sugar

1 teaspoon cinnamon

Bake the Crunchy Piecrust dough as directed. Press 2 cups of the hot crust mixture against the bottom and sides of a 9-inch pie pan, reserving the rest for a topping. Cool. Sift together the flour mixture, brown sugar, cornstarch, and salt into a medium-size saucepan. Drain the pears, reserving ¾ cup of the syrup. Gradually add the reserved pear syrup and milk to the dry ingredients, and blend until smooth. Cook over medium heat, stirring constantly, until the mixture thickens and comes to a boil. Boil 1 minute, then remove from heat. Very gradually stir at least half of the hot mixture into the beaten eggs, then stir egg mixture back into saucepan. Return to heat, and boil 1 minute. Remove from heat. Stir in the butter and vanilla. Pour into the crust. Chill for 3 hours. Whip the cream, and spread it over the chilled pie. Stir together the sugar and cinnamon; dip the pear halves in the cinnamon sugar, and arrange them on the whipped cream. Sprinkle the top of the pie with the reserved crumbs from the crust mixture. *Makes 8 2-inch-thick servings.*

One serving—Calories: 484; Total fat: 29 g; Saturated fat: 5.6 g; Cholesterol: 119 mg; Sodium: 265 mg; Carbohydrates: 53.4 g; Fiber: 1.8 g; Sugar: 37.3 g; Protein: 5.8 g

Caramel Custard Apple Pie

Let the custard cool *completely* before refrigerating. This prevents moisture from forming on top of the pie.

2 tablespoons butter

2 pounds Golden Delicious apples,
    each peeled and sliced into 8 pieces

½ cup light brown sugar

1 12-ounce can evaporated milk

1 egg yolk

⅓ cup pure maple syrup

2 tablespoons cornstarch

1 teaspoon vanilla

1 baked single-crust Flaky Piecrust (See Index.)

½ cup whipping cream

1 tablespoon granulated sugar

¼ teaspoon cinnamon

Melt the butter in a large skillet. Add the apples and brown sugar. Cook, stirring, until the apples are very tender and thickly glazed, about 15 to 20 minutes. Cool to room temperature. Heat the milk in a saucepan until bubbles appear around the edge of the pan. Whisk together the egg yolk, maple syrup, cornstarch, and vanilla in a bowl. Gradually whisk in the evaporated milk. Return the mixture to the saucepan. Stir over low heat until thickened. Remove from heat, and whisk for 1 minute. Spoon the apples into the piecrust. Top with the hot maple custard, and smooth the top. Cool to room temperature. Refrigerate until the custard is firm, about 1 hour. Whip the cream until soft peaks form. Beat in the granulated sugar and cinnamon until stiff peaks form. Spoon the whipped cream over the pie. *Makes 8 2-inch-thick servings.*

One serving—Calories: 532; Total fat: 27.7 g; Saturated fat: 3.9 g; Cholesterol: 102 mg; Sodium: 344 mg; Carbohydrates: 65.9 g; Fiber: 3.8 g; Sugar: 36.1 g; Protein: 7.9 g

Butterscotch Praline Pie

When you spread the meringue, blend up slight swirls of the butterscotch mixture for color.

⅓ cup plus 6 tablespoons butter

1⅓ cups light brown sugar

½ cup chopped pecans

1 baked single-crust Flaky Piecrust (See Index.)

1 cup water

7 tablespoons Gluten-Free Flour Mixture (See the Hints chapter.)

½ teaspoon salt

1⅔ cups milk

2 eggs, separated

1 teaspoon vanilla

¼ cup granulated sugar

Preheat oven to 450°F. Melt ⅓ cup of the butter in a saucepan; stir in ⅓ cup of the brown sugar and the pecans. Heat, stirring, till the sugar is dissolved; spread on the bottom of the piecrust. Bake 5 minutes or till bubbly; set on a wire rack to cool. Melt the remaining 6 tablespoons of butter; stir in the remaining 1 cup of brown sugar and the water. Heat, stirring, till the sugar is dissolved; remove from heat. Sift the flour mixture and salt; stir in the milk till smooth. Slowly stir in the brown sugar mixture. Cook over low heat, stirring constantly, till the mixture thickens and boils 1 minute; remove from heat. Beat the egg yolks slightly; slowly stir three-fourths of the hot mixture into the yolks. Return the mixture to the pan, and continue cooking, stirring constantly, just till bubbly. Remove from heat; stir in the vanilla. Cool slightly; pour over the praline layer in the piecrust.

Preheat broiler to 375°F. With clean, dry beaters, whip the egg whites till double in volume. Gradually beat in the granulated sugar until barely stiff peaks form. Drop the meringue by teaspoonfuls onto the pie. Brown under broiler till the meringe is golden-tipped. Let the pie cool, then refrigerate 3 to 8 hours until serving time. *Makes 8 2-inch-thick servings.*

One serving—Calories: 673; Total fat: 33.8 g; Saturated fat: 1.4 g; Cholesterol: 124 mg; Sodium: 516 mg; Carbohydrates: 71.7 g; Fiber: 2 g; Sugar: 40.4 g; Protein: 7.8 g

Glazed Strawberry Pie

This just may be the world's greatest strawberry pie!

2 tablespoons cornstarch

¾ cup plus 2 tablespoons granulated sugar

4 pints fresh strawberries, cleaned

½ cup water

4 ounces gluten-free cream cheese, softened

Dash salt

½ teaspoon vanilla

1–2 tablespoons plus ½ pint whipping cream

1 baked single-crust Flaky Piecrust (See Index.)

¼ cup confectioners' sugar

Stir together in a medium-size saucepan the cornstarch and ¾ cup of the sugar. Dice 2 pints of cleaned strawberries; stir them and water into saucepan. Cook over medium heat, stirring constantly, until thickened, smashing the strawberries with the back of a spoon as much as possible (there will be small chunks of berries). Barely simmer the glaze for 15 minutes, then remove from heat and cool at least 15 minutes. Whip together the remaining 2 tablespoons of sugar, cream cheese, salt, and ¼ teaspoon of the vanilla. Add 1 to 2 tablespoons of the whipping cream until the mixture becomes spreadable. Spread the cream cheese mixture on the bottom and sides of the piecrust. Cut any large strawberries in the remaining 2 pints in half; arrange the whole and halved berries (cut side down) on top of the cheese mixture. Cover the pie with the glaze, working the glaze down between the berries with the tip of a spoon. Beat the remaining ½ pint of whipping cream with ¼ teaspoon of the vanilla and the confectioners' sugar until peaks form. Cover the pie with the whipped cream. Refrigerate 3 to 8 hours until serving time. *Makes 8 2-inch-thick servings.*

One serving—Calories: 435; Total fat: 25.2 g; Saturated fat: 5.1 g; Cholesterol: 71 mg; Sodium: 282 mg; Carbohydrates: 47.2 g; Fiber: 2.7 g; Sugar: 16 g; Protein: 4.3 g

Chocolate Meringue Pie

For the crowning touch, lay shaved chocolate curls on top of the center of the pie.

    1 4-ounce bar gluten-free German sweet chocolate, melted
    3 tablespoons gluten-free hot coffee
    1 cup whipping cream
    1 tablespoon vanilla
    ¼ cup chopped walnuts
    1 baked Meringue Crust (See Index.)

Melt the chocolate in a double boiler over simmering water. Stir in the coffee. Whip the cream and vanilla until stiff peaks form; fold into the chocolate mixture. Pour into the piecrust, and sprinkle with the nuts. Refrigerate 4 to 8 hours till serving time. *Makes 8 2½-inch-thick servings.*

One serving—Calories: 377; Total fat: 22.6 g; Saturated fat: 13.3 g; Cholesterol: 30 mg; Sodium: 82 mg; Carbohydrates: 40.7 g; Fiber: 2.2 g; Sugar: 18.2 g; Protein: 3.6 g

Easy Key Lime Pie

This pie uses no green food coloring, so the color of the pie is lighter than most commercial key lime pies.

    Dough for single-crust Flaky Piecrust (See Index.)
    3 egg yolks
    1 14-ounce can sweetened condensed milk

½ cup lime juice

½ pint whipping cream

¼ cup confectioners' sugar

1 fresh key lime

Preheat oven to 400°F. Roll out the piecrust and place it in an 8-inch pie plate. Prick the crust well with a fork, and bake 10 minutes. Remove the crust from the oven, and reduce oven temperature to 325°F. Whip together the egg yolks, milk, and lime juice. Pour into the piecrust, and bake 30 minutes. Cool, then refrigerate pie for 2 hours. Whip the cream with the sugar till stiff; cover the pie with the whipped cream. Garnish the pie with thin lime slices. *Makes 8 1¾-inch-thick servings.*

One serving—Calories: 327; Total fat: 16.2 g; Saturated fat: 4.2 g; Cholesterol: 123 mg; Sodium: 179 mg; Carbohydrates: 39.1 g; Fiber: 0.5 g; Sugar: 5.7 g; Protein: 5.7 g

Corn Bread Pie

Don't laugh at this idea. The pie is terrific!

1⅔ cups sugar

¼ cup butter, softened

1 teaspoon vanilla

3 eggs

1 tablespoon cornmeal

1 tablespoon Gluten-Free Flour Mixture (See the Hints chapter.)

¼ cup milk

1 unbaked single-crust Flaky Piecrust (See Index.)

Preheat oven to 200°F. Cream the sugar, butter, and vanilla till fluffy. Add the eggs, and beat well. Add the cornmeal, flour mixture, and milk, and whip till thoroughly mixed. Pour into the unbaked piecrust, and bake 1 hour. *Makes 8 2-inch-thick servings.*

One serving—Calories: 284; Total fat: 8.8 g; Saturated fat: 4.3 g; Cholesterol: 147 mg; Sodium: 338 mg; Carbohydrates: 68.3 g; Fiber: 1.1 g; Sugar: 7.3 g; Protein: 9.7 g

ℒemonade Chiffon Pie

It is essential that the evaporated milk be ice cold and the lemonade mixture thoroughly chilled.

1 cup evaporated milk

1 envelope gluten-free unflavored gelatin

¼ cup cold water

½ cup boiling water

⅔ cup sugar

1 6-ounce can gluten-free frozen lemonade concentrate

1 Toasted Coconut Piecrust (See Index.)

Chill the evaporated milk in the freezer about 1 hour until almost frozen around the edges. In a large bowl, soften the gelatin in the cold water 5 minutes. Add the boiling water, and stir until the gelatin has dissolved. Stir in the sugar and the frozen lemonade concentrate, stirring until the lemonade thaws. Chill the mixture in the refrigerator about 1 hour until very thick but not set. Place a 1-quart bowl and beaters in the freezer for 15 minutes. Put the ice-cold milk into the chilled bowl, and whip at high speed until stiff peaks form. Fold into the chilled lemonade mixture. Pour into the piecrust, and chill 3 hours until firm. *Makes 8 2-inch-thick servings.*

One serving—Calories: 220; Total fat: 10.6 g; Saturated fat: 6 g; Cholesterol: 20 mg; Sodium: 83 mg; Carbohydrates: 27.2 g; Fiber: 1.4 g; Sugar: 11.7 g; Protein: 2.8 g

ℤucchini Pie

This pie is definitely a novel dessert that will bring raves. You don't taste the zucchini!

3 medium zucchini, unpeeled

1 teaspoon salt

2 eggs, slightly beaten

½ cup sugar

½ cup Gluten-Free Flour Mixture (See the Hints chapter.)

⅓ cup Cream of Rice

½ teaspoon cinnamon

½ teaspoon vanilla

1 cup raisins

1 cup chopped walnuts

1 single-crust Flaky Piecrust (See Index.)

Preheat oven to 450°F. Grate the zucchini, and put it in a colander; sprinkle with salt, and mix with a spoon. Leave the zucchini in the colander several hours (or overnight) to drain. Squeeze the zucchini dry, and put it in a bowl. Stir in the eggs and sugar. Sift together the flour mixture, Cream of Rice, and cinnamon; stir into the egg mixture. Stir in the vanilla, then the raisins and nuts. Prick the pie crust all over with a fork. Bake 5 minutes, then pour the filling into the piecrust. Lower oven temperature to 350°; bake 25 minutes or till a knife inserted in the center comes out clean. *Makes 8 2-inch-thick servings.*

One serving—Calories: 388; Total fat: 21 g; Saturated fat: 1.5 g; Cholesterol: 95 mg; Sodium: 85 mg; Carbohydrates: 50.6 g; Fiber: 3.7 g; Sugar: 23.8 g; Protein: 8.4 g

ᴓweet Potato Pie

You may boil your own sweet potatoes, but drained canned sweet potatoes work equally well in this recipe. If you prefer fresh sweet potatoes, cook 1 pound of them to get 1 cup mashed.

1 cup mashed sweet potatoes

½ cup light brown sugar

¼ teaspoon salt

¼ teaspoon cinnamon

¼ teaspoon allspice

½ teaspoon vanilla

2 eggs

1 5-ounce can evaporated milk

1 No-Roll Flaky Piecrust (See Index.)

Preheat oven to 450°F. Whip together the sweet potatoes, brown sugar, salt, cinnamon, allspice, vanilla, and eggs. When smooth, blend in the milk on low speed. Pour the filling into the piecrust and place in the oven. Immediately lower oven temperature to 350° and bake 35 minutes or until a knife inserted near the center comes out clean. *Makes 8 2-inch-thick servings.*

One serving—Calories: 213; Total fat: 9.1 g; Saturated fat: 1.3 g; Cholesterol: 99 mg; Sodium: 170 mg; Carbohydrates: 28 g; Fiber: 1.4 g; Sugar: 10.1 g; Protein: 5 g

Crème de Cacao Pie

Crème de cacao and apricot brandy blend to make this pie irresistible.

2 envelopes gluten-free unflavored gelatin

¾ cup whipping cream

¾ cup scalded milk

¼ cup sugar

3 tablespoons gluten-free apricot brandy

3 tablespoons crème de cacao

1 cup ice cubes (6–8 small cubes)

1 Chocolate Coconut Crust (See Index.)

In a blender, sprinkle the gelatin over the cold whipping cream; let stand 5 minutes. Add the hot milk, and process on the lowest speed until the gelatin is completely dissolved, about 2 minutes. Add the sugar, brandy, and crème de cacao; process at high speed until blended. Add the ice cubes, one at a time; process at high speed until the ice is melted. Pour into the piecrust, and chill until firm. *Makes 8 2-inch-thick servings.*

One serving—Calories: 256; Total fat: 18.7 g; Saturated fat: 11.8 g; Cholesterol: 33 mg; Sodium: 54 mg; Carbohydrates: 17.7 g; Fiber: 2.4 g; Sugar: 10.1 g; Protein: 2 g

$\mathscr{B}$randy Alexander Pie

Several steps in this recipe require time for ingredients to cool, so allow plenty of time to prepare this masterpiece.

1 Chocolate Petal Crust (Recipe follows.)
30 large gluten-free marshmallows
½ cup milk
1 cup semisweet chocolate chips
1 teaspoon vanilla
2 tablespoons gluten-free brandy
2 tablespoons crème de cacao
2 cups heavy cream
Shaved chocolate for garnish

Prepare and bake the Chocolate Petal Crust. Set aside to cool. Combine the marshmallows and milk in a saucepan. Cook over low heat, stirring constantly, until the marshmallows are melted and the mixture is smooth. Pour half of the marshmallow mixture into a small bowl; set aside. Add the chocolate chips to the marshmallow mixture remaining in the saucepan. Return to low heat, and stir until the chocolate chips are melted. Remove from heat; stir in the vanilla. Cool to room temperature. Stir the brandy and crème de cacao into the bowl of reserved marshmallow mixture. Chill until the mixture mounds slightly when dropped from a spoon, about 45 minutes.

Beat the cream in a chilled bowl until stiff peaks form. Fold 2 cups of the whipped cream into the cooled chocolate mixture, then spoon the chocolate and cream mixture into the piecrust. Fold the remaining whipped cream into the chilled brandy mixture. Spread over the chocolate mixture. Chill the pie about 2 hours until firm. Just before serving, garnish the top of the pie with shaved chocolate. *Makes 8 2-inch-thick servings.*

One serving—Calories: 419; Total fat: 32.2 g; Saturated fat: 18 g; Cholesterol: 86 mg; Sodium: 45 mg; Carbohydrates: 40 g; Fiber: 1.2 g; Sugar: 36.7 g; Protein: 3 g

Chocolate Petal Crust

¼ cup butter, softened

½ cup sugar

1 egg

½ teaspoon vanilla

½ cup Gluten-Free Flour Mixture (See the Hints chapter.)

¼ cup unsweetened cocoa

½ teaspoon baking soda

⅛ teaspoon salt

Whip the butter till smooth; add the sugar, egg, and vanilla, beating till fluffy. Sift the flour mixture, cocoa, baking soda, and salt; add to the butter mixture, beating well. Divide the dough in half. Shape each half into a long roll, 1½ inches in diameter. Wrap each roll in plastic wrap; refrigerate until firm (several hours). Preheat oven to 375°F, and butter a 9-inch pie plate. Slice each roll ⅛ inch thick. Arrange the slices, edges just touching, on the bottom and up the sides of the buttered pie plate. (Small spaces in the crust will blend together during baking.) Bake 8 to 10 minutes until the crust is slightly puffed and feels somewhat firm when gently touched with a fingertip. Do not overbake. Cool completely on a wire rack before filling. *Makes 8 2-inch-thick servings.*

One serving—Calories: 123; Total fat: 7 g; Saturated fat: 0.5 g; Cholesterol: 42 mg; Sodium: 106 mg; Carbohydrates: 14.6 g; Fiber: 1.1 g; Sugar: 7.5 g; Protein: 2 g

Chocolate Bar Pie

For company, add a garnish of almond daisies on top of the pie by arranging 6 almonds in a circle, pointed ends at the center of the circle.

20 large gluten-free marshmallows

1 4-ounce gluten-free chocolate almond bar

1 square (1 ounce) gluten-free unsweetened chocolate

⅔ cup milk

1 cup heavy cream

1 Chocolate Crumb Crust (See Index.)

Combine the marshmallows, chocolate bar, unsweetened chocolate, and milk in the top of a double boiler. Heat over hot, not boiling, water until melted, stirring frequently. Cool. Whip the cream until stiff peaks form; fold into the chocolate mixture. Pour into the piecrust, and chill for several hours. *Makes 8 2-inch-thick servings.*

One serving—Calories: 796; Total fat: 44.7 g; Saturated fat: 22 g; Cholesterol: 126 mg; Sodium: 237 mg; Carbohydrates: 90.3 g; Fiber: 1.7 g; Sugar: 80.6 g; Protein: 3.1 g

German Chocolate Pie

Do not substitute walnuts for the pecans. The pecans give this pie a special flavor. Note that the baking directions for the piecrust in this recipe vary from those for the basic No-Roll Flaky Piecrust recipe.

1 4-ounce bar gluten-free milk chocolate

¼ cup butter

1⅔ cups evaporated milk

1½ cups sugar

3 tablespoons cornstarch

⅛ teaspoon salt

2 eggs

1 teaspoon vanilla

1 No-Roll Flaky Piecrust (See Index.)

1⅓ cups flaked coconut

½ cup chopped pecans

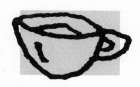

Preheat oven to 375°F. Place the chocolate and butter in a saucepan, and melt over low heat till blended, stirring constantly. Remove from heat, and gradually blend in the milk. Combine the sugar, cornstarch, and salt. Beat in the eggs and vanilla. Blend in the chocolate mixture. Pour into the piecrust. Combine the coconut and pecans, and sprinkle over filling. Bake 45 minutes. Cool at least 4 hours before cutting. (The filling will set while cooling.) *Makes 8 2-inch-thick servings.*

One serving—Calories: 584; Total fat: 35.5 g; Saturated fat: 12.2 g; Cholesterol: 17 mg; Sodium: 282 mg; Carbohydrates: 58.2 g; Fiber: 3.1 g; Sugar: 32.4 g; Protein: 11.6 g

Cheesecake Pumpkin Pie

Let this pie cool completely before refrigerating it. This prevents the layers from separating.

1½ cups canned pumpkin

¾ cup sugar

¾ teaspoon cinnamon

¼ teaspoon ground cloves

½ teaspoon ground ginger

½ teaspoon salt

2 eggs, slightly beaten

1¼ cups evaporated milk

1 teaspoon vanilla

1 No-Roll Flaky Piecrust (See Index.)

Cheesecake Topping (Recipe follows.)

Preheat oven to 400°F. Whip together the pumpkin, sugar, cinnamon, cloves, ginger, and salt. Blend in the eggs, milk, and vanilla. Pour into the piecrust. Pour the Cheesecake Topping over the pumpkin filling, and bake 35 to 40 minutes or until center is set. *Makes 8 2-inch-thick servings.*

Cheesecake Topping

¼ cup sugar

1 teaspoon vanilla

Dash salt

8 ounces gluten-free cream cheese, softened

2 eggs

Whip together the sugar, vanilla, salt, and cream cheese. Add the eggs, one at a time, beating well after each addition. *Makes 1¾ cups.*

One serving (with topping)—Calories: 277; Total fat: 14.2 g; Saturated fat: 4.6 g; Cholesterol: 165 mg; Sodium: 293 mg; Carbohydrates: 31.4 g; Fiber: 1.7 g; Sugar: 17.9 g; Protein: 6.5 g

Chocolate Pie

If you love almonds, use chocolate almond bars in place of the plain chocolate bars.

1 tablespoon water

1 8-ounce gluten-free chocolate candy bar

1 8-ounce container gluten-free nondairy whipped topping

1 Chocolate Crumb Crust (See Index.)

In the top of a double boiler, melt the water and chocolate over hot (not boiling) water. Mix well, then let cool. Fold in the whipped topping; spoon into the piecrust. Cover and freeze at least 3 hours. *Makes 8 2-inch-thick servings.*

One serving—Calories: 593; Total fat: 25.8 g; Saturated fat: 10.1 g; Cholesterol: 30 mg; Sodium: 203 mg; Carbohydrates: 89.5 g; Fiber: 1.3 g; Sugar: 61.7 g; Protein: 2.6 g

*P*ineapple Marshmallow Pie

This is a refreshing pie to serve in the summertime. It is pretty garnished with fresh mint leaves.

    30 large gluten-free marshmallows
    1 cup milk
    1 20-ounce can crushed pineapple, drained
    ½ pint heavy cream
    1 Toasted Coconut Piecrust (See Index.)

Combine the marshmallows and milk in the top of a double boiler. Heat, stirring frequently, until the marshmallows are melted. Set aside to cool. Stir pineapple into the marshmallow mixture. Whip the cream until stiff peaks form; fold into the pineapple mixture. Spoon the filling into the piecrust, and refrigerate 8 hours. Serve cold. *Makes 8 2-inch-thick servings.*

One serving—Calories: 242; Total fat: 13.9 g; Saturated fat: 6.9 g; Cholesterol: 26 mg; Sodium: 78 mg; Carbohydrates: 31.3 g; Fiber: 1.5 g; Sugar: 28.7 g; Protein: 2.3 g

*F*resh Raspberry Pie

Raspberries must be handled very gently. Rinse them, and let them drain dry before adding them to the pie. This pie is excellent topped with a scoop of gluten-free vanilla ice cream.

    1 cup water
    1 cup sugar
    3 tablespoons cornstarch
    ½ cup plus 1 quart fresh raspberries
    1 baked single-crust Flaky Piecrust (See Index.)

Combine the water, sugar, and cornstarch in a saucepan, and cook on medium or low heat until thick, stirring frequently. With a fork, slightly mash ½ cup of the berries; stir into the sugar mixture. Place the remaining berries in the piecrust. Pour the sauce over the berries, and let the filling set. *Makes 8 2-inch-thick servings.*

One serving—Calories: 242; Total fat: 9 g; Saturated fat: 0 g; Cholesterol: 23 mg; Sodium: 126 mg; Carbohydrates: 14.8 g; Fiber: 5.3 g; Sugar: 14.6 g; Protein: 2.3 g

*B*rown Sugar Peach Pie

In place of the fresh peaches, you may substitute 3½ cups of drained canned peaches.

Dough for 1 Flaky Piecrust (See Index.)
6 fresh peaches, peeled and sliced
¾ cup light brown sugar
⅓ cup cornstarch
4 tablespoons light corn syrup
1 tablespoon lemon juice
⅓ cup butter, softened
1 tablespoon milk
2 tablespoons granulated sugar

Preheat oven to 400°F. Roll half the piecrust dough ⅛ inch thick between two sheets of waxed paper that have been sprinkled with flour mixture. Fit the dough into a 9-inch greased pie plate. Place the peaches on the piecrust. Combine the brown sugar, cornstarch, corn syrup, lemon juice, and butter in a saucepan. Cook over low heat for 1 to 2 minutes or until the sugar is completely dissolved, stirring constantly. Cool slightly; pour the sauce over the peaches. Roll out the remaining piecrust dough into a 10-inch circle. Place the top crust over the pie and crimp edges. With a sharp knife, cut several slits in the top crust for steam to escape.

Brush the milk over the crust; sprinkle the crust with the granulated sugar. Bake about 40 minutes till top crust is light golden.
Makes 8 2-inch-thick servings.

One serving—Calories: 302; Total fat: 16.6 g; Saturated fat: 0 g; Cholesterol: 41 mg;
Sodium: 201 mg; Carbohydrates: 36.4 g; Fiber: 1.5 g; Sugar: 11.3 g; Protein: 2.2 g

ℒuscious Lemon Meringue Tarts

To achieve volume, eggs must be at room temperature when you
whip them.

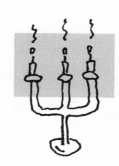

- 3 eggs, separated
- ⅛ teaspoon cream of tartar
- 1¾ cups sugar
- ¾ teaspoon vanilla
- ⅛ teaspoon salt
- 3 tablespoons cornstarch
- 1½ cups boiling water
- Juice of 2 lemons
- 2 tablespoons grated lemon zest
- 1 fresh lemon, thinly sliced

Remove the eggs from the refrigerator to come to room temperature. Preheat oven to 250°F, and cover the bottoms of six
medium muffin tins with rounds of heavy brown paper. (Do not
grease.) Beat the egg whites till foamy. Add the cream of tartar,
and beat till soft peaks form. Add ¾ cup of the sugar, 2 tablespoons at a time, beating well after each addition. Whip in the
vanilla. Pack each muffin tin with the meringue, indenting it in
the center and building up the sides to form a cup. Bake 1¼ hours.
Let stand a few minutes; remove from pans, and let cool. Mix the
remaining 1 cup of sugar with the salt and cornstarch in a
saucepan. Slowly add the boiling water, and cook over medium
heat until thick, stirring constantly. Whip the egg yolks; add the

lemon juice and zest. Beating constantly, slowly add half of the sugar and cornstarch mixture to the egg yolk mixture, then stir this back into the saucepan with the remaining sugar and cornstarch mixture. Cook in the top of a double boiler until thick, about 10 minutes, stirring constantly. Cool. Fill the meringue shells with the custard. Decorate each tart with a slice of fresh lemon. *Makes 6 tarts.*

One tart—Calories: 196; Total fat: 2.5 g; Saturated fat: 0.8 g; Cholesterol: 106 mg; Sodium: 83 mg; Carbohydrates: 39.8 g; Fiber: 0 g; Sugar: 33.8 g; Protein: 3.2 g

7
Puddings

$\mathcal{T}$his chapter features several delicious recipes. To prevent the surface of the puddings from getting "weepy," cool them completely before refrigerating. If using one of the recipes for a pie filling, use approximately ½ cup less liquid.

Chocolate Creme

To make a creamy pudding, this recipe uses half-and-half instead of milk. For an even richer treat, use cream in place of the half-and-half.

> 1 cup sugar
> ⅓ cup cornstarch
> ¼ teaspoon salt
> 3 ounces (3 squares) gluten-free unsweetened chocolate,
>   cut into small pieces
> 3 cups half-and-half
> 1 ½ teaspoons vanilla
> Sweetened whipping cream (optional)

Combine the sugar, cornstarch, salt, and chocolate in a saucepan. Gradually stir in the half-and-half. Cook over medium heat, stirring constantly, until the chocolate melts and the mixture comes to a boil and thickens. Boil 1 minute. Remove from heat; stir in the vanilla. Pour into a 3-cup mold, and cover with plastic wrap. Refrigerate until cold (about 3 hours). When ready to serve, run a knife around the top edge; dip the mold very quickly in warm water, then invert onto a serving platter. Garnish with sweetened whipped cream, if desired. *Makes 6 ½-cup servings.*

One serving (without whipped cream)—Calories: 254; Total fat: 21.6 g; Saturated fat: 13.3 g; Cholesterol: 44 mg; Sodium: 150 mg; Carbohydrates: 15.5 g; Fiber: 2.4 g; Sugar: 4.1 g; Protein: 5.5 g

Greek Rice Halvah

This Greek pudding is thick in texture and has the combined taste of cinnamon and orange.

¾ cup butter, softened

¾ cup sugar

4 eggs

2 cups Cream of Rice

1 teaspoon cinnamon

1 cup coarsely chopped almonds

Halvah Syrup (Recipe follows.)

Preheat oven to 350°F, and grease a 9-inch square pan. Cream the butter and sugar until fluffy. Add the eggs, one at a time, beating well after each. Add the Cream of Rice and cinnamon, and beat until the mixture is creamy. Stir in the almonds. Pour the mixture into the greased pan, and bake 40 minutes. While the halvah is still hot, pour the Halvah Syrup over the top. Cool, then cut into squares. *Makes 9 3-inch-square servings.*

Halvah Syrup

½ pound butter

2 slices fresh orange

2 cups water

1 cinnamon stick

Combine all the ingredients in a saucepan over medium-high heat; bring to a boil. Boil until the mixture reaches the consistency of a thick syrup. Remove the orange slices and cinnamon stick; pour slowly over the halvah. *Makes 9 ⅓-cup servings.*

One serving (with syrup)—Calories: 377; Total fat: 18.8 g; Saturated fat: 1.2 g; Cholesterol: 119 mg; Sodium: 128 mg; Carbohydrates: 44.1 g; Fiber: 1.6 g; Sugar: 10.1 g; Protein: 7.9 g

Caramel Custard Mold

Plain custard sprinkled with nutmeg is good. This custard is bathed in a caramel glaze, which is even better! Do not refrigerate until the custard has cooled completely.

1½ cups sugar

6½ cups milk

9 eggs

5 egg yolks

¾ teaspoon salt

2 teaspoons almond extract

¾ cup whipping cream

¼ cup sliced blanched almonds

Preheat oven to 325°F. Place 1 cup of the sugar in a heavy 10-inch skillet; shake so the sugar is level. Place over high heat; watch for the sugar to begin melting, then immediately lower heat to medium and tilt the pan back and forth slowly to keep the sugar moving. Remove from heat as soon as the sugar has completely melted and is a light golden brown. Pour hot water into a 2½-quart heatproof soufflé dish to warm the dish; throw out the water. Pour the hot melted sugar into the bottom of the soufflé dish. In a large pan, scald the milk. Whip the eggs, egg yolks, and remaining ½ cup of the sugar until completely blended. Pour the egg mixture into the scalded milk, stirring constantly with a wire whisk. Add the salt and almond extract. Set the soufflé dish in a larger pan; place on a rack in the oven. Fill the larger pan with boiling water to within ¾ inch of the top. Pour the custard into the soufflé dish. Bake 1¼ hours or until a knife inserted in the center comes out clean. Cool on a wire rack; refrigerate for 6 to 24 hours.

Run a knife around the edge of the custard. Invert onto a serving platter. (Caramel will collect around the edge of the custard.) Whip the cream until stiff peaks form. Spoon ¼ cup of the caramel syrup from around the edge of the custard and fold it into the whipped cream. Surround the edge of the custard with dollops of (or piped) whipped cream; sprinkle the whipped cream with the almonds. *Makes 12 1-cup servings.*

One serving—Calories: 255; Total fat: 14.5 g; Saturated fat: 7.6 g; Cholesterol: 281 mg; Sodium: 267 mg; Carbohydrates: 23.9 g; Fiber: 1 g; Sugar: 13.7 g; Protein: 11.6 g

*R*um Custard

Just 2 tablespoons of rum transform a plain custard into a true taste sensation.

3 eggs, slightly beaten
¼ teaspoon salt
8 tablespoons sugar
3 cups scalded milk
2 tablespoons gluten-free light rum
Nutmeg

Preheat oven to 350°F. Combine the eggs, salt, and 5 tablespoons of the sugar. In a heavy saucepan, melt the remaining 3 tablespoons of sugar over low heat till caramelized. Stir the caramelized sugar into the scalded milk. Slowly add the milk to the egg mixture, stirring constantly. Stir in the rum. Pour into four custard cups that have been sprayed with gluten-free nonstick spray, and sprinkle with nutmeg. Place the custard cups in a pan of hot water, and bake 30 to 35 minutes or till a knife inserted in the center comes out clean. *Makes 4 1-cup servings.*

One serving—Calories: 237; Total fat: 9.7 g; Saturated fat: 5 g; Cholesterol: 185 mg; Sodium: 285 mg; Carbohydrates: 24.5 g; Fiber: 0 g; Sugar: 23.5 g; Protein: 10.7 g

Hot Coconut Soufflé

Soufflés are truly impressive desserts. This version is best when served as soon as it comes out of the oven.

½ cup quick-cooking tapioca

⅓ cup sugar

2 cups milk

1 cup plus 3 tablespoons shredded coconut

¾ teaspoon vanilla

2 tablespoons butter

3 eggs, separated

¼ teaspoon salt

Preheat oven to 350°F. Cut a 28-inch length of aluminum foil, 6 inches wide. Wrap the foil on the inside of a 5-cup ovenproof soufflé dish, so the foil stands 3 inches above the rim; secure with masking tape. Spray the inside of the foil with gluten-free cooking spray. Combine the tapioca and sugar in the top of a double boiler. Add the milk; cook over boiling water 10 minutes or till thick, stirring frequently. Stir in 1 cup of the coconut and the vanilla and butter. Beat the egg whites till foamy; add the salt, and beat till stiff. In another bowl, beat the egg yolks till thick. Fold the egg yolks into the coconut mixture; fold in the egg whites just till blended. Spoon the mixture into the soufflé dish; sprinkle with the remaining 3 tablespoons of coconut. Bake 45 minutes. Carefully run a knife between the soufflé and the foil, and remove the collar. Serve immediately. *Makes 6 ⅔-cup servings.*

One serving—Calories: 264; Total fat: 15.9 g; Saturated fat: 4.5 g; Cholesterol: 21 mg; Sodium: 211 mg; Carbohydrates: 22.8 g; Fiber: 0.7 g; Sugar: 10 g; Protein: 6.1 g

Scalloped Pineapple Pudding

Let the pudding set for 45 minutes before baking to absorb more moisture. The result will be a creamier pudding.

> 1 20-ounce can pineapple tidbits, drained
> 2 eggs, slightly beaten
> 2 tablespoons light brown sugar
> 1 cup granulated sugar
> ⅓ cup butter, melted
> 1 teaspoon cinnamon
> 6 slices gluten-free bread, cut into small cubes
> ⅓ cup half-and-half
> Sweetened whipped cream for topping

Stir together the pineapple and eggs; mix in the brown and granulated sugars. Stir in, one at a time, the butter, cinnamon, bread cubes, and half-and-half. Pour the mixture into a buttered 5-cup casserole, and let set 45 minutes. Preheat oven to 350°F. Bake 45 minutes or till the top is golden. Serve warm with a dollop of sweetened whipped cream. *Makes 6 ¾-cup servings.*

One serving (without whipped cream)—Calories: 309; Total fat: 14.5 g; Saturated fat: 1.8 g; Cholesterol: 101 mg; Sodium: 254 mg; Carbohydrates: 41 g; Fiber: 1 g; Sugar: 29.9 g; Protein: 4.8 g

Chocolate Bread Pudding

Remove the crusts from the bread before cutting it into cubes. Use as porous a bread as possible.

2 ounces (2 squares) gluten-free semisweet chocolate

3 cups whipping cream

2 tablespoons butter

¼ teaspoon salt

½ cup light brown sugar

2 eggs, separated

1½ teaspoons vanilla

7 slices dry gluten-free bread, cut into ½-inch cubes

¼ cup granulated sugar

Preheat oven to 350°F, and grease a 2-quart casserole or 9-inch square pan. Heat the chocolate, cream, and butter in the top of a double boiler until the chocolate is melted. Add the salt. Whip together the brown sugar and egg yolks; add the chocolate mixture slowly, beating constantly. Add the vanilla. Stir in the bread cubes, and let the mixture set for 35 minutes, stirring occasionally (so the bread may absorb some of the liquid). Whip the egg whites until foamy; add the granulated sugar gradually, beating until stiff. Partially fold the egg whites into the bread mixture, leaving noticeable white streaks. Turn into the greased casserole or pan, and bake 30 minutes or until almost firm. *Makes 9 ¾-cup servings.*

One serving—Calories: 391; Total fat: 27.7 g; Saturated fat: 7 g; Cholesterol: 94 mg; Sodium: 253 mg; Carbohydrates: 21.5 g; Fiber: 1 g; Sugar: 14.4 g; Protein: 3.1 g

𝓑anana Cookie Pudding

To make the cookie crumbs used as the base for this pudding, crush about 10 Banana Cookies with a rolling pin.

2 cups scalded milk

1 cup Banana Cookie crumbs (See Index.)

1 cup mashed banana

2 teaspoons sugar

¼ teaspoon salt

1 teaspoon grated lemon zest

2 teaspoons lemon juice

3 eggs, slightly beaten

Lemon Topping (Recipe follows.)

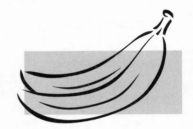

Preheat oven to 350°F, and grease an 8″ × 12″ baking dish. Pour the milk over the cookie crumbs; let stand till mixture cools. Stir in the banana, sugar, salt, lemon zest, and juice. Add the eggs, mixing well. Pour into the greased baking dish; place the dish in a larger pan, and fill the larger pan two-thirds full with hot water. Bake 1 hour or until firm. Remove from oven; let stand 5 minutes. Serve warm with the Lemon Topping. *Makes 12 ⅓-cup servings.*

Lemon Topping

1 cup light corn syrup

1 tablespoon grated lemon zest

1 tablespoon butter

1 tablespoon lemon juice

Bring the corn syrup to a boil; add the lemon zest and butter. Simmer for 2 minutes. Remove from heat, and stir in the lemon juice. *Makes 1 cup (about 12 1⅓-tablespoon servings).*

One serving (with topping)—Calories: 177; Total fat: 4.9 g; Saturated fat: 1.2 g; Cholesterol: 67 mg; Sodium: 100 mg; Carbohydrates: 34 g; Fiber: 0.7 g; Sugar: 3.4 g; Protein: 3.5 g

Peanut Butter and Jelly Pudding

Use your favorite jelly with this recipe. If you bake this pudding in a mold pan, unmold it, and decorate by drizzling 2 tablespoons of warmed jelly over the top.

> 2 eggs
> 1 cup light corn syrup
> 1 cup sugar
> ½ cup gluten-free peanut butter
> 1 teaspoon vanilla
> ½ cup jelly

Preheat oven to 350°F, and grease an 8-inch square pan. Beat the eggs till fluffy; whip in the corn syrup, sugar, peanut butter, and vanilla till blended. With a spoon, partially fold in the jelly; let some jelly streaks remain. Pour into the greased pan, and bake 45 minutes or till set. *Makes 9 ⅓-cup servings.*

One serving—Calories: 386; Total fat: 15.3 g; Saturated fat: 2.1 g; Cholesterol: 47 mg; Sodium:165 mg; Carbohydrates: 57.4 g; Fiber: 1.8 g; Sugar: 25.3 g; Protein: 9.4 g

Chocolate with Chocolate Mousse

This dessert is for those who can't seem to get enough chocolate!

> 1 cup semisweet chocolate chips
> 1 tablespoon butter
> ¼ cup white chocolate chips

⅓ cup whipping cream

2 teaspoons confectioners' sugar

2 teaspoons minced macadamia nuts

3 ounces (3 squares) gluten-free semisweet chocolate

1 teaspoon corn oil

Melt the semisweet chocolate chips and butter in the top of a double boiler over hot (not boiling) water. Remove from heat, but keep the pan over warm water. Spread a thin layer of the melted chocolate over the insides of 12 pleated miniature foil cupcake liners. Refrigerate 1 hour till firm. Gently peel the foil from the chocolate cups; keep the cups refrigerated until ready to fill. In the top of a double boiler, melt the white chocolate with 1 tablespoon of the cream; remove from heat, and cool 20 minutes. Beat the remaining 4⅓ tablespoons of cream and the confectioners' sugar until soft peaks form (do not overbeat). Fold half of the whipped cream into the white chocolate mixture. Fold in the remaining whipped cream and the nuts just till blended; spoon into the chocolate cups. Refrigerate for 1 hour or until serving time. Melt the squares of semisweet chocolate with the corn oil in the top of a double boiler. When ready to serve, drizzle the melted chocolate over the filled cups. *Makes 12 chocolate cups with 1⅓ tablespoons of filling.*

One serving—Calories: 294; Total fat: 21.2 g; Saturated fat: 12.7 g; Cholesterol: 35 mg; Sodium: 35 mg; Carbohydrates: 23.2 g; Fiber: 1.3 g; Sugar: 21.9 g; Protein: 1.8 g

𝒢reek Custard (Galopita)

If you refrigerate this custard before it has completely cooled, it will turn "weepy" with moisture on top.

1 quart milk

1¼ cups plus 2 tablespoons sugar

⅛ teaspoon salt

½ cup Cream of Rice

¾ cup butter

10 eggs, separated

1 teaspoon vanilla

1 ¼ teaspoons cinnamon

Preheat oven to 375°F, and grease a 9″ × 13″ baking pan. Place the milk, 1 cup of the sugar, and the salt in a saucepan. Cook over medium heat till the milk is warmed. Slowly add the Cream of Rice, stirring constantly, till thick and creamy. Remove from heat; stir in the butter till melted. Cool the mixture. Beat the egg yolks till fluffy; beat in the vanilla and ¼ teaspoon of cinnamon. With clean, dry beaters, beat the egg whites till stiff; whip in ¼ cup of the sugar, and fold into the egg yolks. Fold the eggs into the cooled milk mixture. Pour into the greased baking pan; bake 30 minutes. Remove from oven. In a small bowl, mix 2 tablespoons of sugar with 1 teaspoon of cinnamon; sprinkle on top of custard. When completely cool, cut into diamonds, and refrigerate for 2 to 24 hours. *Makes 18 3-inch-square servings.*

One serving—Calories: 197; Total fat: 12.6 g; Saturated fat: 2 g; Cholesterol: 146 mg; Sodium: 158 mg; Carbohydrates: 15.4 g; Fiber: 0 g; Sugar: 10.7 g; Protein: 5.6 g

ℳarmalade Pudding

To test if this pudding is done steaming, insert a knife in the center. If it comes out clean, the pudding is done.

½ cup butter, softened

½ cup sugar

5 eggs

½ teaspoon vanilla

1 cup Gluten-Free Flour Mixture (See the Hints chapter.)

3 teaspoons gluten-free baking powder

5 tablespoons marmalade (any flavor)

Preheat oven to 350°F. Whip together the butter and sugar till fluffy. Add the eggs and vanilla; beat well. Sift together the flour mixture and baking powder; add to the butter mixture. Spread the marmalade in the bottom of a 4-cup mold pan that has been sprayed with gluten-free nonstick spray; pour the batter on top. Cover the mold with foil, and place in a pan of hot water. Bake 1¼ hours or until a knife inserted in the center comes out clean. When cooled, invert and unmold. *Makes 6 ½-cup servings.*

One serving—Calories: 352; Total fat: 20.3 g; Saturated fat: 1.3 g; Cholesterol: 217 mg; Sodium: 212 mg; Carbohydrates: 36 g; Fiber: 0.7 g; Sugar: 20.3 g; Protein: 7.3 g

Brandied Cherry Mousse

The taste-tempting blend of cherry and chocolate is enhanced with a hint of cherry brandy.

1 15-ounce can dark, sweet pitted cherries

¼ cup gluten-free cherry brandy

3 ounces (3 squares) gluten-free semisweet chocolate

1 cup granulated sugar

3 egg yolks, well beaten

2 tablespoons crème de cacao

2 cups whipping cream

½ cup confectioners' sugar

½ teaspoon vanilla

Drain the cherries, reserving ⅓ cup of their juice. Cut the cherries into quarters; place in a small bowl. Pour the brandy over the cherries, and marinate several hours. Melt the chocolate over low heat with the reserved cherry juice, stirring constantly. Add the granulated sugar; cook till dissolved. Gradually stir the hot mixture into the egg yolks. Return the mixture to the saucepan; heat to a boil. Cool. Stir in the brandy (reserving cherries) and crème de cacao. Whip the cream with the confectioners' sugar and vanilla till stiff. Fold the cherries and whipped cream into the chocolate mixture. Pour into an oiled 2-quart bowl. Cover and freeze overnight. Remove from freezer 10 minutes before serving. Loosen with a spatula, and unmold onto a platter. Cut into wedges. *Makes 10 ¾-cup servings.*

One serving—Calories: 322; Total fat: 17 g; Saturated fat: 11.6 g; Cholesterol: 112 mg; Sodium: 22 mg; Carbohydrates: 31.4 g; Fiber: 0.6 g; Sugar: 25 g; Protein: 1.4 g

Almond Pudding

This Lebanese pudding is traditionally served with minced blanched almonds sprinkled on top.

> 1 quart milk
> ¾ cup sugar
> 3 tablespoons cornstarch
> 1 teaspoon almond extract

Bring the milk to a boil over low heat; cook until a crust forms on top. Add the sugar, and stir until the mixture returns to a boil. Remove from heat. Mix the cornstarch with a little water to form a paste; add to the milk, and cook over low heat, stirring constantly, until thickened. Stir in the almond extract, and cook, stirring, for 1 more minute. Pour into 8 custard cups that have been lightly sprayed with gluten-free nonstick spray, and cool. *Makes 8 ½-cup servings.*

One serving—Calories: 131; Total fat: 4 g; Saturated fat: 2.5 g; Cholesterol: 18 mg; Sodium: 61 mg; Carbohydrates: 19.9 g; Fiber: 0 g; Sugar: 16.9 g; Protein: 4 g

Old-Fashioned Rice Pudding

When making this pudding, do not use instant or converted rice. Short-grain rices work well. Be patient while cooking this pudding on the stove; it will take 20 minutes or more to begin thickening.

⅓ cup short-grain rice

⅓ cup boiling water

1 quart warmed half-and-half

¾ cup sugar

Dash salt

2 eggs

2 tablespoons butter

1 teaspoon vanilla

Cinnamon

Cook the rice in a large saucepan, uncovered, in the boiling water until the water is absorbed, about 5 minutes. Add the warmed half-and-half, and cook slowly, stirring frequently, until the rice is tender and the mixture has thickened, about 45 minutes. Add the sugar and salt; stir until dissolved. Remove the pan from the heat. Beat the eggs; stir in a little of the rice mixture very slowly, stirring constantly; continue to stir in the rice mixture slowly until at least half of it has been added to the eggs. Add the butter, and stir till melted. Pour the egg yolk mixture back into the saucepan with the rest of the rice mixture. Replace the pan on medium heat, and stir until creamy and thickened, about 15 minutes. Remove from heat; stir in the vanilla. Pour the pudding into 6 dessert bowls; sprinkle each liberally with cinnamon. When completely cool, refrigerate from 1 to 24 hours. *Makes 6 1-cup servings.*

One serving—Calories: 264; Total fat: 15 g; Saturated fat: 6.3 g; Cholesterol: 110 mg; Sodium: 94 mg; Carbohydrates: 27.5 g; Fiber: 0.3 g; Sugar: 17.2 g; Protein: 5.2 g

$\mathscr{S}$weet Potato Pudding

For a special effect, after baking this pudding, spoon it into hollowed orange halves. Top with the meringue, and brown the meringue as directed.

6 egg yolks

3 egg whites

2¼ cups sugar

2 tablespoons vanilla

2 tablespoons nutmeg

1 tablespoon cinnamon

½ cup butter, melted

1½ cups milk

4 cups peeled and grated sweet potatoes

Meringue

3 egg whites

8 teaspoons sugar

2 teaspoons vanilla

Preheat oven to 350°F, and grease an 8″ × 12″ baking pan. Beat the egg yolks and egg whites with the sugar, vanilla, nutmeg, cinnamon, butter, and milk till well blended and light. Stir in the sweet potatoes. Pour into the greased pan, and bake 1 hour, stirring frequently with a fork. Cool the pudding. Increase the oven temperature to 400°F. To make the meringue, whip the egg whites until almost stiff. Gradually add the sugar and vanilla, and continue beating until stiff peaks form. Spread the meringue over the pudding; bake about 5 minutes or until golden brown. *Makes 12 ¾-cup servings.*

One serving—Calories: 306; Total fat: 15.5 g; Saturated fat: 2.5 g; Cholesterol: 133 mg; Sodium: 360 mg; Carbohydrates: 37.3 g; Fiber: 1.6 g; Sugar: 25.7 g; Protein: 5.5 g

Vanilla Custard Pudding

If you prefer, substitute almond extract for the vanilla, and sprinkle the pudding with ground almonds.

> 1 quart milk or half-and-half
>
> ¾ cup sugar
>
> 2 tablespoons cornstarch
>
> 4 egg yolks, well beaten
>
> 1 teaspoon vanilla

Heat the milk or half-and-half to lukewarm in a large saucepan. Stir in the sugar. In a bowl, dissolve the cornstarch in the egg yolks; slowly stir the egg yolks into the milk mixture. Cook over low heat, stirring constantly, until the mixture thickens. Remove from heat, and stir in the vanilla. Pour into dessert cups. *Makes 6 ¾-cup servings.*

One serving (made with milk)—Calories: 209; Total fat: 8.7 g; Saturated fat: 4.3 g; Cholesterol: 165 mg; Sodium: 86 mg; Carbohydrates: 25.5 g; Fiber: 0 g; Sugar: 22.5 g; Protein: 7.2 g

Maple Pudding

This pudding is delicious served with sweetened whipped cream or a marshmallow sauce.

> 2 cups pure maple syrup
>
> 1 tablespoon butter, softened
>
> 3 tablespoons sugar
>
> 2 eggs
>
> 1 cup Gluten-Free Flour Mixture (See the Hints chapter.)
>
> 3 teaspoons gluten-free baking powder
>
> ¼ teaspoon salt
>
> ½ cup milk

Preheat oven to 400°F, and grease a 5-cup baking dish. Heat the maple syrup to boiling, then pour into the greased baking dish. Cream the butter and sugar till fluffy. Add the eggs, and mix well. Sift together the flour mixture, baking powder, and salt; add alternately with the milk to the butter mixture, beating well after each addition. Pour the pudding into the hot syrup, and bake about 25 minutes. When cooled, turn out onto a serving plate. *Makes 8 ½-cup servings.*

One serving—Calories: 310; Total fat: 2.9 g; Saturated fat: 0.5 g; Cholesterol: 57 mg; Sodium: 119 mg; Carbohydrates: 67.7 g; Fiber: 0.5 g; Sugar: 57 g; Protein: 3.6 g

Dessert Mélange

This chapter is brimming with tortes, doughnuts and cream puffs, cheesecakes of all kinds, and other specialty desserts. You can never have too much dessert!

Tortes

Tortes are rich cakes with extras . . . perhaps a cream topping layered with fruits, or several layers separated by rich nut fillings, or a fresh fruit glaze, or a decadently rich texture like that of fudge. Each of the tortes in this section has a unique feature to distinguish it from the others.

Strawberry Torte

This torte's meringue filling and topping is baked right onto the base.

1 cup Gluten-Free Flour Mixture (See the Hints chapter.)

1 ½ teaspoons gluten-free baking powder

¾ teaspoon salt

½ cup butter, softened

1 ½ cups sugar

4 eggs, separated

¼ cup milk

1 ½ teaspoons vanilla

½ teaspoon cream of tartar

Strawberry Filling (Recipe follows.)

Strawberry Sauce (Recipe follows.)

Preheat oven to 350°F, and grease two 8-inch round cake pans. Sift the flour mixture, baking powder, and ¼ teaspoon of the salt. Cream the butter and ½ cup of the sugar till fluffy. Beat the egg yolks till thick; add to the creamed mixture. Stir in the milk and 1 teaspoon of the vanilla. Add the dry ingredients; beat until the batter is smooth. Spread the batter in the greased pans. Beat the egg whites, the remaining ½ teaspoon of salt, and the cream of tartar till soft peaks form. Add the remaining 1 cup of sugar, 1 tablespoon at a time, beating well, and the remaining ½ teaspoon of vanilla. Lightly pile half of the meringue over the batter in each pan, smoothing the top so it is level. Bake 35 to 40 minutes. Remove the cake from the oven; loosen the sides. Cool 5 minutes; remove from pans, and cool on a wire rack with the meringue side up. When the layers are cool, spread the Strawberry Filling over one layer; cover with the second layer. To serve, cut into wedges, and drizzle the Strawberry Sauce over the wedges. *Makes 12 1¼-inch-thick servings.*

Strawberry Filling

½ cup whipping cream

3 tablespoons confectioners' sugar

1 cup sliced fresh strawberries

Whip the cream and sugar together until stiff. Fold in the strawberries. *Makes 2¼ cups.*

One serving (torte with filling)—Calories: 235; Total fat: 12.6 g; Saturated fat: 2.6 g; Cholesterol: 101 mg; Sodium: 255 mg; Carbohydrates: 26.2 g; Fiber: 0.7 g; Sugar: 17.5 g; Protein: 3.3 g

Strawberry Sauce

1 10-ounce package frozen strawberries, thawed

1 teaspoon sugar

1¼ teaspoons cornstarch

1 tablespoon water

Heat the strawberries (with their syrup) and sugar to boiling. Stir together the cornstarch and water; stir into the strawberries. Return to boiling, stirring constantly. Boil and stir for 1 minute till thickened, then cool. *Makes 1¼ cups (about 13 1½-tablespoon servings).*

One serving—Calories: 298; Total fat: 0 g; Saturated fat: 0 g; Cholesterol: 0 mg; Sodium: 1 mg; Carbohydrates: 7 g; Fiber: 0.4 g; Sugar: 0.2 g; Protein: 0.1 g

Apple Torte

One bowl, one spoon, one paring knife—that's all you need to make this dessert. Just add a dollop of whipped cream!

½ cup light brown sugar

¼ cup granulated sugar

Dash salt

1 egg, slightly beaten

½ cup Gluten-Free Flour Mixture
     (See the Hints chapter.)

1¼ teaspoons gluten-free baking powder

1 teaspoon vanilla

1 cup peeled, minced McIntosh apples

1 cup chopped walnuts

Preheat oven to 350°F, and grease a 9-inch pie plate. Stir the brown and granulated sugars and the salt into the egg in a large bowl. Sift the flour mixture and baking powder; stir into the egg mixture. Stir in the vanilla, apples, and walnuts. Spread in the greased pie plate. Bake 30 to 35 minutes till golden brown. *Makes 8 2-inch-thick servings.*

One serving—Calories: 188; Total fat: 10.5 g; Saturated fat: 0.8 g; Cholesterol: 27 mg; Sodium: 9 mg; Carbohydrates: 21.5 g; Fiber: 1.7 g; Sugar: 13.5 g; Protein: 15.4 g

*P*each Wine Torte

This dessert tastes best when left to "ferment" overnight in the refrigerator.

> Batter for Sugar Sponge Cake, without topping (See Index.)
> 12 tablespoons gluten-free white wine
> 2 cups peach preserves
> 9 tablespoons finely chopped pecans
> 12 pecan halves

Preheat oven to 350°F, and grease two round 9-inch cake pans. Bake the Sugar Sponge Cake according to directions. Cool; with a serrated knife, split each layer in half horizontally. Place one layer, crust side down, on a serving plate. Sprinkle with 3 tablespoons of the wine; spread with ¼ cup of the preserves; sprinkle with 3 tablespoons of the pecans. Repeat with the next two layers. Top with the last layer, crust side up; sprinkle with the remaining 3 tablespoons of wine. In a saucepan, melt 1 cup of the preserves. With a pastry brush, glaze the sides of the torte with the melted preserves. Spread the remaining ¼ cup of preserves on top of the cake, and decorate with the pecan halves. Cover and refrigerate overnight. *Makes 12 1¼-inch-thick servings.*

One serving—Calories: 197; Total fat: 8.9 g; Saturated fat: 1.1 g; Cholesterol: 71 mg; Sodium: 68 mg; Carbohydrates: 26.7 g; Fiber: 1.3 g; Sugar: 18.6 g; Protein: 3.8 g

Frozen Walnut Cream Torte

Put one of these tortes in the freezer so you will always be prepared for unexpected company. It will keep up to a month in the freezer.

> 2 teaspoons Gluten-Free Flour Mixture (See the Hints chapter.)
>
> 5 eggs, separated
>
> ¾ cup granulated sugar
>
> 3 teaspoons vanilla
>
> ¼ cup fresh gluten-free bread crumbs
>
> 1 cup ground walnuts
>
> 2 cups whipping cream
>
> ¼ cup confectioners' sugar
>
> 3 ounces (3 squares) gluten-free semisweet chocolate

Preheat oven to 350°F, and grease two 9-inch round cake pans. Line the bottom of each pan with waxed paper, and grease the waxed paper. Sprinkle each lightly with 1 teaspoon of flour mixture; shake out the excess flour mixture. Beat the egg yolks, granulated sugar, and 1 teaspoon of the vanilla in a bowl until triple in volume. Lightly toast bread crumbs in the oven at 350°F for 4 minutes; stir them into the yolks. Stir in the walnuts. With clean, dry beaters, whip the egg whites until stiff enough to hold firm peaks; fold into the egg yolk mixture. Pour the batter into the greased pans; bake 12 to 15 minutes till the cake begins to shrink away from edge of each pan. Cool the cake in the pans on wire racks. When cooled, remove the cake from the pans, and peel off the waxed paper. Whip the cream until soft peaks form. Beat in the confectioners' sugar and the remaining 2 teaspoons of vanilla. Continue beating till barely stiff peaks form. Place a cake layer on a serving plate; spread with one-fourth of the whipped cream. Top with the second cake layer. Frost the sides and top with the remaining whipped cream. Melt the chocolate; drizzle over the cake with the tip of a spoon. Freeze about 1 hour; wrap the frozen cake in foil, and return it to the freezer. One hour before serving, remove the foil, and place the cake in the refrigerator. *Makes 8 2-inch-thick servings.*

One serving—Calories: 156; Total fat: 10.9 g; Saturated fat: 3.6 g; Cholesterol: 77 mg; Sodium: 32 mg; Carbohydrates: 12.8 g; Fiber: 0.8 g; Sugar: 10.7 g; Protein: 3.6 g

Chocolate Almond Decadence

Make the torte base to this sumptuous dessert the day before serving.

> 1 8-ounce can almond paste
> 1 cup unsalted butter, softened
> ¾ cup unsweetened cocoa
> ¼ cup confectioners' sugar
> 3 eggs
> Bittersweet Glaze (Recipe follows.)

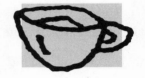

Preheat oven to 350°F, and grease a 9-inch round cake pan. Line the bottom with parchment, then grease the parchment. Whip together the almond paste, butter, cocoa, and sugar until smooth. Add the eggs, one at a time, beating well after each. Spoon the batter into the cake pan, and smooth the top. Bake 20 minutes or until set and just beginning to pull away from the sides of the pan. (The top may crack slightly.) Cool the cake completely in the pan. Run a knife around the edge of the cake. Invert onto a sheet of plastic wrap; wrap tightly, and refrigerate for 4 hours or overnight. Transfer the torte to a wire rack, and lay a sheet of waxed paper under the rack. Pour the warm Bittersweet Glaze over the cake, allowing the excess to drip onto the waxed paper. Tap the rack on the counter several times to smooth the glaze. Refrigerate 30 minutes to set the glaze. Using two large spatulas, carefully transfer the torte to a serving platter. *Makes 8 2-inch-thick servings.*

Bittersweet Glaze

> 8 ounces (8 squares) gluten-free bittersweet chocolate
> ½ cup unsalted butter

Finely grate the chocolate. Transfer to a mixing bowl. Melt the butter; slowly add the melted butter to the chocolate while whipping at medium speed. If the mixture is too thick to pour, place it in the top of a double boiler, and stir just until smooth and pourable. *Makes 1½ cups (about 8 3-tablespoon servings).*

One serving (cake with glaze)—Calories: 587; Total fat: 56.5 g; Saturated fat: 29.2 g; Cholesterol: 252 mg; Sodium: 76 mg; Carbohydrates: 40 g; Fiber: 5.7 g; Sugar: 19.7 g; Protein: 14.4 g

Patchwork Torte

Experiment with different flavors (and colors) of preserves. A 9-inch springform pan may be used to make this torte.

> 1 4-ounce can blanched almonds
> 1¼ cups Gluten-Free Flour Mixture (See the Hints chapter.)
> ¼ cup sugar
> 2 eggs
> ½ cup butter, softened
> 1 tablespoon grated lemon zest
> ½ teaspoon almond extract
> ¾ cup apricot preserves
> ¼ cup raspberry preserves

Preheat oven to 350°F. Finely grind the almonds in a blender. Sift together the flour mixture and sugar; stir in the ground almonds. Separate 1 egg. Stir the egg yolk and the remaining whole egg into the flour mixture. Beat in the butter, lemon zest, and almond extract until the mixture forms a ball. Flatten one-third of the dough, and wrap it in waxed paper; refrigerate. Press the remaining two-thirds of the dough into the bottom and ½ inch up the sides of a greased 10-inch flan pan with a removable bottom. Spread ½ cup of the apricot preserves evenly over the dough. Roll out the refrigerated dough into a 9-inch circle between two pieces of waxed paper that have been lightly dusted with additional flour mixture. Cut the circle of dough into 10 strips, each ½ inch wide; place the strips of dough across the top of the torte lattice style. Seal the strips at the edges. Trim off the edges evenly with a knife. Whip the reserved egg white with a whisk; brush on the lattice strips. Spoon the remaining ¼ cup of apricot preserves and the raspberry preserves in alternate spaces between the strips. Bake 30 minutes or until the crust is golden. Cool 10 minutes; remove sides of pan. Serve warm or at room temperature. *Makes 12 1¼-inch-thick servings.*

One serving—Calories: 256; Total fat: 9.8 g; Saturated fat: 0.6 g; Cholesterol: 55 mg; Sodium: 93 mg; Carbohydrates: 31 g; Fiber: 1.4 g; Sugar: 19.3 g; Protein: 4.4 g

Praline Vienna Torte

As a time-saver, you may wish to make the Almond Praline several days before preparing the torte and store it in a reclosable plastic bag at room temperature.

> 6 eggs, separated
> ½ cup sugar
> ½ cup butter, softened
> 6 ounces (6 squares) gluten-free semisweet chocolate
> Almond Praline (Recipe follows.)
> ¾ cup Gluten-Free Flour Mixture (See the Hints chapter.)
> 1¼ teaspoons gluten-free baking powder
> 1 12-ounce jar apricot preserves
> Vienna Glaze (Recipe follows.)

Preheat oven to 325°F, and grease an 8-inch round springform pan. Beat the egg whites at high speed till foamy. Sprinkle ⅓ cup of the sugar, 1 tablespoon at a time, over the egg whites, beating thoroughly after each addition, until soft peaks form; set aside. In a small bowl, beat the butter till fluffy; add the egg yolks and the remaining 2⅔ tablespoons of sugar; beat till fluffy. Melt the chocolate; let it cool. Add the melted chocolate and ½ cup of the Almond Praline to the egg yolk mixture; beat at low speed. Sift together the flour mixture and baking powder; resift directly into the egg mixture with a whisk. Fold in the egg whites with a whisk just until blended. Pour the batter into the greased pan; bake 1¼ hours or until a toothpick inserted in the center comes out clean. Cool 10 minutes in the pan on a wire rack. Loosen the edges, and remove the ring from the pan. Cool completely. Even off the top of the cake, then split the cake horizontally into two layers. Spread half of the preserves on the bottom layer; replace the top. Brush the remaining preserves on the top and sides of the cake. Let stand at least 2 hours for the preserves to soak in and partially dry. Pour all but 2 tablespoons of the Vienna Glaze over the cake, letting it drip down the sides, smoothing the top with a warm spatula. Sprinkle with the reserved Almond Praline. Drizzle the reserved glaze over the praline from the tip of a spoon. *Makes 8 1¾-inch-thick servings.*

One serving—Calories: 436; Total fat: 22.2 g; Saturated fat: 5 g; Cholesterol: 189 mg; Sodium: 169 mg; Carbohydrates: 57.1 g; Fiber: 1.6 g; Sugar: 45.1 g; Protein: 6.7 g

Almond Praline

½ cup sugar
½ cup slivered almonds

Butter a cookie sheet. In a small, heavy skillet, heat the sugar over medium heat just till melted and starting to turn golden. Add the almonds. Continue cooking until the almonds start to "pop" and the mixture is deep golden. Pour onto the buttered cookie sheet; cool completely. Break into small pieces; crush finely in a blender. *Makes ¾ cup.*

One serving—Calories: 52; Total fat: 2.6 g; Saturated fat: 1.9 g; Cholesterol: 0 mg; Sodium: 0 mg; Carbohydrates: 6.3 g; Fiber: 0.6 g; Sugar: 5.3 g; Protein: 1 g

Vienna Glaze

> 2 tablespoons water
> 2 tablespoons light corn syrup
> 1½ cups sifted confectioners' sugar
> 1½ ounces (1½ squares) gluten-free unsweetened chocolate

Blend the water and corn syrup in the top of a double boiler. Stir in the sugar and chocolate. Set over hot (not boiling) water, and heat, stirring, until the chocolate melts and the glaze is thin enough to pour over the cake. *Makes 1¾ cups (about 8 3½-tablespoon servings).*

One serving—Calories: 113; Total fat: 2.9 g; Saturated fat: 1.7 g; Cholesterol: 0 mg; Sodium: 8 mg; Carbohydrates: 27.8 g; Fiber: 0.8 g; Sugar: 21.7 g; Protein: 0.5 g

Chocolate Oblivion

This torte is like dense fudge when chilled; at room temperature, it is like a truffle. Serve it either way, but cut the pieces thin because it is very rich.

> 16 ounces (16 squares) gluten-free bittersweet chocolate,
>   coarsely chopped
> 1 cup unsalted butter
> 6 large eggs
> Confectioners' sugar for garnish

Preheat oven to 425°F, and grease an 8-inch springform pan. Line the bottom of the pan with waxed paper, and grease the paper. Wrap the outside of the pan with a double layer of foil. Melt the chocolate and butter in the top of a double boiler over low heat, stirring occasionally. Break the eggs into a large bowl; set the bowl over simmering water for 3 minutes or just until the eggs are warmed through. (Stir constantly to prevent the eggs from scrambling.) Remove from heat; beat the eggs 6 minutes or until triple in volume and soft peaks form. Fold half of the eggs into the melted chocolate till partially incorporated. Fold in the remaining eggs just until no streaks remain. Scrape into the prepared pan; smooth the top. Place the springform pan in a larger pan; pour hot water into the larger pan to come two-thirds up the sides of the springform pan. Bake 5 minutes. Cover loosely with lightly buttered foil; bake 35 minutes longer. (The cake will look soft but will set as it chills.) Cool on a wire rack 1 hour; cover and refrigerate 3 hours until very firm. Run a knife around the edge of the cake; remove the sides of the pan. Line a plate with plastic wrap; carefully invert the cake onto the plate. Remove the pan bottom and waxed paper. Place the cake right side up on a serving platter, and remove the top plastic. Gently press a paper doily on the cake, and sift the confectioners' sugar over the top. Carefully lift off the doily. *Makes 16 ¾-inch-thick servings.*

One serving—Calories: 276; Total fat: 28.9 g; Saturated fat: 16.9 g; Cholesterol: 111 mg; Sodium: 29 mg; Carbohydrates: 7.3 g; Fiber: 4.3 g; Sugar: 0.8 g; Protein: 5.4 g

Chocolate Hazelnut Torte

To keep the dough from sticking to your fingers, sprinkle your hands with a little Gluten-Free Flour Mixture.

Hazelnut Crust

> 2 cups confectioners' sugar
>
> 1 cup butter, softened
>
> 2 eggs
>
> 2¼ cups Gluten-Free Flour Mixture (See the Hints chapter.)
>
> 1 teaspoon gluten-free baking powder
>
> 1¾ cups ground hazelnuts

Chocolate Filling

> 7 ounces (7 squares) gluten-free semisweet chocolate,
> cut into pieces
>
> ½ cup butter, softened
>
> ½ cup confectioners' sugar
>
> 2 eggs

Preheat oven to 350°F. Generously grease a 9-inch springform pan, and lightly flour with Gluten-Free Flour Mixture. To make the crust, beat together the sugar and butter until light and fluffy. Add the eggs one at a time, beating until blended. Sift the flour mixture and baking powder; add to the butter mixture, and blend well. By hand, mix in the hazelnuts. Reserve 1 cup of the dough. Press the remaining dough over the bottom and ¾ inch up the sides of the greased and floured pan.

To make the filling, melt the chocolate in a small saucepan over low heat, stirring constantly until smooth. In a small bowl, beat the butter and sugar until light and fluffy. Add the eggs, one at a time, beating well after each addition. (The mixture may look curdled, but it's OK.) Stir in the melted chocolate, and pour the filling into the Hazelnut Crust. Divide the reserved dough into six equal pieces, and roll each to form an 8-inch rope. Lay the ropes over the filling in a crisscross pattern. Bake 50 to 55 minutes or until crust is golden. Cool 1 hour; remove the sides of the pan. Cool completely. Store covered in refrigerator from 3 to 24 hours. *Makes 12 1¼-inch-thick servings.*

One serving—Calories: 554; Total fat: 40.7 g; Saturated fat: 4.1 g; Cholesterol: 131 mg; Sodium: 264 mg; Carbohydrates: 44.8 g; Fiber: 3.3 g; Sugar: 25.3 g; Protein: 7.5 g

Raspberry Walnut Torte

This recipe may also be served as bar cookies. Just cut smaller pieces, and omit the Raspberry Sauce.

1¼ cups Gluten-Free Flour Mixture (See the Hints chapter.)
⅓ cup confectioners' sugar
½ cup butter, softened
1 10-ounce package frozen raspberries, thawed
¾ cup chopped walnuts
2 eggs
1 cup granulated sugar
½ teaspoon salt
¾ teaspoon gluten-free baking powder
1 teaspoon vanilla
Raspberry Sauce (Recipe follows.)

Preheat oven to 350°F, and spray the bottom of a 9-inch square pan with gluten-free nonstick spray. Sift together 1 cup of the flour mixture and the confectioners' sugar. Beat the butter till fluffy; add the sifted ingredients, and blend well. Press the butter mixture onto the bottom of the prepared pan. Bake 15 minutes. Cool. Drain the raspberries, reserving their juice for the Raspberry Sauce. Spread the berries over the crust, and sprinkle with the walnuts. In a small bowl, combine the eggs, granulated sugar, remaining ¼ cup of flour mixture, salt, baking powder, and vanilla at low speed. Pour the batter over the walnuts. Bake at

350°F for 35 minutes or till golden brown. Cool; cut into squares. Serve with the Raspberry Sauce. *Makes 9 3-inch-square servings.*

Raspberry Sauce

½ cup sugar

2 tablespoons cornstarch

½ cup water

Juice reserved from raspberries in Raspberry Walnut Torte

1 tablespoon lemon juice

In a saucepan, stir together the sugar, cornstarch, water, and raspberry juice. Simmer, stirring constantly, until thick and clear. Remove from heat, and stir in the lemon juice. Cool. *Makes 1 cup (about 9 1¾-tablespoon servings).*

One serving (with sauce)—Calories: 162; Total fat: 9.2 g; Saturated fat: 0.4 g; Cholesterol: 37 mg; Sodium: 127 mg; Carbohydrates: 18.5 g; Fiber: 1.3 g; Sugar: 6.8 g; Protein: 2.4 g

Swedish Almond Torte

This torte is best served the same day it is made.

½ cup butter, softened

½ cup sugar

1 egg yolk

1¼ cups Gluten-Free Flour Mixture (See the Hints chapter.)

Almond Filling (Recipe follows.)

Sugar Glaze (Recipe follows.)

Preheat oven to 325°F, and grease an 8-inch springform pan. Cream the butter and sugar till fluffy. Add the egg yolk, and blend well. Sift the flour mixture; whip into butter mixture. Knead the dough to form a smooth ball. Add a few drops of cold water if needed to hold the dough together. Press the dough gently onto the bottom and sides of the greased pan. Pour the Almond Filling into the shell; bake 45 minutes or until the filling is set. Set on a wire rack to cool. When cool, remove the sides of the pan. Drizzle the Sugar Glaze over the torte from the tip of a spoon in a lattice pattern. *Makes 10 1¼-inch-thick servings.*

Almond Filling

> 1 cup sifted confectioners' sugar
> ¾ cup ground blanched almonds
> ¼ teaspoon almond extract
> 2 eggs

Combine all the ingredients in a bowl, and beat until the mixture is smooth. *Makes 2¼ cups.*

Sugar Glaze

> ½ cup sifted confectioners' sugar
> 2 teaspoons milk
> ¼ teaspoon vanilla

Combine all the ingredients in a bowl, and stir until smooth. *Makes ½ cup (about 10 1½-teaspoon servings).*

One serving (torte with filling and glaze)—Calories: 311; Total fat: 16 g; Saturated fat: 0.8 g; Cholesterol: 67 mg; Sodium: 115 mg; Carbohydrates: 37.5 g; Fiber: 1.6 g; Sugar: 24.4 g; Protein: 5.5 g

Chocolate Cookie Torte

This moist, layered torte holds well for several days.

> 2 cups semisweet chocolate chips
> 1 14-ounce can sweetened condensed milk
> 1 tablespoon butter
> 1 teaspoon vanilla
> 2 cups Gluten-Free Flour Mixture (See the Hints chapter.)

¼ teaspoon salt

½ teaspoon baking soda

1 cup chopped walnuts

Cookie Torte Filling (Recipe follows.)

Preheat oven to 350°F, and grease an 8″ × 12″ baking pan. Melt the chocolate with the milk in a double boiler. Remove from heat; stir in the butter and vanilla. Sift the flour mixture, salt, and baking soda; stir into the milk mixture. Stir in the nuts. Spread two-thirds of the dough in the greased pan. Spread the Cookie Torte Filling over the dough in the pan; cover with the remaining cookie dough. (The filling will be very thick.) Bake 25 minutes. Cool; cut into bars. *Makes 15 2½- by 2¼-inch servings.*

Cookie Torte Filling

1 egg white

⅓ cup honey

1 teaspoon vanilla

2 cups finely chopped walnuts

1 tablespoon plus 2 teaspoons Gluten-Free Flour Mixture
    (See the Hints chapter.)

¼ teaspoon salt

Beat the egg white till stiff peaks form. Add the honey gradually, then add the vanilla. Mix the walnuts, flour mixture, and salt in a separate bowl; fold into the egg white mixture. (This mixture will be very thick.) *Makes 2⅔ cups.*

One serving (torte with filling)—Calories: 119; Total fat: 7.2 g; Saturated fat: 1.9 g; Cholesterol: 9 mg; Sodium: 120 mg; Carbohydrates: 46.3 g; Fiber: 3.5 g; Sugar: 19.3 g; Protein: 8 g

Swedish Coffee Torte

To prepare a grand finale, decorate the top of this torte with gluten-free chocolate leaves or gluten-free chocolate candies.

2 cups ground pecans

2 tablespoons gluten-free
     instant-coffee powder

7 eggs, separated

1 cup sugar

⅛ teaspoon salt

Coffee Filling (Recipe follows.)

Preheat oven to 350°F. Cut waxed paper to fit the bottoms of two 9-inch round cake pans. Grease the pans; line with the waxed paper, and grease the top of the waxed paper. Mix the pecans with the instant coffee. Beat the egg yolks and sugar until thickened and paler yellow; set aside. Beat the egg whites and salt until peaks form. Gently fold the egg yolk mixture into the egg whites. Fold in the pecan mixture. Pour the batter into the cake pans, and bake 25 to 30 minutes. Cool; remove from pans, and remove the waxed paper. Place one layer on a plate, and spread with one-third of the Coffee Filling. Top with the second layer; frost the top and sides with the remaining Coffee Filling. Refrigerate 2 to 8 hours until serving time. *Makes 10 1½-inch-thick servings.*

Coffee Filling

4 teaspoons gluten-free instant-coffee powder

2 cups heavy cream

16 large gluten-free marshmallows

Mix the coffee with ⅓ cup of water. Whip the cream until stiff peaks form; chill. Melt the marshmallows with the coffee in the top of a double boiler. Chill 1 hour. With a wire whisk, fold the coffee and marshmallow mixture into the cream. *Makes 5 cups.*

One serving (torte with filling)—Calories: 429; Total fat: 31.1 g; Saturated fat: 11 g; Cholesterol: 199 mg; Sodium: 94 mg; Carbohydrates: 26.4 g; Fiber: 2.3 g; Sugar: 20 g; Protein: 7.7 g

ℳeringue Torte

As the cake bakes, it will form a hollow in the center for filling.
Use a very sharp knife to slice off the top of the cake.

  9 egg whites
  ¼ teaspoon cream of tartar
  3 cups granulated sugar
  ½ teaspoon vanilla
  1 teaspoon apple cider vinegar
  2 20-ounce packages frozen sweetened strawberries, thawed
  ½ pint heavy cream
  ¼ cup confectioners' sugar

Preheat oven to 275°F, and butter a 9-inch springform pan. Beat
the egg whites till very stiff. Add the cream of tartar; gradually
add 1½ cups of the granulated sugar, beating till well blended.
Whip in the vanilla and vinegar. Fold in the remaining 1½ cups
of sugar. Place in the buttered pan, and bake 1 hour or until
cracks appear on top of the meringue. Cool. With a sharp knife,
cut off the top fourth of the meringue to make two layers. Just
before serving, drain the strawberries, and place the fruit on the
thick meringue layer. Whip the cream and confectioners' sugar
until stiff peaks form. Spread the whipped cream over the fruit;
replace the top layer. *Makes 10 1½-inch-thick servings.*

One serving—Calories: 232; Total fat: 2.3 g; Saturated fat: 1.4 g; Cholesterol: 8 mg;
Sodium: 57 mg; Carbohydrates: 50 g; Fiber: 2.4 g; Sugar: 37.9 g; Protein: 3.8 g

ℬanana Torte

If you need a make-ahead dessert, this is the perfect one. It will
hold in the refrigerator up to 3 days.

  Batter for ½ Sugar Sponge Cake, without topping (See Index.)
  1 10-ounce jar strawberry preserves
  2 medium, ripe bananas

1 cup heavy cream
3 tablespoons confectioners' sugar
1 tablespoon sliced almonds

Bake the Sugar Sponge Cake at 325°F in a greased 8½″ × 4½″ loaf pan for 45 minutes or until a toothpick inserted in the center comes out clean. Cool; cut into ½-inch-thick slices. Line the bottom of a shallow 8″ × 12″ baking dish with waxed paper cut to overhang the edges slightly. Arrange one-third of the cake slices over the waxed paper to cover the bottom of the dish. Spread with half of the preserves. Slice 1 of the bananas, and lay the slices evenly over the preserves. Repeat the three layers; finish with a top layer of cake slices. (Fit small pieces of cake into the corners and around the edges.) Cover the dessert with a plate to press it down compactly; refrigerate, covered, for 6 to 24 hours to blend the flavors. Whip the cream with the sugar till stiff peaks form. Remove the cake from the refrigerator; unmold onto a serving plate, and remove the waxed paper. Frost with the whipped cream, and decorate the top with the almonds. Refrigerate until ready to serve. *Makes 12 2½- by 3-inch servings.*

One serving—Calories: 246; Total fat: 10.1 g; Saturated fat: 5.1 g; Cholesterol: 81 mg; Sodium: 24 mg; Carbohydrates: 37 g; Fiber: 1 g; Sugar: 25.8 g; Protein: 3.2 g

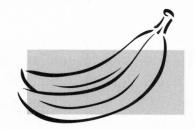

Doughnuts and Cream Puffs

Cooking temperatures are given with each doughnut recipe because the secret to making fried doughnuts that are not greasy is to have the oil hot enough so it won't be absorbed by the doughnut, yet cool enough that the oil won't start to smoke. Drain fried doughnuts on paper towels before frosting them to remove any excess oil.

𝒫olish Doughnuts

Had you given up trying to find a good gluten-free doughnut recipe? Here is one you will love.

3¾ cups Gluten-Free Flour Mixture (See the Hints chapter.)
1¾ teaspoons baking soda
½ teaspoon salt
½ teaspoon nutmeg
1 egg
1 cup buttermilk
2 tablespoons corn oil plus corn oil for frying
1¼ cups sugar
½ teaspoon vanilla
2 teaspoons cinnamon

Sift the flour mixture, baking soda, salt, and nutmeg. Beat together the egg, buttermilk, 2 tablespoons of the corn oil, 1 cup of the sugar, and the vanilla; add the sifted dry ingredients, and beat well. Knead the dough on a cutting board that has been liberally dusted with additional flour mixture. Place the dough between two sheets of waxed paper dusted with flour mixture. Roll out the dough ½ inch thick; cut with a doughnut cutter (or the rim of a drinking glass) dipped in flour mixture. Heat 1½ inches of corn oil to 360°F in a medium-size skillet. Fry the doughnuts, four at a time, for 4 minutes or until lightly browned on both sides. Drain on paper towels. Stir together the remaining ¼ cup of sugar and the cinnamon. Roll the warm doughnuts in the cinnamon sugar. *Makes 48 doughnuts.*

One doughnut—Calories: 58; Total fat: 1.3 g; Saturated fat: 0.2 g; Cholesterol: 4 mg; Sodium: 29 mg; Carbohydrates: 10.3 g; Fiber: 0.3 g; Sugar: 3.3 g; Protein: 1.3 g

ℬuttermilk Drop Doughnuts

Experiment with toppings. You can spread these doughnuts with chocolate frosting, then sprinkle with nuts, or spread with a confectioners' sugar glaze, then sprinkle with coconut. The possibilities are endless.

    2 eggs
    ½ cup sugar
    2 tablespoons butter, softened
    2 cups plus 1 tablespoon Gluten-Free Flour Mixture
        (See the Hints chapter.)
    1½ teaspoons gluten-free baking powder
    1 teaspoon baking soda
    ½ teaspoon salt
    ¼ teaspoon cinnamon
    ½ cup buttermilk
    Corn oil for frying
    Granulated or confectioners' sugar

Whip the eggs till fluffy. Beat in the sugar and butter. Sift together the flour mixture, baking powder, baking soda, salt, and cinnamon. Whip the dry ingredients into the egg mixture alternately with the buttermilk till blended. Heat 1½ inches of corn oil to 360°F in a medium-size skillet. Drop the dough by teaspoonfuls, four at a time, into the hot oil; fry, turning once, until lightly browned. Drain on paper towels. While the doughnuts are still warm, roll them in granulated or confectioners' sugar. *Makes 48 doughnuts.*

One doughnut (plain, unsugared)—Calories: 40; Total fat: 1.9 g; Saturated fat: 0.2 g; Cholesterol: 10 mg; Sodium: 34 mg; Carbohydrates: 5 g; Fiber: 0.2 g; Sugar: 1.4 g; Protein: 0.8 g

ream Puffs à l'Orange

Delicate, light, airy cream puffs—no one will suspect they are gluten-free!

> ½ cup water
> 3 tablespoons sugar
> ¼ cup butter
> ⅛ teaspoon salt
> ½ cup Gluten-Free Flour Mixture
>   (See the Hints chapter.)
> 2 eggs
> Grated zest of 1 orange
> Chocolate Cream Filling (Recipe follows.)
> Cream Puff Glaze (Recipe follows.)

Preheat oven to 450°F. Bring the water, sugar, butter, and salt to a boil in a medium-size saucepan. Sift the flour mixture; add to the pan, stirring briskly over medium heat about 1 minute or till the mixture leaves the sides of the pan and forms a smooth ball. Remove from heat; stir in the eggs, one at a time, beating well after each addition. Beat in the orange zest. Drop the dough by teaspoonfuls onto an ungreased baking sheet. Bake 12 minutes or till the bottoms are lightly browned. Immediately place the puffs on a wire rack to cool. While still warm, cut off the top third of each puff, and remove the soft center with a spoon. When cooled, fill with the Chocolate Cream Filling, and replace the top of each puff. Drizzle the tops with the Cream Puff Glaze; refrigerate up to 8 hours. *Makes 52 miniature cream puffs.*

Chocolate Cream Filling

> ½ cup semisweet chocolate chips
> 2 tablespoons orange juice
> ⅓ cup finely chopped almonds

½ cup whipping cream

2 teaspoons confectioners' sugar

Melt the chocolate chips in a double boiler over hot (not boiling) water. Stir in the orange juice. Remove from heat, and stir in the almonds. Beat the cream and sugar until stiff; fold into the chocolate mixture. *Makes 2½ cups.*

Cream Puff Glaze

5 ounces (3 squares) gluten-free semisweet chocolate

2 tablespoons butter

Melt the chocolate and butter in the top of a double boiler over hot (not boiling) water, stirring till smooth. *Makes 9 tablespoons (about 52 ½-teaspoon servings).*

One cream puff (with filling and glaze)—Calories: 48; Total fat: 3.5 g; Saturated fat: 1.2 g; Cholesterol: 14 mg; Sodium: 21 mg; Carbohydrates: 3.1 g; Fiber: 0.3 g; Sugar: 3 g; Protein: 0.7 g

Cheesecakes

A gluten-free diet need not prevent you from treating yourself to a luscious slice of cheesecake every now and then. A homemade cheesecake may sound difficult to make, but it isn't if you know the basics. The following tips tell how to avoid the most common pitfalls.

Make sure all the ingredients are at room temperature. Using ingredients at room temperature produces a cheesecake with a smoother texture. Use regular gluten-free cream cheese unless the recipe specifically calls for "soft" or "light" cream cheese.

Thoroughly combine the cheese with the eggs before adding any other ingredients. Lumps are almost impossible to remove once other liquid ingredients have been added. If your mixer has a paddle attachment, use it instead of beaters. Beaters may add too much air to the mix, causing cracks in the cheesecake. If you use beaters, mix the ingredients at low speed. When mixing, frequently scrape down the sides of the bowl and the paddle or beaters to ensure no lumps are in the batter. Fold in, rather than stir, the whipped cream or beaten egg whites gently and slowly with a wire whisk or rubber spatula. A spoon or stirring motion will deflate the volume.

To make it easier to remove the cake from the pan, grease the bottom and sides of a springform pan. After baking, run a knife around the sides of the cake to loosen it from the pan. If the top browns too quickly during baking, cover the cheesecake with foil, then finish baking. If too much steam is released too quickly while the cheesecake cools, the cheesecake may crack. Cool the cheesecake away from drafts. If possible, when the cake is done baking, turn off the oven, open the oven door, and let the cheesecake cool on the oven rack. Be sure the cheesecake has thoroughly cooled to room temperature before refrigerating it. Putting it in the refrigerator before it is at room temperature may cause the top to crack. Remove the sides of the springform pan before refrigerating, leaving the cheesecake on the pan bottom to serve.

Cottage Cheese Torte

The texture and flavor is slightly different from a traditional cheesecake, with the flavor of roasted pistachio nuts.

   Dough for 1 ½ Cookie Crusts (See Index.)
   4 eggs
   2 cups sugar
   Dash salt
   Juice and grated zest of ½ lemon
   1 teaspoon vanilla
   ½ pint whipping cream

24 ounces gluten-free cottage cheese

½ cup Gluten-Free Flour Mixture (See the Hints chapter.)

¼ cup chopped pistachios

Preheat oven to 325°F, and butter a 9-inch springform pan. Press three-fourths of the crust mixture on the bottom and slightly up the sides of the pan. Beat the eggs with the sugar until light. Add the salt, lemon juice and zest, and vanilla. Stir in the cream, and mix well. Stir in the cottage cheese. Sift the flour mixture; add to the cream mixture. Strain the mixture through a fine sieve. Stir until smooth. Pour into the crust; sprinkle with the nuts. Bake 1 hour. Turn off the heat, and let the cheesecake stand in the oven, with the oven door open, 1 hour or until mostly cooled. Remove from oven, and finish cooling completely on a wire rack. Remove the sides of the pan. Cover and refrigerate for 3 to 24 hours. *Makes 16 1-inch-thick servings.*

One serving (made with Snickerdoodle cookie crust)—Calories: 262; Total fat: 15.5 g; Saturated fat: 5.1 g; Cholesterol: 101 mg; Sodium: 185 mg; Carbohydrates: 23 g; Fiber: 0.6 g; Sugar: 17.3 g; Protein: 7.4 g

Apple Cheesecake

Starting on the outer edge of the torte, lay thin apple slices in concentric circles, slightly overlapping, arriving at the center. The result will be a beautiful apple chrysanthemum.

Dough for 1 Cornflake Nut Crust, substituting chopped almonds
　　for the walnuts (See Index.)

8 ounces gluten-free cream cheese, softened

¼ cup plus ⅓ cup sugar

1 egg

½ teaspoon vanilla

¾ teaspoon cinnamon

6 cups thinly sliced, peeled apples

¼ cup sliced almonds

Preheat oven to 450°F, and grease a 9-inch springform pan. Pat the Cornflake Crust onto the bottom of the pan. Whip the cream cheese and ¼ cup of the sugar until smooth. Add the egg and vanilla, and beat on low speed until well blended. Pour over the crust. In a large bowl, combine the cinnamon and the remaining ⅓ cup of sugar. Add the apples, and toss until well coated. Arrange the apples over the cheese layer in an attractive pattern. Tuck the almonds between apple slices. Bake 10 minutes. Reduce oven temperature to 400°F, and continue baking 35 minutes or until the apples are tender. Cool thoroughly; refrigerate. Remove the sides of the pan. *Makes 16 1-inch-thick servings.*

One serving—Calories: 213; Total fat: 15.6 g; Saturated fat: 7.3 g; Cholesterol: 56 mg; Sodium: 207 mg; Carbohydrates: 15.9 g; Fiber: 1.4 g; Sugar: 6.4 g; Protein: 3.7 g

𝒫eanut Butter Chocolate Chip Cheesecake

This cheesecake freezes beautifully. Merely thaw in the refrigerator for 24 hours before serving.

  1½ cups finely ground gluten-free cornflakes
  ⅓ cup sugar
  ¼ cup unsweetened cocoa
  ⅓ cup butter, melted
  24 ounces (1½ pounds) gluten-free cream cheese, softened
  1 14-ounce can sweetened condensed milk
  1 10-ounce package gluten-free peanut butter chips, melted
  4 eggs, at room temperature
  2 teaspoons vanilla
  1 cup mini semisweet chocolate chips

Preheat oven to 300°F. Grease the bottom of a 9-inch springform pan. Stir together the cornflake crumbs, sugar, cocoa, and butter. Press onto the bottom of the greased pan. Whip the cream cheese until fluffy. Gradually beat in the milk, then the melted peanut butter chips until smooth. Add the eggs and vanilla, beating well. Stir in the chocolate chips. Pour over the crust. Bake 55 to 65 minutes till the center is set. Cool completely; refrigerate for 3 to 24 hours. *Makes 16 1-inch-thick servings.*

One serving—Calories: 471; Total fat: 31.6 g; Saturated fat: 17 g; Cholesterol: 126 mg; Sodium: 319 mg; Carbohydrates: 39.6 g; Fiber: 2.4 g; Sugar: 10.2 g; Protein: 9.8 g

Fudge Truffle Cheesecake

Cut thin slices. This is a rich dessert!

- 1½ cups gluten-free puffed-rice cereal
- ¼ cup unsweetened cocoa
- 4½ tablespoons confectioners' sugar
- 6 tablespoons butter, melted
- 24 ounces (1½ pounds) gluten-free cream cheese, softened
- 1 14-ounce can sweetened condensed milk
- 4 eggs
- 2 cups semisweet chocolate chips, melted
- 2 teaspoons vanilla

Preheat oven to 300°F, and grease a 9-inch springform pan. Place the cereal in a blender, and blend into fine crumbs. Pour the crumbs into a bowl. With a fork, stir together the crumbs, cocoa, and sugar; stir in the butter. Press the crumb mixture firmly onto the bottom of the greased pan. Beat the cream cheese until fluffy. Gradually beat in the milk until smooth. Add the eggs, melted chocolate, and vanilla; mix at low speed till blended. Pour over the crust, and bake 1 hour or until the center is set. Cool completely; refrigerate for 3 to 24 hours. *Makes 16 1-inch-thick servings.*

One serving—Calories: 416; Total fat: 29 g; Saturated fat: 16.3 g; Cholesterol: 75 mg; Sodium: 259 mg; Carbohydrates: 37.3 g; Fiber: 1.7 g; Sugar: 15.8 g; Protein: 6.9 g

✐lmond Cheesecake

To dress up this cheesecake for company, press sliced almonds completely around the outside. This takes patience, but the effect is worth it.

12 ounces (¾ pound) gluten-free cream cheese, softened

¾ cup sugar

1 teaspoon almond extract

1 teaspoon lemon juice

2 eggs

Almond Crust (Recipe follows.)

Sour Cream Topping (Recipe follows.)

3 tablespoons chopped almonds

Preheat oven to 350°F. Whip the cream cheese till fluffy. Slowly add the sugar, almond extract, and lemon juice; beat until creamy. Add the eggs, and beat on low speed until blended. Pour into the Almond Crust. Bake 30 minutes or until center is set. Cool 5 minutes. Spread the Sour Cream Topping over the cheesecake, and sprinkle with the almonds. Bake 10 minutes more. Remove from oven, and cool completely on a wire rack. Remove the sides of the pan, and refrigerate the cheesecake for 3 to 24 hours. *Makes 16 1-inch-thick servings.*

Almond Crust

¼ pound butter, softened

½ cup sugar

3 eggs

2 cups Gluten-Free Flour Mixture (See the Hints chapter.)

2 teaspoons gluten-free baking powder

Pinch salt

3 tablespoons ground almonds

Whip together the butter, sugar, and eggs. Sift the flour mixture, baking powder, and salt; blend into the butter mixture until it forms a soft dough. Add the almonds, mixing well. Press into a greased 9-inch springform pan. *Makes 16 1-inch-thick servings.*

Sour Cream Topping

- 3 tablespoons sugar
- 1 teaspoon lemon juice
- 1 teaspoon almond extract
- 1 cup gluten-free sour cream

Whip all the ingredients together until smooth and creamy. *Makes 1⅛ cups (about 16 1-tablespoon servings).*

One serving (cheesecake with crust and topping)—Calories: 243; Total fat: 14.6 g; Saturated fat: 4.8 g; Cholesterol: 99 mg; Sodium: 124 mg; Carbohydrates: 23.6 g; Fiber: 0.7 g; Sugar: 12.3 g; Protein: 4.9 g

Specialty Desserts

When a cake or pie just won't fit the occasion, you can create something special from the following dessert crepe, trifle, torte, and dumpling recipes.

ℳake-Ahead Filled Crepes

This is the perfect dessert to make a week ahead and freeze. Just thaw and warm the filled crepes, and spoon on the topping. Filled crepes also make an impressive statement when served at a Sunday brunch.

4 eggs

¾ teaspoon salt

1½ teaspoons plus 1 tablespoon sugar

¾ cup water

¾ cup plus 2 tablespoons milk

½ teaspoon vanilla

1¼ cups Gluten-Free Flour Mixture (See the Hints chapter.)

¾ teaspoon gluten-free baking powder

16 ounces gluten-free small-curd cottage cheese

Grated zest of 1 lemon

¼ teaspoon cinnamon

1 teaspoon Cream of Rice

1 21-ounce can gluten-free cherry pie filling

Beat 3 of the eggs till fluffy. Gradually beat in ½ teaspoon of the salt, 1½ teaspoons of the sugar, and the water, milk, and vanilla. Sift the flour mixture and baking powder; beat into the egg mixture. Lightly brush a warmed 5½-inch skillet with butter. Pour in enough batter, while tipping the skillet, to *thinly* coat the bottom of the pan (about 2 tablespoons). Cook the crepe till dry on top and slightly browned on bottom. Turn crepe over and cook underside for about 10 seconds, just to brown it. Turn out on a paper towel to cool. Repeat with the remaining batter, brushing the skillet with butter as needed.

Press the cottage cheese through a strainer into a bowl. Stir in the lemon peel zest, 1 slightly beaten egg, the remaining 1 tablespoon of sugar, the remaining ¼ teaspoon of salt, and the cinnamon and Cream of Rice. Place a heaping tablespoon of the cheese mixture at the edge of one crepe; roll up jelly-roll fashion. Repeat with the remaining crepes. Lay the filled crepes side by side, seam side down, in a lightly greased 9″ × 13″ baking pan. Cover with foil, and freeze. The day before serving, thaw the crepes in the refrigerator. Just before serving time, bake the crepes, uncovered, at 350°F for 20 minutes or till heated through. Warm the pie filling, and spoon over the crepes. *Makes 12 2-crepe servings.*

One serving (filled crepes with topping)—Calories: 130; Total fat: 2.3 g; Saturated fat: 0.5 g; Cholesterol: 56 mg; Sodium: 132 mg; Carbohydrates: 131.6 g; Fiber: 0.7 g; Sugar: 0.9 g; Protein: 3.6 g

ℐeachy Bake

This fruit dessert is best served warm, topped with sweetened whipped cream or a scoop of gluten-free vanilla ice cream.

1 layer (½ recipe) Sweet Cream Cake, without filling (See Index.)
1 cup milk
2 eggs, slightly beaten
1 cup chopped peaches
1 cup raisins
1 tablespoon vanilla
1 teaspoon cinnamon

Let the cake sit out for 12 hours or overnight, uncovered, to dry out. Preheat oven to 350°F, and grease a 3-quart casserole dish. Break the dried cake into medium-sized pieces about the size of golf balls. Place in a bowl with the milk, eggs, peaches, raisins, vanilla, and cinnamon; fold to blend. Pour into the casserole, and bake about 45 minutes until firm. *Makes 12 ¾-cup servings.*

One serving—Calories: 269; Total fat: 10.2 g; Saturated fat: 5.7 g; Cholesterol: 102 mg; Sodium: 101 mg; Carbohydrates: 39.2 g; Fiber: 1.5 g; Sugar: 24.8 g; Protein: 5.4 g

ℐrifle

Trifle is so pretty when served in a large glass compote bowl.

1 Sugar Sponge Cake, without topping (See Index.)
6 tablespoons gluten-free sherry

   1 12-ounce jar raspberry jam

   1 pint whipping cream

   ½ cup confectioners' sugar

   ¼ cup chopped walnuts

Cut the cake into ½-inch pieces. Line a 9″ × 13″ glass dish (or glass compote bowl) with half of the cake pieces. Sprinkle with 3 tablespoons of the sherry. Carefully spread half of the jam over the cake. Beat the whipping cream and sugar together until peaks hold their shape. Spread half of the whipped cream over the jam layer. Repeat the layers of cake, sherry, jam, and whipped cream. Sprinkle with the nuts. Cover and refrigerate several hours or overnight. *Makes 18 3- by 2-inch servings.*

One serving—Calories: 185; Total fat: 6.4 g; Saturated fat: 2.2 g; Cholesterol: 80 mg; Sodium: 45 mg; Carbohydrates: 34.1 g; Fiber: 0.5 g; Sugar: 21.5 g; Protein: 3 g

𝒫each Cream Torte

Torte may be served warm or thoroughly chilled. The fruit helps keep this dessert moist.

   2 cups Gluten-Free Flour Mixture (See the Hints chapter.)

   ¾ cup sugar

   ½ teaspoon gluten-free baking powder

   ¾ teaspoon salt

   ½ cup butter

   1 15-ounce can sliced peaches, well drained

   1½ teaspoons cinnamon

   2 egg yolks

   1 cup gluten-free sour cream

Preheat oven to 400°F, and grease a 9-inch square pan. Sift together the flour mixture, ¼ cup of the sugar, the baking powder, and salt. Cut in the butter with two knives until the mixture resembles fine crumbs. Press the dough firmly against the bottom and sides of the greased pan. Arrange the peach slices evenly over the bottom crust. Stir together the remaining ½ cup of sugar and the cinnamon; sprinkle over the fruit. Bake 15 minutes. Beat the egg yolks, and blend in the sour cream. Spoon over the partially baked torte. Continue baking 20 minutes or until light golden brown. *Makes 9 3-inch-square servings.*

One serving—Calories: 306; Total fat: 12.2 g; Saturated fat: 2.4 g; Cholesterol: 62 mg; Sodium: 239 mg; Carbohydrates: 36.8 g; Fiber: 1.7 g; Sugar: 12.6 g; Protein: 3.2 g

ℬutterscotch Dumplings

This perfect fall and winter dessert is best when served hot from the oven.

- 3 cups boiling water
- 2 cups light brown sugar
- 1½ teaspoons vanilla
- 2 tablespoons butter
- 1 cup Gluten-Free Flour Mixture (See the Hints chapter.)
- 3 teaspoons gluten-free baking powder
- ½ cup milk
- ½ cup chopped walnuts
- ½ cup raisins

Preheat oven to 350°F. In a 9″ × 13″ metal baking pan, mix together the water, 1 cup of the brown sugar, 1 teaspoon of the vanilla, and 1 tablespoon of the butter. Put on the stove to barely simmer. Sift together the flour mixture, baking powder, and remaining 1 cup of brown sugar. Stir in the milk, remaining ½ teaspoon of vanilla, and 1 tablespoon melted butter till a smooth batter is formed. (Add a few extra drops of milk if needed.) Stir in the nuts and raisins. Drop the batter by spoonfuls into the hot butterscotch sauce, and bake 20 minutes. *Makes 12 2-dumpling servings.*

One serving—Calories: 191; Total fat: 5.6 g; Saturated fat: 0.5 g; Cholesterol: 6 mg; Sodium: 28 mg; Carbohydrates: 33.7 g; Fiber: 1 g; Sugar: 25.1 g; Protein: 2.3 g

Index